THE

ROAST PENGUIN

CHRONICLES

Hoosh, Scurvy Days, Sleeping with Vegetables,
and Other Adventures in Antarctic Cuisine

THE ROAST PENGUIN CHRONICLES

Hoosh, Scurvy Days, Sleeping with Vegetables,
and Other Adventures in Antarctic Cuisine

Jason C. Anthony

The Roast Penguin Chronicles is a work of non-fiction. References to historical incidents were researched and depicted to the best of the author's ability. The descriptions of all individuals reflect a faithfulness to historical accuracy.

For my mother, Joanne Anthony, and in memory of my father, Vaughn Anthony. And for Nicholas, who made Antarctica better.

CONTENTS

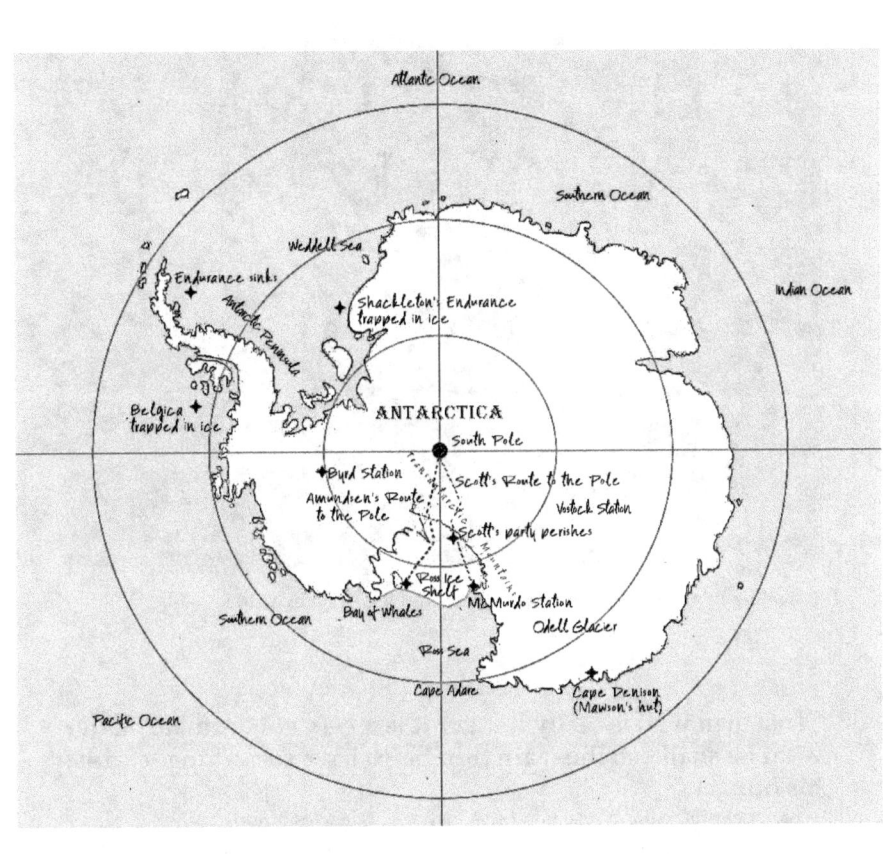

Traveling by dogsled in front of a weathered iceberg, circa 1911

"To a man who is really hungry it is a very subordinate matter what he shall eat; the main thing is to have something to satisfy his hunger."
—Lieutenant Kristian Prestrud of the 1910–12 *Fram* expedition

PROLOGUE: A Recipe for Something

A day before I flew by Twin Otter from Ross Island into the Transantarctic Mountains for a three-month deep field assignment, my friend Robert Taylor led me quietly into the McMurdo Station kitchen and surprised me with a dozen loaves of his exquisite bread. A slender, soft-spoken baker with a penchant for mischief, he knew he was helping me escape to the hinterlands with some of the best food in the United States Antarctic Program (USAP).

Into my knapsack went bundles of illicitly made olive, sweet potato, and plain sourdough, moist but with a firm crust.

"This is beautiful, Robert," I said. "How can I repay you?"

"You can't," he said, smiling sweetly. "Just have a good time, and when you come back tell me some stories."

Ask anyone for stories of Antarctic cuisine, and they're likely to go as blank as the ice continent itself. Antarctica lies somewhere beyond their imagination, or exists as the strange white mass smeared across the bottom of their cylindrical-projection world map.

Often they'll confuse it with the Arctic, where polar bears and Santa Claus roam the sea ice. With a little prompting, they may at least know Antarctica as the media depict it — the frigid home of penguins, icebergs, and undaunted scientists.

For me, it has been both a second home and a dreamlike otherworld of ice. For eight Antarctic summers, I lived and worked in the starkest landscape on Earth. I slept on a mass of ice larger than India and China combined, woke up flying over glaciers that overflow mile-high mountains, and ate meals in a tent shaken so wildly by katabatic winds that I thought its destruction was imminent.

Antarctic ice is three miles deep in places. The growth of sea ice around the continent each winter is the greatest seasonal event on the planet, while the largest year-round terrestrial animal is microscopic and plant life is confined to a few stony pockets within the 0.4 percent of Antarctica not covered in permanent snow or ice. Ninety percent of the planet's ice sits in Antarctic ice caps so hostile to human life that *nobody* stood on them until the twentieth century.

The existence of Antarctica, the only significant realm actually discovered by colonizing Europeans, was not proved until 1820, and the continent's coastline was not fully sketched until the late 1950s.

You may ask, therefore, if there is really such a thing as a venerable Antarctic cuisine. In a word, no. Since the dawn of time, as far as we know, no human ate so much as a snack in the Antarctic region until Captain James Cook and his frostbitten sailors nibbled on biscuits as they dodged icebergs below the Antarctic Circle in 1773.

Seal hunters made the first brief Antarctic landings by the austral summer of 1819–20, but no one sat down for a regular meal on the continent until 1898.

Then, as now, what visitors to the Antarctic — and we are *all* visitors — sit down to are imported meals. There is no Antarctic *terroir*.

The land does not provide, cannot provide, because there isn't a square foot of arable soil on the entire 5.4-million-square-mile continent in which to plant a garden.

There have been, however, two sources of Antarctic cuisine: the flavors people bring with them and the flavors of the Southern Ocean, meaning the flesh of seals, penguins, and sea birds raising their young on the Antarctic shoreline. Antarctic culinary history comprises a mere century of stories of isolated, insulated people eating either prepackaged expedition meals or butchered sea life.

In recent decades, with kinder, more complex menus, each nation's research base enjoys a limited version of its own home cuisine.

If the mother of Antarctic cuisine was necessity, its father was privation. Hunger was the one spice every expedition carried.

In the words of Lieutenant Kristian Prestrud of the 1910–12 *Fram* expedition, "To a man who is really hungry it is a very subordinate matter *what* he shall eat; the main thing is to have *something* to satisfy his hunger." Rations for sledging expeditions looked and tasted much alike.

Sustenance ruled over sensitivity. Thus, the heroes and stoics of Antarctic history scribbled in their journals about seal steaks and breast of penguin, about pemmican and biscuit crumbs boiled in tea. About dog flesh and caches of pony meat. About "hoosh," the bleak Antarctic soup of meat and melted snow. About scurvy and dying hungry.

Properly defined, hoosh is a porridge or stew of pemmican and water, often thickened with crushed biscuit. Ship's biscuit, also known as hardtack, had fed sailors for centuries. Pemmican is a Native American high-energy food made of dried, shredded meat mixed with fat and flavored with dried berries. Antarctic pemmican differed in substance—commercial beef and beef fat rather than wild meat—and appearance—compacted, uniform, measured blocks.

The word *hoosh* is a cognate of *hooch*, itself a corruption of the Tlingit *hoochinoo*, meaning both a Native American tribe on Admiralty Island, Alaska, and the European-style rotgut liquor that they made. Hooch became common slang throughout North America for bootleg liquor, particularly during Prohibition, while for British polar explorers in both the Arctic and Antarctic, hoosh came to mean the meat stew of the ravenous.

"Hoosh—what a joyous sound that word had for us," said Frank Worsley, captain of the *Endurance*. And indeed, the onomatopoeic sound of it, like the *whoosh* of the Primus stove bringing their stew to a boil, must have been music to their ears. All of which shows how Antarctica's sad state of culinary affairs has been framed by a truly rich history on this *terra incognita*.

Here, at the bitter end of terrestrial exploration, where year-round occupation preceded the invention of the microwave oven by only a few years, food has rarely had a more attentive, if helpless, audience. Cold, isolation, and a lack of worldly alternatives have conspired to make Antarctica's captive inhabitants desperate for generally lousy food.

My Antarctic captivity—quite voluntary—occurred between 1994 and 2004. I worked various jobs in the USAP (waste management specialist, fuels operator, cargo handler, field camp supervisor) as part of the U.S. community from which scientists ventured out to gather data.

Occasionally, I worked more closely with these researchers, but like most Antarctic residents, I had little to do with science. This surprises most people to whom I tell my Antarctic stories. They hear in the media that Antarctica is lightly populated with teams of bold researchers, funded by the National Science Foundation (NSF) to bring home information for the benefit of humanity.

There is some truth in this, certainly, as the entire population of the continent in the busy, summer research season (nearly five thousand) is smaller than that of a small town back home and there are many bold and useful science projects being done by brilliant scientists under difficult conditions.

What few people know, however, is that only 20 percent of residents are there for scientific research. The rest of us create and maintain the infrastructure that makes this science possible. In Antarctica, where children are as rare as flowers, it takes a village to raise a scientist.

By far the largest "village" in Antarctica is McMurdo, the USAP hub on Ross Island in the Ross Sea, 2,400 miles due south of our deployment point in Christchurch, New Zealand. (The second largest base, the Amundsen-Scott South Pole Station—with up to 240 summer residents—is also an American installation.)

Most Antarctic bases are populated by ten to one hundred multitaskers. McMurdo, however, bustles with up to *twelve hundred* people in the austral summer months (October through February, when the northern half of the planet is in winter). The vast majority of them are dining-room attendants, carpenters, plumbers, general assistants, shuttle drivers, and so on.

They bake the bread, clean the dormitory and office toilets, operate bulldozers, handle radio communications, and shovel snow. For the most part, my experience was their experience. Although by the end of my decade I'd had my share of excitement in the Antarctic wilderness, most of my time was spent in McMurdo, working ten hours a day and six days a week with friends in a workaday triangle between dormitory, job, and cafeteria.

And though it seems strange to say, this mundane experience makes my perspective on Antarctica unusual. While most books from the Antarctic have been written by explorers, journalists, historians, and scientists, those notables have made up only a small minority of Antarctica's inhabitants.

Even though many of the working residents have stayed longer and seen more, over the last century, only a few support workers (out of tens of thousands) have published books.

In the history of the USAP, the largest community on the ice, Jim Mastro (*Antarctica: A Year at the Bottom of the World*, 2002) and Nicholas Johnson (*Big Dead Place*, 2005) were the first to give voice to our neglected majority. These books look beyond the harsh weather and cute penguins of a typical Antarctic travelogue. Jim, Nicholas, and I write from the wealth of experience gathered during long austral stints, returning year after year to a community rich in oral history and deeply connected to the strange Antarctic landscape.

We share our occupation of the barren landscape with the ghosts of early exploration. Men (and they were all men for the first eighty years) from four different expeditions during the early twentieth century struggled across the volcanic gravel McMurdo has since bulldozed for its roads and buildings.

The wind-worn wooden shed on Hut Point—just beyond our massive cargo pier—is a remnant of Robert Falcon Scott's 1901 *Discovery* expedition, complete with rusting tins of meat on the interior shelves and a ninety-year-old seal carcass outside.

As if in response, across town from Hut Point and looming over McMurdo like the final note in a fugue, a large jarrah-wood cross standing atop Observation Hill commemorates the deaths of Scott and his men on their 1912 *Terra Nova* expedition.

On that final journey, starvation, malnutrition, and severe weather laid the men down just one hundred and thirty miles south of the hut and eleven miles away from their next cache of food.

In between *Discovery* and *Terra Nova*, Sir Ernest Shackleton led his *Nimrod* expedition across Hut Point en route to the South Pole, which, in the end, lay just ninety-seven miles beyond his grasp. He struggled and starved his way back to the hut, just in time to set a shed ablaze as a signal to his northbound ship.

Later, in 1915, the men of the *Aurora* (the second ship of Shackleton's *Endurance* expedition, who planned to cross the continent to Ross Island via the Pole), passed under the shadow of Ob Hill (Observation Hill) as scurvy and storm claimed three of their lives.

Some forty years later, the modern age of Antarctic exploration began in earnest and the roots of McMurdo were put down in a massive operation by the U.S. Navy. Despite storm and cold, thousands of burger-fed sailors from several steel ships moved the makings of a tent city, and eventually a small permanent prefab town, onto the ice-free shores of the southward-pointing Hut Point peninsula of Ross Island. McMurdo became the southernmost port on Earth, and Antarctica was at the doorstep.

During my time on ice, our banter around the dining tables in McMurdo's galley (as the navy-built cafeteria has long been called) often includes reference to these outsized stories of Antarctic exploration. The early tales of men like Shackleton, Scott, and Roald Amundsen, and the navy's hard-won settlement of the ice, remind us of the harshness of the place in which we now enjoy soft-serve ice cream.

Douglas Mawson, an Australian who knew more about Antarctic suffering than most, said that, in the midst of his deprivation, "cocoa was almost intoxicating and even plain beef suet, such as we had in fragments in our hoosh mixture, had acquired a sweet and aromatic taste scarcely to be described . . . as different as chalk is from the richest chocolate cream."

Are we Mawson's descendants or his antithesis? Either way, we revel in our cozy existence in a place that once sponsored such raptures over the benefits of starvation.

As on other frontiers, the successes, the failures, and the noble and ignoble exploits of our pioneers become essential narratives for those of us who have settled into their footprints.

As we find opportunities to leave McMurdo for more remote parts of the ice, and then sense the same human insignificance and fragility they experienced amid the Antarctic austerity, their storied past provides a literary and historic language by which to understand our experience.

This book is my love letter to that storied past and to all that Antarctica has fed me: beauty, wonder, friendship. It is the weaving of my own small story within the wilder tales of hunger and survival from an incredible cast of characters. And *The Roast Penguin Chronicles* is a culinary history of a continent without its own cuisine.

Why? Because no matter where we are on Earth, food is how we taste the world, past and present.

My little exploit, the one Rob's bread was meant to feed, took place in the austral summer of 2001–2. I had been asked to take the lead in a new two-person camp in the Transantarctic Mountains, where we would build and maintain a runway on a minor seven-mile-wide thread of ice called the Odell Glacier. I was told to pack everything we'd need for the full one hundred days on the Odell, because no one knew if there would be a resupply plane or helicopter available to send out an extra stick of butter.

Still reeling from the task of planning three hundred meals—plus snacks—ahead of time, I was particularly pleased when Rob led me between the oversized cauldrons and gleaming bread racks of McMurdo's industrial kitchen toward his secret cache of sourdough.

Looking surreptitiously behind us, he slipped into the walk-in freezer to grab two large bags.

I just stared at him. "This is real food, Robert. We may have to make an altar out of cardboard or ice or something and worship this while we munch on granola bars."

Rob rolled his eyes and smiled. "I hope you find a better use for it than that, Jason."

"I'm sure we will. Let's see, twelve loaves over a hundred days, that's . . . a loaf every eight days.

Oh man, we are all set. This is great. Thank you so much."

"Of course. I'm happy to help. Just be careful out there and let me know how it goes."

I knew I'd have stories for Rob. Something was bound to happen. Two guys, three months, four tents, one glacier, and fifteen boxes of food. It was a recipe for something.

Frank Hurley (skinning penguin) and Ernest Shackleton at Patience Camp

"Our food lies ahead, and death stalks us from behind."
–Sir Ernest Shackleton, *The Heart of the Antarctic*

All Thinking and Talking of Food   1

My dining companion on the Odell Glacier would be Julian Ridley, another Antarctic veteran. Julian had worked in the USAP off and on since 1988, but unlike me hadn't made a life of it. Instead, every few years or so, Julian would quit a software job in California and find a summer gig in McMurdo or at Palmer Station, the small American base on the Antarctic Peninsula. He helped lay the foundation for the Crary Lab, McMurdo's world-class science facility, spent another summer transporting liquid nitrogen to the South Pole, and he entertained himself at Palmer by waterskiing through ice chunks and slush while hoping not to become food for leopard seals. Julian cherished the Antarctic experience so much that he refused to turn it into a mere job. While I returned yearly like a yo-yo, Julian made the journey south only when it felt like a new adventure.

As the date of our departure to the Odell approached, we worked closely to plan and pack our gear and food supplies and were both deeply grateful for the gift of Rob's bread. We each had several years' experience on the ice and could speak to the unpredictability of our meals in far-flung places.

We were also both well versed in the historic Antarctic tales of hungry triumph, hungrier incompetence, and starving tragedy. Julian, in fact, is a living reminder of that history, being a direct descendant of Lieutenant William Colbeck, a member of the 1898–1900 *Southern Cross* expedition, the first to spend a year on the Antarctic continent. Julian's ancestor had suffered acutely amid the difficulty and isolation, and his story was a reminder of the value of good companionship and decent food.

Only a small fraction of the Antarctic coast (and none of the interior) had been mapped, yet the *Southern Cross* set ten men and their hut on the desolate shoreline of Cape Adare, on the edge of the Ross Sea, before sailing away through the ice. With no guarantee that the ship would return safely a year later, and no communication beyond the windswept beach they occupied, the men of the *Southern Cross* expedition were perhaps the most isolated on Earth as the new century dawned. William Colbeck soon tasted the dark emptiness of Antarctic seclusion where, unlike the Arctic, it is nearly impossible to live off the stark and mesmerizing land. His companions (Norwegian, Sámi, and British) were his entire world.

As it turned out, pleasant company was in short supply. The leader, Carsten Borchgrevink, who surreptitiously drank much of the crew's liquor, transmogrified through the dark winter months from odd duck into infuriating tyrant. Trapped with him on the darkened edge of the Earth, his stressed group of young men put up with random declarations of power and a demand for oaths of loyalty. While admitting no fault, Borchgrevink felt the stress too. "We were getting sick of each other's company," he wrote. "We knew each line in each other's faces."

Worse, as gales, anxiety, and resentment shook their small hut for months, Colbeck's meals followed each other in a sad monotony: porridge with buttered bread and either bacon or ham at breakfast, dinners of milk soup or sweet soup, pressed/tinned meat or dried fish, and tinned or dry vegetables. Meals "lasted, on great occasions, ten minutes; often less than five minutes on ordinary occasions," admitted Borchgrevink. Each bland tin of food could only remind them of their own confinement. Borchgrevink's one attempt at baking produced an inedible loaf that Colbeck's comrade Louis Bernacchi later wrote was "still in the Antarctic regions on the left hand top corner of the shelf inside the hut."

On some days, expedition members merely lay in their bunks through their waking hours. Bernacchi described them listening to a Sámi companion singing "in the most sepulchral tones. One 'sucks' melancholy from these songs as a weasel sucks eggs."

One hundred and one years later, with such history in mind, Colbeck's great-grandson and I made our preparations to camp together deep in Antarctica's otherworldly landscape. Julian began a journal he titled "100 Days after 100 Years." We each sensed what might go wrong—disagreements or misunderstandings intensified by close quarters—in a two-person camp over a long Antarctic summer. Like most of the men of the *Southern Cross* expedition, Julian and I began our journey as strangers, having met just two weeks earlier. The friend I had hired dropped out at the last minute, and Julian, on the recommendation of a mutual acquaintance, was able to fill in. Julian, who was living in New Zealand, quit his computing job to meet me at a bar in Christchurch on my way south.

Born English, but a Californian since childhood, Julian is a well-mannered gentleman with a passion for surfing. He smiles at least once in every conversation and manages to wear even puffy insulated Antarctic clothing like a pressed suit. At six feet five inches, Julian is four inches taller than I am and has a slight tall-man's stoop that gives the impression that he bows gently when speaking.

In our first pleasant, careful meeting over Christchurch microbrews, we laid the groundwork for the diplomacy and adventure before us. We smiled, talked of mutual acquaintances and our ice histories, listened closely to each other's answers, but did not talk business. Rather, we genially toasted our future success. Neither of us had done as long or as isolated an Antarctic journey as we had before us, and we were both excited. I left for McMurdo the next day and Julian followed a week later.

Out on the Odell, we'd have two goals: first, to build and maintain an emergency runway for planes weathered out of landing in McMurdo and too short on fuel to go anyplace else. The New York Air National Guard (NYANG)—who fly the USAP's cargo in large LC-130 Hercules aircraft from New Zealand to McMurdo and then distribute it to sites around the continent—wanted an alternate landing site. Many times each summer, a storm or fog makes landing in McMurdo dangerous. Julian and I would be in charge of NYANG's "last chance" landing field.

Our other goal: to be good company, with only each other to look at for ninety days. Sanity in an Antarctic field camp starts with good food or, failing that, a good attitude toward the food you've got. Luckily, Julian and I would have access to the best supplies in the USAP and, more importantly, we'd share a similar approach to cooking: Start with dessert, make simple meals, and keep the food coming.

Unlike the *Southern Cross* expedition, we were not bringing a ton of compressed potatoes or butter in hundredweights.

Nor were we packing chartreuse, champagne, or twenty-eight tons of Spratt's dog biscuits. We would be well supplied, however, with provisions generally familiar to Julian's great-grandfather: a modern mix of carbs, fats, sweets, and yes, plenty of cans. We had no intention of ending like so many historic Antarctic travelers: overzealous, underfed, scurvy-ridden, and chewing on their dogs. Chewing on our snowmobiles would be of little use, in any event, so we padded our food lists and considered praying to the ghost of Sir Ernest Shackleton to see us through.

A legendary leader, gifted storyteller, lover of poetry, and a survivor of sagas, Shackleton has become Antarctica's symbol and patron saint. He was tough, intuitive, and charming enough to talk his way out of the merchant navy and into the elite world of polar exploration.

It's worth exploring Shackleton's adventures in depth, because his incredible tales convey not just drama, but an understanding of how food (and the desperate lack of it) informs Antarctic history.

the high-water mark of gastronomic luxury

Although he is the most famous of Antarcticans, Shackleton struggled and starved his way through three major expeditions and died without his Christmas dinner at the start of his fourth. He may, therefore, not be the most auspicious saint of Antarctic cuisine.

On his first journey—as a secondary figure on Robert Falcon Scott's *Discovery* expedition—he was invalided home after a bout with scurvy during an abortive sledging trip across the Ross Ice Shelf. (The captain of the resupply ship that brought Shackleton home was none other than William Colbeck, who despite his dark year with Borchgrevink, still craved the Antarctic experience—a craving inherited by his great-grandson.)

But whatever the odds, Shackleton was a survivor. I love his remarkable narrative of the last weeks of his second venture, the 1907–9 *Nimrod* expedition. He and his three companions—Jameson Adams, Dr. Eric Marshall, and Frank Wild—were trudging back to McMurdo Sound after a remarkably stoic attempt to reach the South Pole.

Each day stretched their rations and brought the men to the brink of starvation. In four months, they had only one full meal.

During the climax of this drama, Shackleton scrawled very brief diary entries that always noted his group's overpowering hunger:

> February 7, 1909: "Blowing hard blizzard. Kept going till 6 p.m. Adams and Marshall renewed dysentery. Dead tired. Short food; very weak."
>
> February 8: "Started from camp in blizzard. Adams and Marshall still dysentery; Wild and I all right. Feel starving for food. Talk of it all day. Anyhow, getting north, thank God. Sixty-nine miles to Chinaman [pony meat] depot."
>
> February 9: "Strong following blizzard, and did 14½ miles to north. Adams not fit yet. All thinking and talking of food."

February 10: "Strong following wind. Did 20 miles
300 yards. Temperature plus 22 degrees Fahr. All
thinking and talking of food."

The group's thin hooshes of pemmican, crushed biscuit,
pony fodder, and rancid pony meat could not compensate for
the thousands of calories burned daily while hauling their
heavy sledge. When each man was down to a ration of just
four "miserably thin" biscuits per day, Shackleton gave one
of his to the dysentery-weakened Frank Wild.

"I do not suppose that anyone else in the world," wrote
Wild in his diary, "can thoroughly realize how much
generosity and sympathy was shown by this. I do by god I
shall never forget it."

Hjalmar Johansen and some of the forty-two thousand biscuits he counted and packed

Wild was less generous in his comments on Adams and
Marshall, who he called "those two grub-scoffing, useless
beggars." Marshall, in particular, "does not pull the weight of

his food, the big, hulking, lazy hog," though it was Marshall who found the strength to reach a depot when the other men had collapsed after forty starving hours.

Marshall had earlier handed out cocaine- and caffeine-based Forced March tablets from the medical kit when the food ran out, but to little avail.

Shackleton understood how close they all were to the edge. "Our food lies ahead," he scribbled with a frostbitten hand, "and death stalks us from behind."

By the end, their limbs clumsy with cold, Shackleton's team were a collection of shivering vital organs moving desperately forward. They had wagered their lives on the idea that they could sustain themselves with the skimpy depots of food and fuel they had cached at intervals between the Pole and home.

"We could not joke about food," Shackleton said, but he and his companions schemed and argued about it daily and dreamed about it at night.

On the march, they described previous feasts and fantasized about the banquets they would lay out for each other if they reached civilization.

One fantasy included a day of feasting at home with six huge, elaborate meals—upon waking, then at 8:00 a.m., 11:00 a.m., 1:00 p.m., 3:45 p.m., and 6:00 p.m.—and then at midnight a really big meal, just before we go to bed.

There will be melon, grilled trout and butter-sauce, roast chicken with plenty of livers, a proper salad with eggs and very thick dressing, green peas and new potatoes, a saddle of mutton, fried suet pudding, peaches *a la Melba*, egg curry, plum pudding and sauce, Welsh rarebit, Queen's pudding, angels on horseback, cream cheese and celery, fruit, nuts, port wine, milk and cocoa.

They kept up this very serious fantasizing for hours throughout the day, and for days throughout the death march. They tightened their belts and looked forward, sitting down at each meal, not to angels on horseback (oysters wrapped in bacon), but to small portions of hoosh with stringy, dysentery-inducing pieces of a pony named, appropriately enough, Grisi.

The long marches were also spent inventing new courses for the others to appreciate or critique. "No French chef ever devoted more thought to the invention of new dishes than we did," Shackleton later wrote.

At the "high-water mark of gastronomic luxury" was Frank Wild's "Wild roll": a generous portion of mincemeat wrapped in rashers of fat bacon, set into a thick pastry, and fried in a pan full of fat. Shackleton's personal best, "which I must admit I put forward with a good deal of pride as we marched over the snow," was a sardine pasty made with at least ten tins of sardines.

Shackleton later admitted that they forgot about Antarctica in their suffering.

The "glory of the high mountains" and the "majesty of the enormous glaciers," which they were the first humans to see, did not excite them. Instead, in the final days of the *Nimrod* expedition, their calorie-starved bellies grumbled their daily prayers amid the wilderness of ice.

It is a keen reminder to those of us who would venture into that wilderness that while beauty may be in the eye of the beholder, appreciation of it begins with a full belly.

◖ penny cookery ◗

But like all Antarcticans, actual and armchair, Julian and I both prefer the extraordinary drama of Shackleton's third and most famous expedition, the 1914–17 *Endurance* saga, a tale of shipwreck, castaways, desperate rescue journeys, and superb leadership. Few published adventures can compare. Leaving aside that the expedition never actually made it to the continent, and that Shackleton's *Endurance* tale really has more in common with the long and noble history of Arctic shipwrecks than Antarctic terrestrial exploration, it is a good thing to honor the story.

Julian and I would be wise to emulate the expedition's greatest survival tools: boundless patience and relentless optimism. That the *Endurance* crew all survived is the stuff of legend; *how* they survived is food for thought. With the ambitious goal of crossing the Antarctic continent, Shackleton left England at the onset of World War I. When the *Endurance* arrived at the whaling station on the subantarctic island of South Georgia, the venerable, hard-bitten Norwegian sailors there told Shackleton that the ice of the Weddell Sea was too extensive, too dangerous that year. But with the now-or-never realities of an indebted expedition, Shackleton drove his ship south regardless. The ice opened to the *Endurance*, then closed around it just sixty miles away from the continent.

By the following summer, all that remained was a pile of magnificent splinters sent to the bottom of the Weddell Sea.

Their last meal on board was eaten in silence as the ship's great timbers broke beneath them. The greatest endurance shown In the *Endurance* expedition was not in the arduous moments of crisis—though there were plenty of those—but rather in the long, hungry months of waiting, initially on the broken ice floes of the Weddell Sea.

Although it is hard for us today to imagine true disconnect from the world, place yourself among the encampment of these sailors and scientists on the shifting, snow-covered sea ice, over a thousand miles from the nearest humans, several thousand feet above the sea floor, with no method of communication beyond their thin voices. (A wireless radio on the ship had failed.)

The fragmented gyre of Weddell Sea pack ice they occupied was like a flat white Europe in demented motion, not unlike the World War I landscape the men had left behind. As they rotated slowly through the Antarctic summer, the men sat, slept, and fought fear and boredom on a slushy, transient surface. The soft, often ruptured ice made travel impossible. One sailor wrote in his journal that it was a "hard, rough, jolly life, this marching and camping ... working as hard as the human physique is capable of on a minimum of food." When Shackleton ordered the crew to step into harness like beasts of burden and "manhaul" their boats toward the Antarctic Peninsula, they managed a mere seven and a half miles after seven days of extreme effort. They stopped and awaited their fate for the next 103 days in the aptly named Patience Camp.

Their average day's food consisted of half a pound of seal with three-quarters of a pint of tea for breakfast, one four-ounce bannock (flat unleavened bread) with milk for lunch, and three-quarters of a pint of seal hoosh for supper. Seal blubber was eaten raw, fried, and boiled. Shackleton kept his men's spirits up by planning slightly different menus each week, and by occasionally mixing in one of the remaining treats saved from the ship—jam, or anchovies in oil, for example.

At Christmas, he broke out canned peaches, cold mutton, curried prawns, jam, figs, and onions. Still, men were hungry. Some combed the snow for crumbs, others fantasized aloud about food, and eventually Shackleton ordered the last of the sled dogs killed and butchered. The last of the cocoa was drunk, and old seal flippers and heads were dug out of the slush for their remnants of rancid fat.

One problem was that there were simply too many men. The *Endurance* sailors were never intended to winter over with the expedition team. With stores salvaged from the crushed ship and steady success killing seals and penguins, they could live for some time. But when hunting grew inconsistent, rations decreased.

Thomas Orde-Lees, anxious keeper of the stores, wrote that "no housewife ever had more to do than we have in making a little go a long way."

Perhaps the most valuable food in the hold of the *Endurance* was the supply of half-pound Bovril rations, bricks of condensed sledging food meant for the transcontinental crossing, each one calculated as a one-man, 2,864-calorie meal. An amalgam of lard, oatmeal, beef and vegetable protein, salt, and sugar, the Bovril rations melted in hot water into a thick hoosh like a dense pea soup.

Much of it was saved, however, for the difficult times ahead; Shackleton knew that their time on the ice, however trying, was merely prelude for the trials to come.

Indeed, five months later the ice fragmented and melted beneath the twenty-eight men. They crowded into three small boats and desperately launched into a chaos of ice and storm. Ironically, their last meal before jumping into the boats was their first full meal in months.

Some food wouldn't fit in the boats, and Shackleton figured "every pound eaten [was] a pound saved."

For five days they fought for their lives against crushing floes, gales, hypothermia and frostbite, wild currents, freezing spray, hunger, and dehydration.

The men slept little, piled together in the bottom of the boats and hugging each other for warmth when they weren't rowing for their lives. Hot meals were makeshift and far between, made by their cook, Charles Green, with his improvised blubber stove on unsteady ice floes while the crew worked to keep the boats off the crushing ice edge. "Never did a cook work under more anxious scrutiny," observed Shackleton.

Their only water came as ice chips from bergy bits picked up in passage. Dehydration worsened until lips cracked and tongues hardened. Though chunks of bloody seal meat seemed at first to quench thirst, their saltiness only made it worse. Some men were so miserable with seasickness that they could not eat. Frank Worsley, captain of the *Endurance*, wrote that the crew could only watch jealously while sea birds dove into the waters around them for small fish, "picking them up like sardines off toast."

Worsley also noted Shackleton's great leadership skills in crisis: "He seemed to keep a mental finger on each man's pulse. If he noted one with signs of the strain telling on him he ordered hot milk and soon all would be swallowing the scalding, life-giving drink to the especial benefit of the man, all unaware, for whom it had been ordered."

Throughout the hundred-hour ordeal, nearly all the men kept up appearances, making jokes when they could— bartering matches for future bottles of champagne—but Shackleton noted that when on the third day he asked men to keep an eye out for a suitable floe to cook on, he could gauge each man's hunger by how eagerly they pointed out suitable ice.

In the end, when they scraped up onto the rocks of Elephant Island, Green was immediately offloaded to begin an all-day cooking session for men who were either "crazed by their privations," as photographer Frank Hurley put it, or at least drunk with pleasure at stepping onto solid land for the first time in nearly five hundred days. Ten days after arrival, knowing that no rescuer would ever think to look for them on Elephant, Shackleton took five men with him in the twenty-two-foot *James Caird* to seek help. It became the most celebrated small-boat journey in modern history, a seventeen-day, eight-hundred-mile miracle back to South Georgia through the worst seas on the planet.

But those twenty-two men he left behind knew only that his mission was a likely death sentence. Their lives were desperately tied to his. Blind to Shackleton's fate, they remained on the barren shoreline of Elephant Island for more than four months after his departure, not knowing if he had died at sea or if they too should put to sea with little sustenance and no safe destination.

Every day they hoped against hope, harvested the occasional seal or penguin, scraped limpets off rocks at low tide, and scanned the horizon for a ship. Their hero during this time was their leader, Frank Wild, who kept their misery at bay with a hard schedule and a harder optimism. Each day he woke the men, rolled up his sleeping bag, and said, "Get your things ready, boys, the boss may come today."

And well he should cheer them on. The Elephant Islanders lived an impossible existence under two small, overturned boats, their faces and clothes blackened by blubber smoke, their diet a pathetic litany of small hooshes littered with sand, penguin feathers, and reindeer hairs shed from the sleeping bags of the men living atop the thwarts.

Meat and fat were everywhere. Their improvised stove burned ten blubbery penguin skins a day. Orde-Lees, sleeping on the ground near their indoor abattoir, once found half a pound of putrefying meat under his sleeping bag, and another time a pool of penguin blood. Despite the filth, the expedition doctors used the greasy hoosh pot to sterilize instruments for the amputation of former stowaway Perce Blackborow's gangrenous frostbit toes.

Breakfast consisted of a small piece of seal or half a penguin breast each. Lunch might be a biscuit or chunks of blubber already squeezed for oil to supply the lamps.

A favorite dessert was pudding made with two days' biscuit ration saved in a canvas bag, crushed into powder, then boiled with a little sugar. Supper was minced seal or penguin fried up in seal blubber. The men all craved carbohydrates, particularly dumplings.

Somehow a small "penny cookery book" had survived the journey, and from it each night one — only one — recipe was read aloud, like a passage from the Bible. Serious discussion followed, with amendments proposed and debated before they slept and dreamed of unattainable meals

On Midwinter Day, the still-celebrated Antarctic milestone that in temperate regions is called the summer solstice, they gorged happily on a pudding of "powdered biscuit boiled with twelve pieces of moldy nut-food."

Soon they were gnawing on old seal bones and harvesting inedible seaweed. Four months was a long time to wait, cheerfully starving, for someone who set off in a small boat across eight hundred miles of the world's worst ocean.

The *James Caird* crew—Shackleton, Frank Worsley, Thomas Crean, Tim McCarthy, John Vincent, and Harry McNeish—had rounded Elephant, slipped between uncounted icebergs, then put themselves at the mercy of the mighty westerly winds of the Southern Ocean.

At times, great rollers towered over their little mast, blocking the gales and turning the sail slack. Mostly, however, they were driven like ghosts before the dawn. Shackleton carried just one month's food for six men.

There was no need to deprive the Elephant Islanders of more, as after a month the men of the *James Caird* would either be drowned, blown past South Georgia into certain death in the wide South Atlantic, or safe and warm for the first time in seven months.

Frank Worsley's navigation skills somehow reckoned them accurately toward the small island. Waves broke over the *Caird* constantly, wetting the men day and night.

Time ticked by, measured not in sleep (which they rarely got in their sodden sleeping bags laid across angular ballast stones), nor in the passage of the sun (which hid behind clouds), but in the meals they somehow made aboard their battered little cork.

To cook, Worsley and Crean wedged themselves on either side of the boat with the cooker pressed firmly between their feet. Worsley held the hoosh pot and raised it "whenever the boat gave a madder leap than usual." They all ate it straight after boiling, preferring a burnt mouth to a lukewarm body.

Eating was maddening, as they were crouched so low beneath the decking that their chests pushed down onto their stomachs.

Alternatively, Worsley said, they could lie loose on rough stones and the corners of boxes like "a Roman emperor reclining luxuriously at an epicurean banquet." At night, Shackleton ordered relief in the form of scalding milk every four hours, which they kept up until they ran out of water in the last days of the journey.

Just offshore of South Georgia, thirst and hurricane winds savaged them for a day in which the hoosh pot was good only for desperate, constant bailing. The next day, they slipped between reefs to a landing, then fell to their knees to drink from pools of glacial meltwater.

They were ragged and weak and trapped on the wrong side of the mountainous island, but they did not care. Manna from heaven arrived in the form of fourteen-pound albatross chicks, nesting in the tussock grass above their stony beach.

An adult albatross like a guardian angel had floated behind them much of the way from Elephant Island, and Worsley had estimated that the bird, with the fierce westerlies at its back, could have made their eight-hundred-mile trip in ten hours. Now, as if ritually consuming their talisman, they ate everything—succulent flesh, soft bone, and jellied broth—in a hoosh that they would remember for the rest of their lives.

There was a law against killing albatross, but these men were "a law unto themselves, and looked it." There was a note of compassion, but it didn't last. "The first time I killed one I felt like a murderer," Worsley wrote, "the second time a little less bad, and after that I just thought what a fine meal they would make, and what a glorious feed the first had been."

Vincent and McNeish were near death, and the others were as feeble as invalids. After recovering on a diet of albatross and elephant seal, Shackleton, Crean, and Worsley began the last leg of their odyssey across the unknown interior of South Georgia to a whaling station on the other side. Each man carried three days of Bovril sledging rations and biscuits stuffed in a sock.

The carpenter's adze became an ice axe. As they climbed up and down the ragged, wind-blasted peaks of mountains that stood in the way of the planet's fiercest weather, each quick hoosh was made by chipping a hole in the snow for the Primus stove, firing it up and waiting for the boil. Sometimes they lay around the hole as an additional windbreak.

They made jokes but were careful not to laugh. "Laughter was in our hearts," said Shackleton, "though not on our parched and cracked lips."

Soon they abandoned the empty Primus, descended the mountains, and arrived at the Norwegian whaling station where they were received first like dangerous troglodytes, then like hungry heroes. They were given cake, bread, scones, jam, and coffee.

For one hundred days after his salvation, Shackleton tried and failed repeatedly—once stopped by the ice a mere eighteen miles away—to rescue the Elephant Islanders with borrowed ships. In his anxiety for their safety, he aged and turned gray. Only on the fourth mission did they succeed.

On August 30, 1916, the twenty-two castaways were preparing a lunch hoosh of limpets, seaweed, and stewed seal bones under the overturned boats. When the shout of "Ship

O!" came from outside, the beloved hoosh pot was kicked over in a mad rush. Wild gave the word to Frank Hurley to light the beacon, "and soon," wrote Hurley, "a goodly pile of penguin skins and seal blubber was sending a dense, oily smoke-signal across the sky."

On board and heading home, Shackleton was rejuvenated in the presence of his entire crew. Not a man was lost, and every man could eat to his heart's content. In *South*, his magnificent account of the expedition, Shackleton closes the tale with these lines: "You readers can imagine my feelings as I stood in the little cabin watching my rescued comrades feeding."

Indeed we could.

Arrival on Elephant Island: first food and drink in three and a half days

Suggested Menu: Breakfast, Lunch, Dinner, Dessert

For breakfast:
Seal brain on toast with fried bacon, baked tomatoes, stewed fruit, cereal, porridge, tea and coffee.

For lunch:
Casserole of seal liver, creamed potatoes, French beans, cheese, roll and butter.

For dinner:
Casserole of cormorant, creamed potatoes, baked tomatoes, and green peas.

For dessert:
Fruit salad and cream, devils on horseback

The Secret Society of Unconventional Cooks

2

Neither Julian nor I have ever been cooks by trade or habit. We're definitely not chefs or gourmands. Perhaps we emulate writer and naturalist Henry David Thoreau, who when asked by Ralph Waldo Emerson during a meal which dish he preferred, said simply, "The nearest."

I have a long and peaceable relationship with gruel, having done a few thousand miles of backwoods canoeing and hiking. I can chew on the same things for weeks.

These days, my wife Heather and I enjoy simple, healthy, country fare, mostly vegetables from our garden, chicken and turkey raised by family or local farms, and venison and moose hunted in the Maine woods. That said, I also value the play of fine food in my mouth and am willing to work at it once in a while. More importantly, I honor those who cook it for me.

But Julian wasn't clamoring to be the lead cook for our expedition. In fact, it was pretty clear I was in charge. Julian, who ate whatever was put in front of him, told me he was elated when he learned that I liked to cook, and was therefore "happy owning the latter part of the cooking process, being the dishes."

Years of burned grilled cheese sandwiches and cookies had taken their toll on his confidence in the kitchen. And besides, he said, he had a "dysfunctional perfectionism" when it came to dishes, which would be a challenge in a tent on a remote Antarctic glacier.

So we were both content, knowing what to expect from each other, and knowing we would have no complaints. I'd make big simple meals, we would both demolish them as only tall skinny men can do, and he would scrub the pots.

Despite our mutual fascination with Antarctic history, we could not hope to dine on galantine of seal, black pudding made with seal's blood, or Adélie penguin cutlets.

Not that we had a choice: For one thing, cooking Antarctic wildlife is illegal these days, and even if it weren't, there was no wildlife to cook. During our three months on the glacier, Julian and I constituted nearly the entire biomass of the region.

Yet there was plenty for us to feast on in the stories of early Antarctic exploration, the era known as the "heroic age," which in recent years has been represented most often by Shackleton's exploits.

The heroic age (a nostalgic term perhaps first applied in 1956) began in the late 1890s with the *Belgica* and *Southern Cross* expeditions and ended in 1922 with Shackleton's death aboard the *Quest* and his burial in a grave on South Georgia. But Shackleton's tales and a few other dramatic efforts to be the first to stand at the blank spot known as the South Pole are only appetizers for a far greater history.

Early Antarctic exploration offers a collection of deeply compelling stories of human endeavor, in which crushing sea ice, hurricane-force blizzards, frostbite, crevasses, starvation, and scurvy all flavor a history of humans hurling themselves against the white wall of the Antarctic for geographic conquest, scientific discovery, and personal adventure.

"Nowhere in Western literature," as historian Stephen Pyne wrote, "is there a more compelling, sustained chronicle of life, humanity, and civilization reduced to their minima." Julian and I (and our fellow modern Antarcticans) have certainly been compelled by these astonishing chronicles, many of which we consume like cultural pemmican: a dense, rich broth of local history.

Were they heroes? If the requirements for heroic status include a willingness to attempt the unknown, extreme effort without recourse to assistance, a desire to risk one's life for one's country, or inspiring leadership in crisis, then there were plenty of heroes in the heroic age.

If, however, such status requires abilities beyond the reach of normal men, or the capacity to plan appropriately according to the best available knowledge, or that the work they were doing was actually necessary, then the list dwindles.

In *Slicing the Silence: Voyaging to Antarctica*, Tom Griffiths peels back some layers: "The heroic era of Antarctic exploration was 'heroic' because it was anachronistic before it began, its goal was as abstract as a pole, its central figures were romantic, manly and flawed, its drama was moral (for it mattered not only what was done but how it was done), and its ideal was national honour." The heroism, as it's been perceived, often owes as much to how well the explorers told their story as to what they accomplished. A century later, the most popular Antarctic explorers are those who wrote most lyrically about the experience in their books.

It's easy enough to love Shackleton's stories, for example, but perhaps the search for heroes should take us deeper into the full menu of Antarctic characters.

A good place to start is in the kitchen, because even on a ship of heroes, the cook is still working harder than anyone else. Perhaps that makes the Antarctic cook a superhero.

ᘿ like someone from a novel ᖰ

Certainly there are rarer, more unusual stories to tell. Few people know about Jean-Baptiste Charcot's 1903–5 French Antarctic Expedition, which settled in for a year to practice excellent science and boldly reveal new lands along the Antarctic Peninsula with little drama.

Fewer will mention Rozo, Charcot's mysterious cook. No one knew his real name or age. His bare feet tucked into worn slippers, Rozo padded up and down the corridors of the *Français* as it lay frozen in a tiny harbor at Booth Island. All through the harsh winter, he baked bread three times a week and perfect croissants on Friday and Sunday for demanding Frenchmen while the Antarctic night raged around them.

When the sun and wildlife returned, Rozo used cormorant and penguin eggs to bake fine cakes and custards. An enigma, he had joined the southbound expedition in Buenos Aires at the last minute and disappeared afterward back into his itinerant life, another example of how the soul of the kitchen leaves only a faint trace in the mouth of history.

Rozo, summed up by Charcot as "an unusual man," seemed to his shipmates to have been everywhere and done everything. "He was certainly well educated and would walk around everywhere, watchfully observant," said Charcot. "He was like someone from a novel, and we almost expected him to arrive one day and announce . . . that he knew a very easy way to the Pole itself."

Rozo carried on conversations with his friend Toby, the expedition's pet pig, and refused to wear socks. (At home, where fashion was a concern, he attached the top of a pair of stockings to his boots so that he could look appropriate if his pant legs were pulled up.)

Rozo, an unusual man

Rozo roasted penguin cutlets, made black pudding from seal's blood and liver (which "ranked among our *plats de fête*," wrote Charcot), surprised the crew from time to time with new *patisseries*, and generally served up fare from cans and wildlife alike that pleased all palates. Charcot's final analysis: Rozo "was extremely resourceful, an excellent cook and baker, hardworking and obliging, an outstandingly good seaman, and we certainly could not have done better."

Like Rozo, Bill Smith of William Bruce's 1902–4 Scottish National Antarctic Expedition put on a fine display of talent and idiosyncrasy. Smith was a rogue and a storyteller—"At yarning it was a case of one man first and the rest nowhere," wrote a shipmate—but he took excellent care of his crew in Omond House, their small stone hut built on the shore of Laurie Island in the South Orkneys.

Smith cooked fine meals of seal and penguin meat daily, Gentoos being the favorite species among the several hundred penguins stacked like frozen cordwood outside the door. And the Scotsmen needed feeding; during the penguin nesting season, Smith served up to fifteen penguin eggs *per man* per day.

Smith's solid build told the story of his own good cooking, and his wild tales of his itinerant cook's life—real or invented—relayed his salty experiences and adventures around the globe. A good cook and the keeper of the social flame, Smith was the one to maintain a flow of good spirits, his Zen-like philosophy politely quoted as "Life's too—short for a funeral."

The least-known cook of the heroic age might be Chikasaburo Watanabe of Nobu Shirase's 1910–12 Japanese *Kainan Maru* (Southern Pioneer) expedition.

The expedition itself was an anomaly at the time and remains little known, with Shirase's account remaining untranslated until 2011.

The crew of the *Kainan Maru* ate some foods common to European expeditions — rice, potatoes, biscuits, peas, and onions, for example — and had picked up some canned New Zealand beef on their way south, but the larder was stocked with items unique in the heroic age, including miso, dried cuttlefish, and pickled plums.

As for Watanabe, it's known that the twenty-seven-year-old cook played a role in one of the expedition's few successes. In their exploration of the Alexandra Mountains on the Edward VII Peninsula, a corner of West Antarctica, crewmembers split into several groups.

Watanabe climbed with his steward, Genzō Nishikawa, as partner. Their only food a tin of beef and another of condensed milk, they navigated a series of steep ice slopes and crevasses until a blizzard overtook them at midnight.

At their limit, they erected a board commemorating the "Dai-Nippon South Polar Expedition Coast Landing Party." Looking inland from their final vantage point, according to the brave two-man kitchen crew who were the first to stand on this point in the Antarctic emptiness, "not a dust mote was to be seen."

In the mystique of Rozo, Smith, and Watanabe resides an Antarctic ideal: the peripatetic eccentric, the multitasker amid extremity, the angel at the blubber stove. So many of us in this century of Antarctic exploration and settlement are deep travelers, unresolved adults, mystics, misfits, wandering philosophers, romantics, curmudgeons, or seekers. Men like Rozo led the way.

Neither scientist nor leader, he was the classic Antarctic generalist, a creative talent who wore many hats but served few masters. And like him, the transient Antarctic residents in his shadow will leave few marks of their contributions to exploration and science but the odd photograph or occasional anecdote. Antarctic culture, from the penguin-eating

Frenchmen aboard the *Français* to the cheerful snow-shovelers at today's South Pole, has been sustained by the Rozos, who over a century of time and frigid space have cobbled hot meals out of thin air.

the most important personage on the ship

Yet it must be admitted that the Antarctic expedition cook did not always live up to this ideal, or even to basic expectations. Those whose names do not brighten heroic age history fall into two categories: troublemakers or incompetents.

Adrien de Gerlache's 1897–99 *Belgica* expedition sacked two cooks before reaching Antarctic waters, due to fighting and drunken insubordination.

Gerlache reported that their only remaining choice, the ship's steward, Louis Michotte, was "quite unconsciously prepared to violate the most basic rules of cooking." His pastries were "boardlike," the success of his breads "a matter of chance," and his only success was soup, though that amounted to opening a can.

As the ill-prepared crew of the *Belgica* spent an unplanned winter trapped in the sea ice, according to expedition doctor Frederick Cook, Michotte began "racking his brain to devise some new dishes to appease our fickle appetites."

Gerlache, as a scrupulous leader, had written out a twenty-eight-day menu composed of various tinned meals, but Michotte insisted on mixing the already tasteless foods. "His soups are full of 'mystery,'" said Cook, "and the 'embalmed meats' are on every tongue for condemnation."

But there is a certain authority in a cook, even one as bad as Michotte. When Captain Georges Lecointe saw the form of a beautiful woman in a nearby iceberg, everyone gently agreed. Then the ship's naturalist imagined it to be a polar bear; the sailors swore it was on the prowl. But soon Michotte giggled and said, "No, it's a pot of boiling soup."

"Next to the Captain the cook is the most important personage on the ship; there are short instances when he even rises above the Captain," noted Cook. "It was so in this case." Everyone soon agreed the likeness to a pot of soup was obvious. "We dared not do otherwise, for it meant no soup to-morrow."

Robert Falcon Scott's 1902-4 *Discovery* expedition also went through two cooks before settling on a third. The first, Sydney Roper, "became too big for his boots" while the ship was stocking up in New Zealand, according to Scott.

The replacement, Henry Brett, was worse, a lousy cook, scoundrel, teller of tales (some of the crew estimated Brett as having lived almost six centuries' worth of adventures and voyages), and a "thorough knave" to whom the men, if they had their way, would do "something slow with boiling oil." Brett's biggest offense, in Scott's view, was that "he is dirty — an unforgivable crime in a cook."

Things had gone badly early with Brett, an insolent civilian in Scott's naval hierarchy. Feeling bound to naval discipline, and with nowhere to banish a man already at the end of the Earth, Scott locked Brett in irons for eight hours, which "brought him to his senses and a condition of whining humility."

In 1903, when Lieutenant Colbeck arrived on the *Morning* with Scott's relief expedition, Brett shipped out. Neither Roper nor Brett earned a mention in Scott's account of the *Discovery* journey.

Robert Falcon Scott in the Cape Evans hut, October 1911

Taking Brett's place in the *Discovery* galley was the popular baker and cook's mate, Charles Clarke. Even before Brett left, Clarke was beloved for his fine bread and what Scott called his "toothsome cakes." Little was said about his qualities as a cook, however.

Although Clarke was nominally in charge of the galley, he focused on baking, and the cooking was "conducted more or less by a committee of taste," wrote Scott, putting the best possible spin on the situation.

Volunteers took turns serving as Clarke's mate or taking charge of meals, which sometimes failed, sometimes worked admirably, but to Scott's relief were at least "prepared with a proper regard for cleanliness."

German expeditions suffered at least as much as their British and Belgian counterparts. Richard Lehmann was apparently one of the ringleaders of some trouble brewed up early on the voyage of the 1901–3 German South Polar Expedition, causing expedition leader Erich von Drygalski to boot him off the *Gauss* in Capetown, South Africa.

A decade later, Wilhelm Filchner, leader of the 1911–12 Second German South Polar Expedition, had to cope with his cook Karl Klück siding against him during the ugliest psychological battle of the heroic age.

The *Deutschland* crew had joined their insane, scheming Captain Vahsel (apparently suffering the final mental ravages of syphilis) in his perverse loathing for the expedition leader. Filchner was diplomatic, offering a sentence or two to praise Klück as the best possible cook of seal meat and to describe his excellent three-course lunches (e.g., milk soup, seal meat sauerbraten with cauliflower, chocolate pudding with vanilla sauce) and dinners (such as seal stew with roast potatoes, Baltic herring roll-ups, and penguin heart and liver stew). "We could be extremely satisfied with our cook," said Filchner, though the mutinous Klück scarcely exists in the official account.

Likewise, William Roberts of the 1907–9 *Nimrod* expedition earned just a few bland mentions in Shackleton's *Heart of the Antarctic* account. Years later, a visitor to the Cape Royds hut whose kitchen was Roberts's domain thought that

"Shackleton's men must have fed like turkey cocks for all the delicacies here: boiled chicken, kidneys, mushrooms, ginger, Garibaldi biscuits, soups of all kinds," so we know at least that Roberts did not lack for variety.

Elsewhere, Roberts, nicknamed "Bobs," is described as a talented cook but rough and antagonistic. In short, Bobs never seemed to like anybody. And some didn't like him. Alistair Mackay, a short-tempered surgeon, nearly choked Roberts to death for repeatedly setting his boots up on Mackay's locker. An expedition member who revisited the cold, silent hut several years later almost expected to hear "Bobs' raucous voice cursing me for my clumsiness." Not surprisingly, Roberts is the only *Nimrod* member whose post-expedition life is a complete mystery. Like Rozo, he simply disappeared.

galantine versus hotcakes

The two best-documented cooks of the heroic age were those involved in the "race" to the South Pole between Britain's Robert Falcon Scott and Norway's Roald Engebreth Gravning Amundsen.

No human had reached the South Pole, and there was fame and national honor at stake. Hundreds of miles apart but heading to the same point (90° South), each team would sledge partway to lay some initial caches of food and fuel (to utilize on the return portion of the Pole journey) during the summer of their arrival in Antarctica.

They would then return to their huts to make final plans over the long winter before heading south again early the next summer. Neither group would know how their competition fared until one made it to the Pole before the other. While their bosses carried their nations' torches southward, their cooks fed the fire. *How* they cooked said much about the likelihood of success or failure. "The fate of nations," explained the eighteenth-century French politician and gourmet Jean Anthelme Brillat-Savarin, "depends on the way they eat."

Supporting the team for Scott's 1910–12 *Terra Nova* expedition, T. C. Clissold was the typical Antarctic generalist: a trained mechanic, a skilled carpenter, a surprisingly good dog trainer, and a "first-class baker," according to Scott. Clissold cleverly managed his dough in a hut with uneven temperatures (freezing near the floor and walls, too hot near the stove and ceiling), and then, while baking, placed a small metal disc on top of each rising loaf.

Thomas Clissold in kitchen at the Cape Evans hut

The disc closed an electrical circuit inside the stove as the loaf reached the proper height, setting off a red light and alarm to pull him back from his other tasks. Clissold's mechanical skills were so impressive that Scott planned to pull him from the kitchen the following summer to help maintain the primitive motorized vehicles meant to haul supplies for the assault on the Pole.

"Clissold the cook has started splendidly," Scott wrote, with "seal, penguin, and skua stew, and I can honestly say that I have never met these articles of food in such a pleasing guise."

Scott was particularly impressed by the lack of fishiness in some seal rissoles—a deep-fried mince-filled pastry dressed with bread crumbs—Clissold prepared that were "so extraordinarily well cooked that it was impossible to distinguish them from the best beef rissoles. . . . It is the first time I have tasted seal without being aware of its particular flavour . . . he really is excellent."

As the entire expedition settled into their first winter, when expectations of variety from the cook were greatest, Clissold produced another novelty of pinniped cuisine: an excellent seal galantine, for which the meat is deboned, stuffed with forcemeat, poached, and then served cold coated in aspic (a clear jelly made of stock and gelatin).

One possible origin for the term *galantine* is the French *galant*, meaning "urbane and sophisticated." That it should be served on the edge of McMurdo Sound in 1911 is a tribute to Clissold.

Another of Clissold's roles around the hut was to pose dramatically atop the Matterhorn, an alpine-looking iceberg often visited by Herbert Ponting, Scott's lyrical photographer.

There came a day of reckoning, however, when Clissold made "a light thud" after dropping about eighteen feet onto a sharp angle in the ice. The poor cook lay lifeless on his back while Ponting frantically tried to revive him by hand and voice.

Although an examination found no broken bones, a badly bruised back and a severe concussion laid Clissold out for the next six weeks, keeping him from both the kitchen and the trail. Now there was no masterful mechanic/cook to nurse Scott's motor sledges toward the Pole. Ideally, these machines could have each pulled three tons of food and fuel at four and a half miles per hour, assuming that soft snow, crevasses, design flaws, or lack of tools and spare parts didn't end their run.

They might have crossed the Ross Ice Shelf to the foot of the Beardmore Glacier in as little as three days, guaranteeing Scott early access to, and full supplies for, the Pole. Instead, the machines were abandoned after a mere fifty miles — one possible cause of the deaths five months later of Scott and his party. Poor Clissold would have reason for regret.

Meanwhile, about four hundred miles away, on the edge of the Ross Ice Shelf, the Norwegian team of Roald Amundsen's 1911–12 *Fram* expedition had their own fine cook, baker, and pastry chef. Adolf Lindstrøm had already been hardened to polar life during four years in the Canadian Arctic with the great Norwegian explorer Otto Sverdrup, and three history-making years with Amundsen as part of the first crew to sail the Northwest Passage.

During the Antarctic winter, the cheerful, reliable Lindstrøm was the heart of Framheim, their hut buried beneath the snow of the Ross Ice Shelf. Amundsen had not intended to let the hut drift over, but in perhaps the funniest oversight in Antarctic history, he forgot to bring snow shovels.

The men made replacements, but by then thought better of digging out the whole hut. Fighting the wind-driven snowdrift would be a constant Herculean task, and they could benefit by living below the surface with a warmer building free from storms and an endless supply of snow in which to tunnel out a warren of workshops and storage rooms.

Lindstrøm simply pulled his seal steaks and cans from snowy shelves in snowy rooms, and to provide water for the kitchen he dug out snow from the end of an unused, ever-lengthening corridor. That snow was guaranteed to be clean, unlike the surface snow sullied by men and roaming dogs.

Not to be outdone by Clissold and his galantines, Lindstrøm was adored for his stacks of buckwheat pancakes, which he had learned to make in his North American travels, and which he slathered with Norwegian whortleberries and cloudberries.

To properly warm the pancake batter in its large bowl on a high shelf above the stove, Lindstrøm lit a fierce fire with wood, paraffin, and coal each morning after waking at 6:00 a.m. By 7:30, the batter was ready and the cook played his other morning role: alarm clock.

He set the table loudly, deliberately rattling plates and silverware. According to Amundsen, Lindstrøm was most effective at this when he was "flinging the teaspoons into the enamel mugs."

Of all the cooks from the heroic age, Lindstrøm earned the largest presence in an expedition account. In *The South Pole*, Roald Amundsen devoted nearly twenty pages to cheerfully following Lindstrøm around on his daily duties. The cook was treated as a professional, a companion, and a crucial part of the mission's success.

LINDSTRÖM WITH THE BUCKWHEAT CAKES.

Adolph Lindstrøm and his beloved hotcakes

For lunches and dinners throughout the year, Lindstrøm applied his near decade of polar cooking skills to highlight the taste of seal meat in stews — the Norwegians did not use the word "hoosh" — and steaks. He served the seal flesh lightly cooked, avoiding the high heat that would destroy the much-needed vitamin C in the meat. Lindstrøm also experimented successfully with a banquet of skua gulls, tough Antarctic avian scavengers that other expeditions had thought unclean.

When Amundsen headed to the Pole, Lindstrøm would be alone for most of two months, a great rarity in Antarctic history. Unfazed by the dangers, he spent his solo time at Framheim as the majordomo, glad to be rid of the owners, cleaning the hut, organizing stores, playing solitaire, shoveling snow, and feeding the dogs that had been left behind.

But before Lindstrøm could enjoy his long solo sojourn, Amundsen returned after just a few days. His boss's far-too-early departure — the cook had *told* him to wait — was aborted by temperatures so cold they burst liquor bottles and made frozen bloody messes of the dogs' paws. Amundsen made the mistake because he was afraid Scott's motor cars would give the British Pole party an unbeatable advantage. It would be Amundsen's only serious blunder in his otherwise brilliant trip to the Pole, but Lindstrøm's message to the party as it limped back into camp was a simple, "I told you so."

Roland Huntford, a key chronicler of the "race" to the South Pole, lionized Amundsen and dismantled Scott. To this end, he cited Brillat-Savarin on the relevance of national cuisine, and found Britain wanting. The fare at Framheim — simple, traditional, hearty — symbolized the clear-headed Norwegian plan for the southern assault on the Pole. At Cape

Evans, in contrast, the *galant* menu reflected Scott's Byzantine sledging plan, an awkward collection of relays pulled by pony, dog, man, and machine. Through the long winter before they set out on their fatal task, Scott and his men ate "in a princely fashion things which would be considered delicacies even in civilization," according to their ski instructor, Tryggve Gran.

When Amundsen led his successful team back into Framheim, he did so quietly one morning, strolling in as a prank to catch Lindstrøm in bed. The cook responded by calling him "the first cuckoo of spring." The first celebratory meal was, of course, hotcakes and coffee. Lindstrøm followed this up with a victory feast, surprising everyone with bottles of champagne he had hidden in his bed for an entire year.

Huntford asks: "How then, are we to judge Lindstrøm, the cook at Framheim?"

We'll let Amundsen, his close friend and admirer, provide the final praise: "A better man has never set foot inside the polar regions . . . He has done Norwegian polar explorations greater and more valuable services than anyone else."

doughballs

Lindstrøm and Clissold worked nobly under the duress of life in an Antarctic hut, but to attain superhero status a cook requires trial by ice. And as on any hero's journey, the cook must suffer and then thrive against all odds, as happened during the *Endurance* saga to Shackleton's favorite cook, Charles Green.

Despite his extraordinary optimism and work ethic, Green

collapsed from exhaustion a week after the half-dead crew landed on Elephant Island. Upon arrival, Green had immediately served a pan of hot milk to each of his ruined companions and began cooking up steaks and blubber from the seals that had innocently awaited their arrival.

"There was no rest for the cook," Shackleton wrote. "The blubber stove flared and sputtered fiercely as he cooked, not one meal, but many meals, which merged into a daylong bout of eating."

The days that followed were no better for Green, who soon could do no more. Green, like the French Antarctic Expedition's peripatetic and enigmatic Rozo, had joined his expedition in Buenos Aires after the first cook was sacked. Some of the sailors nicknamed Green "Doughballs" because of his high-pitched voice—"D'ye think he's had his pockets picked?" they'd ask with a grin—but they respected him enough not to "exercise their time-honoured right of growling at the cook," said Frank Worsley, especially as Shackleton admired and protected him.

In fact, Shackleton praised Green at every opportunity, particularly at Patience Camp on the sea ice, where even during blizzards the cook had produced hooshes in thirty-five minutes. "Small wonder that the cook's face was sooty, but his cheerful grin never deserted him," said Worsley.

After Green's collapse on the shores of Elephant, Shackleton ordered him to rest for a few days and, in the interim, replaced him with an unnamed sailor "who had expressed a desire to lie down and die." The discipline of cooking the hoosh for his shipmates brought the sailor "back to the ordinary cares of life."

The crew moved into their makeshift hut—living

underneath two overturned boats perched upon short stone walls — and Green went back to work at the blubber stove. It wasn't easy, as he sometimes went blind from the greasy soot in the confined space.

The men had to put up with his runny nose dripping into the pot, but there was praise all around for the new hoosh flavor created when Green sliced up the seal meat on a board also used for cutting tobacco. The only meals Green wasn't in charge of were the food fantasies conjured up by the castaways during long evenings. Most men imagined themselves back in civilization at banquets or markets, but one of Lionel Greenstreet's fantasies was so desperately sad (or perhaps simply pragmatic) that he dreamed only that they might sail to *another* desolate island.

On it, they would find an abundance of seals and penguins. In this bleak paradise, they would stuff an eviscerated seal with eviscerated penguins, then cover it all with stones and a large blubber fire.

After a day hungrily watching it cook, they would eat not the seal but the penguins, "which had thus lost none of their own juices, but received those of the seal as well," said Frank Wild. "Can you not imagine us sitting with tightened belts listening to the proposal, with our mouths watering at the very prospect?"

The Elephant Island party never got their feast of seal-infused penguin, but miraculously Shackleton appeared from the imprisoning sea ice in the *Yelcho* and rescued them. Green's work was not yet done, however, as Shackleton asked him to help cook aboard the small Chilean vessel. "That was a bit thick, I thought!" Green later wrote, but he willingly chopped up fresh mutton and potatoes, whipped up some dumplings, and made twelve pounds of macaroni and cheese so rich it made the *Endurance* men ill.

Green may have felt less like a conquering hero when he returned to England to find that his parents had cashed in his life insurance and his girlfriend had married someone else. So perhaps it's not surprising that, like Frank Wild, Frank Worsley, and five other *Endurance* alumni, Green followed Shackleton back to the Antarctic for the fateful 1922 *Quest* expedition. Like Wild, he had forgotten nothing about what it meant to live there. When Wild smiled and asked Green if his memory would fail him when it came time to cook up seal and penguin meat, he replied, "Not likely! If I was to live to be a hundred, I would not forget that."

unconventional cooks and crook cooks

Mawson had quizzed the men in their job interviews, sometimes as his first question, about whether they could cook. Charles Laseron, prospective zoological collector and taxidermist, replied honestly: "I admitted that I had made dampers [rough loaves of bread] on various camping excursions but confessed that my first efforts at least were probably still in the bush in a state of semi-petrification. For some reason this admission seemed to please him." Probably Mawson thought Laseron's honesty and humor made him a fine fit for the rigors of difficult life and simple food amid constant close company.

As Laseron later wrote, in a keen observation of life *in extremis*, "the smallest qualification became of value if it administered in any way to the general welfare." And the men of the AAE certainly were *in extremis*: They built their hut on an unknown coast which, as it turned out, was the windiest place on Earth.

The wind averaged fifty miles per hour over the first year, with some monthly averages much higher. Peak winds topped two hundred miles per hour. Nonetheless, the Australians worked in hurricane-force winds regularly, crawling out from the vibrating hut to read meteorological instruments or gather ice to melt for cooking.

When collecting ice, one man swung the pick while another held "like grim death" onto a box to hold the ice, according to Laseron. Often, chunks disappeared downwind; sometimes the box was ripped from a man's hands and blown out to sea.

Inevitably, in a hut full of young men, cooking became a game. During the AAE's first winter, a small group formed the Secret Society of Unconventional Cooks, in which inexperience was judged less harshly than a failure to impress Photographer Frank Hurley's inedible pastry earned him the rank of founding member, because he stiffened his bread for sculptural purposes "so that it would stand up in the form of a ship or some grotesque shape."

Laseron, another founding member and proud of his pastries, explained that over time nearly every member of the expedition was "elevated with due ceremony to this aristocracy of chefs. . . ."

But even to the end there were a few who still ranked as 'crook cooks,' and even gloried in the title." Belgrave Ninnis, for example, bore the "plebian stigma" of crook cook because he mistakenly used eight ounces each of pepper and salt in a salmon kedgeree (a breakfast dish usually made with fish, rice, and boiled eggs).

He had badly interpreted the meaning of a line in the recipe—*add two ounces of butter, pepper, and salt*—then multiplied by four to provide an overspiced lunch for eighteen hungry men.

Mawson rests at the side of sledge, Adelie Land, Antarctica, 1912

As for Mawson, he had Antarctic cooking experience as a member of Shackleton's *Nimrod* expedition, which made him both admirably willing to contribute to the daily toil and too willing to butt in on the other cooks' work.

His membership, therefore, in what became known as the Society of Muddling Messmen, "made him unpopular with the cook of the day, particularly as we gained in skill and began to fancy ourselves," wrote Laseron. Mawson himself noted that "most cooks adopted an attitude of surly independence."

Some "championships," as these young men called their mishaps and mistakes, included the explosion of cans thawing in the oven, a roly-poly pudding made without suet ("a recipe for synthetic rubber" that was turned down even by the hungriest dogs), and, best of all, a loaf of soda bread baked without baking powder.

The unnamed crook cook responsible for the soda bread, after suffering much derision, quietly launched the stony loaf through the trap door into the gale, but it was found by a prankster and returned for show-and-tell. The next time the offending loaf was tossed out, it was returned again, this time by the dogs.

Over the next two years, the loaf was recovered in the ice tunnels, in the airplane hangar, "and almost the last thing we saw," wrote Mawson, "when abandoning the Hut, nearly two years later, was this same petrifaction defying the blizzard on an icy pedestal near the Boat Harbour."

the blubber kings of inexpressible island

As with Mawson's AAE, Lieutenant Victor Campbell's Northern Party (an arm of Robert Scott's 1910–12 *Terra Nova* expedition trial by ice even more severe than that of Charles Green on Elephant Island) The Northern Party spent an unplanned winter without adequate food or shelter, cooking communally around an improvised blubber stove in the dark, in one of the most extraordinary survival stories in polar literature. It is also, for those of us breaking Antarctic bread together, a beautiful tale of companionship and singing amid gastronomic suffering.

Their site of suffering was a tiny ice cave in Terra Nova Bay on the Victoria Land coast. Today, there are new space-age stations built by China and South Korea and a beautiful, well-appointed Italian base nearby, in which fine, modern cuisine is consumed by healthy, happy Antarcticans.

The culinary gap is simply extraordinary, similar to the technological leap from dogsled to helicopter. But what is more remarkable is how, despite their months of excruciating conditions on the brink of starvation, in "Hell with a capital H," the Northern Party maintained their own happiness.

After spending a year in a hut at Cape Adare—where Borchgrevink and Julian's great-grandfather Colbeck had spent their winter fourteen years earlier—the Northern Party was scheduled to rejoin the rest of Scott's expedition at Cape Evans. The *Terra Nova* picked them up at Cape Adare in early January but dropped them off at Terra Nova Bay for what was intended to be a six-week survey. They accomplished much in that time, despite high winds—"If a cook wants snow he dare not dig without being tied to something or somebody," said Campbell—and snow blindness: "

Only one eye among the three of us and that belongs to Dickason. He tells me it is a lovely day and that he can see to cook hoosh, but after hoosh that goes and we do no more cooking that day."

Their tents, already so battered and thin they let in drifting

58

snow, were ruined in the extreme weather that heralded the onset of winter. By the middle of March, their hungry, shivering optimism that the *Terra Nova* would make its way through the close-packed ice to rescue them had faded. Campbell, Raymond Priestley, Murray Levick, George Abbott, Frank Browning, and Harry Dickason were on their own, with little winter equipment or clothing, and with almost nothing in the way of food. Death seemed almost certain.

A ship could not possibly reach them until the following January, but if they could survive the winter, they could make a do-or-die two-hundred-mile run down the Victoria Land coast to Cape Evans in October.

What food they possessed—a few weeks' worth of pemmican, biscuits, cocoa, and tea—was mostly set aside for that spring journey. Thus their winter diet consisted almost entirely of what they could kill.

They carved out an ice cave, roughly nine by twelve feet in area, five and a half feet tall, on a barren isle they called Inexpressible Island. The cave entrance was covered by a frozen sealskin. They navigated the passage from entrance to cave on hands and knees, passing through a doorway framed by biscuit tins. The passage, roofed in part with sealskins and bamboo poles, was later expanded to include meat storage and other spaces, including an emergency toilet, useful during blizzards.

Their living space was more pentagonal than square, widened to include a cooking area just inside the door. Otherwise, the room was filled entirely by their six decayed sleeping bags.

Three officers lay on one side, feet to feet with the three

sailors on the other, "like six big maggots in a nest." Their only light sources were homemade blubber lamps, which each gave off the equivalent light of half a match. To insulate themselves from the ice floor, they laid down pebbles, seaweed, and finally a canvas floor cloth. Snow blocks insulated them from the ice walls and served as shelving.

Sometimes they called their home a cave, sometimes a hut, and sometimes an igloo. Regardless, it was an ingenious survival shelter, cold enough for snow blocks but warm enough to lie around in and talk about food. The Northern Party's experience was more a hibernation than a winterover, and Priestley was wise enough to plan their "menu" carefully for the next eight months. He sorted through their meager pile of sweets—chocolate, sugar, cocoa, raisins—and set them aside in tiny amounts for weekly and monthly treats, for holidays, and for division between six upcoming birthdays.

He managed to "serve out 12 lumps of sugar to each man every Sunday, 1½ oz. of chocolate every Saturday and every alternate Wednesday, and 25 raisins [each] on the last day of each month." The wisdom of such celebrations cannot be overestimated.

The men looked forward to each small reward and remembered them with fondness long afterward. They developed a three-day work cycle: cook, messman, and day off. At first, cooking was easy. Whoever was on duty used their Primus stove (an ancestor to today's camping stoves), which fired up hooshes quickly and simply with fuel oil.

This procedure differed little from making sledging meals. When it became necessary to conserve the Primus fuel, however, they were obliged to invent blubber stoves. These quickly proved so awkward and inefficient that they took up all the time of the cook *and* the messman.

Blubber had to be heated, melted, and kept burning intensely enough to boil the hooshes. This process required constant attention, a steady supply of blubber strips, and a careful evolution of their stove technology.

Not until early May were Campbell and Levick able to cry "Eureka!" Old, dry seal bones from the beach served as marvelous wicks in the stove, sucking up hot oil and burning fiercely to heat the hoosh in two-thirds the usual time.

For the first two months, the stove had no chimney because the men feared it would undermine the snow roof. Thus the cave became a smokehouse filled up with greasy blubber smoke they called "smitch."

The volatilized oils also filled their lungs "so that we were no cleaner within than we were outside," said Priestley. Even after they built a biscuit-tin chimney, poor burning in the stove and drifting snow outside often caused the smitch to once again fill the cave.

Meat and thoughts of meat filled the men's waking hours. Priestley calculated that fifteen seals would be an absolute minimum to survive the winter on half-rations. They found eighteen. But when they ate seal, it now meant eating blubber as well. Whereas previous expeditions had mostly worked to remove every trace of fat from their cooked seal steaks, the Northern Party's hunger led them inexorably toward that thick layer of insulation, whether in the hoosh or in raw chunks. "It was hard at first to conquer the physical distaste when one bit on a juicy piece of the fat and the oil spirted [sic] in all directions into one's mouth," Priestley wrote, but they quickly grew attached to this food source.

Abbott and Dickason even asserted that the taste of

crabeater seal blubber was reminiscent of melon. Abbott later claimed the title of Blubber King because he gobbled down slabs several inches long.

Campbell described their stark two-meal menu in early April: "Breakfast—1 mug of penguin and seal hoosh and 1 biscuit; supper 1½ mugs of seal, 1 biscuit and ¾ pint of thin cocoa. We were always hungry on this." They had no vegetable matter except the occasional piece of inedible seaweed, which they tried to imagine was like cabbage. But biscuits were their greatest food obsession. They even gambled, by random method, for the crumbs at the bottom of a biscuit tin, which were actually a mixture of "biscuit, granite, paraffin, snow, ice, and frozen meat." Priestley's dissertation on the psychology of hunger for carbohydrates is instructive:

When we awoke in the morning in March, April, May, or June, our first thought was: "Is it a two-biscuit or a one-biscuit morning?" Later, in July or September, when there were no two-biscuit mornings, we said to ourselves: "In half an hour I shall have my biscuit." Only in the worst month of all— August—our mornings were clouded by the thought that there was no biscuit to come to us until the month was past. . . .

If the beginning of the month revealed a box of biscuits which were even a little burnt, loud and deep were the curses called down on the baker's head. Do not let him blame us either until he has starved for a few months on half-rations of tasteless meat and too tasty blubber and one miserable biscuit per diem. If the biscuits were underdone, however, it meant at least thirty bright spots in the coming month. . . .

Then came the question of a fair division. Even if the

biscuits were whole they might differ slightly in size. If a division were made by the server according to his own ideas, although he might be scrupulously fair, not only he himself but all the others would feel continually that the portions were not, in fact could not be, equal.

As for the work rotation, the cook managed the blubber stove and made the two daily hooshes—8:15 a.m. and 3:30 p.m.—while the messman chiseled off pieces of frozen seal by the light of a faintly flickering "reading lamp."

The messman sat shivering in front of the drafty curtained doorway, trying not to hit his numb hand with the hammer. Icy meat flew from the chisel into the dark. "Every now and then an exclamation would betray the fact that some one had been hit on the hand or the face by a flying fragment," said Priestley.

Not until May did they think to warm larger chunks by the heat of the stove. The messman's job description soon included hanging slabs of seal and a whole Adélie next to the fire, as well as gathering ice (both salt and fresh), chopping meat, dicing blubber, clearing snow from the chimney, and plugging the chimney with a rolled penguin skin at night.

The joy that accompanied a day off was twofold; they relaxed in their greasy bags while enjoying the spectacle of others at work.

For the cook, variety in meals was hard to manage. Imagination was the key, but not so much in devising new flavors as in convincing the men that they were tasting something different. Ginger tablets from the medical kit combined with a lump of sugar *might* taste like preserved ginger. Every Sunday three teaspoons of tea were thrown into a blubber-ringed pot of water. "A man with sufficient imagination could taste tea quite distinctly in the first brew," wrote Priestley, but when on Monday they reboiled the same three teaspoons, "I fear not even imagination could flavour [it]." Not flinching from further experimentation, the smokers in the group dried the twice-used tea, mixed it with wood chips, and stuck it in their pipes.

They were already in the process of consuming the teak sledge meter, one pinch of fine shavings at a time. In the depths of an otherwise nearly smokeless winter, Dickason was heard "ruminating as to whether he could possibly convert a pair of hair-socks into tobacco."

But variety in the hoosh was the gold standard. Adélie meat was mixed into breakfast hooshes, to rave reviews. Brains, livers, and kidneys were treasures set aside for special occasions. Saltwater was used as a replacement for salt, to everyone's pleasure but Browning's, whose digestion was always disturbed by it.

Seaweed was put in to "swell the hoosh," but much depended on the condition of the plant, according to Campbell. "When fresh, this was not bad," he wrote, "but most of it had deteriorated in the summer owing to the sun and penguins walking over it." Two unwanted—but not rejected—additions to hooshes during the winter included a penguin flipper (a forgotten pot scrubber) and some Stockholm tar from a two-foot piece of rope.

There were two particularly bright moments amid their culinary monotony. The first was a discovery by Browning, who in slaughtering a Weddell seal found thirty-six undigested fish in its stomach and gullet. (Charcot's *Français* expedition likewise found more than one hundred fish in a crabeater seal's extended belly, one of which had another fish in *its* mouth.) These were fried up and eaten with great pleasure. From then on, when a seal was spotted, the men would yell, "Fish!" But never again did they have such luck.

The second great discovery was the great mass of seal blood that poured into the snow during the butchering. A Weddell seal weighs up to a thousand pounds (twice that of the crabeater) and has about sixty liters of blood, a remarkable 16 percent of its body weight. The men used frozen blood to replace the ice in the hoosh, and the resulting gravy was thick enough "to stand a spoon upright," wrote Priestley. "After a pot and a half of this gravy we did feel as if we had had a meal, if but a small one, and we were fit for quite a good day's work."

When it came time for the traditional Antarctic Midwinter feast, the Northern Party spent weeks excitedly discussing the menu and came up with the most pathetic celebratory bill of fare in Antarctic history: liver hoosh, four biscuits, four sticks of chocolate, twenty-five raisins, and a sip of Wincarnis (tonic wine) each. Even so, they reveled in this taste of luxury.

They found little respite from hunger in their dreams. Every night they "sat at a banquet and saw the provisions whisked away from before our eyes as we commenced to eat," wrote Priestley, or they suddenly remembered that they were home and for all the food and tobacco they could want, they only needed to walk around the corner. But alas, the shop was closed, closed to all but Levick, the lucky one among the six who got to eat his dreamed-up meals. The others were jealous.

They were otherwise unified by their starvation, particularly during meal preparation. They all sang, especially while the hoosh was on the boil, because by midwinter they had exhausted much of their stock of conversation.

They took to singing choral songs, sailor songs, nursery rhymes, hymns, traveler's songs, ditties, and little phrases, whatever they could dredge up from adult experience and childhood memory. Failing that, they made up their own topical songs. "The thing which went farthest towards making our evenings pass pleasantly," wrote Priestley, "was the ability to make a 'cheerful noise.'"

Amundsen's sled depot at 83° South

Even decades later in his comfy chair at Cambridge, he felt some regret that he would never again taste such harmony. He related an experience of singing in England in which "The Battle-Cry of Freedom" brought the Inexpressible Island days vividly back to mind. Tellingly, it was not the image of the cave and his friends that came back most clearly, but rather "the scent of a well-cooked hoosh."

As summer returned, the men were emaciated and showing pre-scurvy symptoms of edema. At the end of September, they made a break for Cape Evans, forty days away. They found salvation in old food depots, first at Cape Roberts, then at Butter Point, where they could eat biscuits to their hearts' content. Their survival assured, they felt human again, but when the party reached Cape Evans, physicist Charles Wright described them as "creatures who had crawled up from the depths of the earth."

Through all the troglodytic misery, ennui, and desperation ("the dismal misery of this dark filthy hole," as Levick described it), their hunger had bound them together, as Priestley noted when using his Northern Party experience to write the first psychological study of Antarctic winterovers. He was sure that if the six of them had possessed plenty of meat, fat, and carbohydrates while trapped in the tiny, difficult space, "we should have become dull and plethoric, and probably before the end of the six months the peace which ruled in the snow-cave would have departed, never to return." Living on the edge of starvation and scurvy kept the men busy and compassionate. And while the Northern Party diet cannot be recommended as a self-help panacea, it is worth noting that six men in smitchy, blubber-soaked clothes emerged blinking from their ice cave happier than most satiated consumers cruising today's supermarket aisles. Priestley summed up the experience as proof that "the luxuries of civilization only fulfill the wants they create.

Frank Wild and M. H. Moyes slay a Weddell seal

"Six seals with a layer of fat three inches thick appeared near the ship yesterday morning. Their fate requires no further explanation."-Roald Amundsen, *Belgica Diary*

Slaughter and Scurvy   3

Seven years before Julian and I started packing for the Odell, I first arrived in Antarctica as a polar novice with open eyes, an open notebook, a habit of wandering, and a notable lack of career ambition. I had spent the previous two years reading and writing poetry in graduate school. The writer/photographer Jim Mastro, who I met in grad school, had been working for years as a diver in the U.S. Antarctic Program, and put in a good word for me with my application.

Julian, likewise, had heard about working on the ice from a guy who had once been the South Pole station manager, and who knew about Julian's family history. Surprisingly, he told Julian not to say a word about that history. ITT Antarctic Services, the contractor at the time, "wanted nothing to do with sentimental, soul-searching applications . . . only those which portrayed wickedly hard-working individuals."

Julian managed to convey his diligence by pestering ITT with a polite but endless stream of communication—with phone calls to ask if they'd received his letters, and then letters thanking them for taking his calls, ad infinitum, until they sent him $700 tickets to New Jersey for an interview, in which his future boss "held up a manilla folder as thick as a book and said, 'Will you now please stop writing to us!'" The next season, Julian landed "with watering eyes" in the region first visited by his great-grandfather.

Why was I interested in wandering to the end of the Earth? Unlike Julian, I didn't have a longstanding fascination with Antarctica rooted in family history. Nor did I have a particular interest in the polar regions. I hadn't read about Shackleton or Rozo or the Northern Party. In fact, I was ignorant of the ice continent's heroic and bloody history. But because of Jim's stories, it seemed like a strange and beautiful adventure, and because of Jim's extraordinary photographs, I was curious to see Antarctica's wildlife and otherworldly landscape bathed in polar light. Finally, I suppose, I had long been intrigued by the blank spaces on maps. And Antarctica was, and remains, the most wondrous of blank spaces.

I immediately fell in love with its ferocious beauty: the way light and wind sang across the ice as windchill cut to the bone, and the way the landscape invited me outward but offered no safe haven. I could, and did, stare for hours across the frozen sea to the ice-filled mountains, but I did so from the warmth of a dormitory lounge. I took walks in –100°F windchill but returned to dine on hot lasagna in a cafeteria.

I soon learned I was at the tail end of a remarkable history that had turned Antarctica from a lunar zone that had never supported human life into a destination fit for scientific exploration and settlement. I was a modern footnote to that history, wandering south with pencil poised over paper, but I was a participant nonetheless. What I had yet to understand was what that history said about the high cost—to both wildlife and men—of our desire to know.

Here's something I know now: A quick course in the history of Antarctic cuisine shows that living off the land was de rigueur. Untold thousands of seals, penguins, and seabirds were consumed by men shivering on the coast, too far from home. The menus were as stark as the men were desperate. And the men were often desperate, struggling to fend off starvation and nutritional deficiencies.

Often throughout the human exploration of the south polar region, Antarctica and the Southern Ocean were described as cruel, because high seas, deep cold, pitiless wind, glacial dangers, and distance from home posed real threats to survival.

But those were simply the terms on which Antarctica agreed to let humans in. The glacial eternity and climatic brutality of the ice predate our species. The only sustenance Antarctica has to offer is air to breathe, snow to melt, and fresh meat on its shoreline. The ice is antithetical to life, except for that life which spends most of its time at sea and only comes ashore to breed. And it is that life which, throughout Antarctic history, fed the men who called the continent cruel.

The cruelty, as it turns out, was all ours. The slaughter was both easy and ghastly because these animals evolved amid an absence of terrestrial predators (polar bears live in the Arctic), and so did not fear humans. (This is still true today; I have strolled up to apathetic seals and kneeled quietly while curious Emperor penguins waddled up to me.)

Hungry and sometimes conflicted men shot at point-blank range or simply clubbed the quarter-ton crabeater seals and half-ton Weddell seals. This wasn't hunting; it was a betrayal of trust.

At the same time, the quest for knowledge that drove the explorers and scientists who stepped ashore at the turn of the twentieth century was often accompanied by a crucial ignorance about how to feed themselves. Scurvy, a disease of vitamin C deficiency, haunted the era, and the stories of heroic age cuisine tend to toggle between killing to eat and killing to heal their disease. In other words, it was slaughter if the men planned well, or scurvy if they didn't. The learning curve was steep, sometimes fatal, and it's worth reading deeper into the story of scurvy to better understand the dependency on wildlife that fed the sagas of the heroic age.

embarking with nutritional deficiencies

The slaughter of Antarctic wildlife was logistical before it became existential. Expedition leaders needed to secure large amounts of free local food, and they wanted to provide fresh variety for their men amid a bland litany of canned meat. These logistics require a brief explanation before exploring the more desperate side of the story.

First, food awaiting Antarctic explorers was food they did not have to purchase or transport. Expeditions often departed under bright flags and a cloud of debt. Exploration is a gamble, after all, and few investors like to throw good money at eccentric men wagering with their lives for rarified goals. Expedition leaders thus begged, cajoled, proselytized, politicked, lectured to universities and the public to awaken government interest, wrote inspiring articles, offered exclusive commercial contracts for food and gear, fibbed about their plans, and promised rich donors the everlasting glory of geographical nomenclature. (Shackleton named the Beardmore Glacier and the *James Caird* for a steel baron and a jute manufacturer, respectively.)

They could little afford enough fresh meat for so many men for a year or two in the Antarctic, much less find space for it aboard their undersized, underpowered wooden ships.

These ships were commonly so overloaded on the way south—dangerously top-heavy on deck, and crammed to the gills below with food, gear, and men—that they had little room for live sheep or cattle available in New Zealand or Australia. "Like most expedition ships, she was grossly overladen," wrote R. W. Richards of the *Aurora* in 1914. "We left with a heavy deck cargo of coal and cases of petrol stacked on top of the cook's galley(!) and on deck, where, incidentally, a fire broke out while at sea." Thus, the local meat that awaited those crowded ships in Antarctic waters was as crucial to an expedition's logistics as it would be to the crew's diet.

Second, the fresh meat of seals and penguins, while unfamiliar, also provided an opportunity to vary the menu. Canned goods had become popular (after some troubling germ-filled decades in the late 1800s), as common in the home market as they were in military contracts. By the 1870s, American kitchens had been transformed by the availability of a myriad of cheap cans, described sanguinely as: a kitchen garden where all good things grow, and where it is always harvest time . . . where raspberries, apricots, olives, and pineapples, always ripe, grow side by side with peas, pumpkins, and spinach; a garden with baked beans, vines and spaghetti bushes, and . . . through it running a branch of the ocean in which one can catch salmon, lobsters, crabs and shrimp, and dig oysters and clams.

But popularity didn't guarantee good taste or texture. Wilhelm Schwarz, cook of the 1901–3 German South Polar Expedition, doled out fibrous tinned meat the men called "rope-yarn." So tasteless were these tins of food that it was easier for the Germans to distinguish the same product (e.g., canned beef) from different companies than it was to distinguish different meats from the same company.

Given the manifold psychological challenges of surviving at the end of the Earth, monotony in meals only exacerbated the intense isolation. Although some men — and these were the ones any leader would be grateful for — kept their *joie de vivre* regardless of harsh weather, hard work, frequent injury, difficult companions, or poor food, some did not. Part of the problem was that the men came south with culinary expectations common at the dawn of the industrial age, and they tired easily of gruel. The "addition of a few delicacies adds little to the cost of an expedition, but means a great deal to those engaged in it," wrote Dr. Alexander Macklin of the *Endurance* and *Quest* journeys.

Sometimes those delicacies came in the form of tinned pheasant and sometimes in the shape of an Adélie squawking at their icy doorstep. It is hard for us now to understand the value of a perfectly cooked seal rissole to expedition members biding their time through the long polar winter, or of summer's first penguin egg to a voracious, gastronomically bored sailor.

Now, finally, imagine instead that the would-be egg or rissole eater had no fresh meat or vegetables at hand for months and began to suffer aching joints, skin lesions, and swollen limbs. Imagine dark, hemorrhaging gums protruding from his mouth. Imagine his teeth loosening, his old wounds weirdly reappearing, his mind succumbing to diet-induced depression.

Then imagine his weakness increasing until death. These are the symptoms of scurvy, a simple if acute vitamin C deficiency, for centuries the bane of badly fed Europeans —

particularly soldiers, sailors, and polar explorers.

Scurvy had become the mysterious, morbid companion to European voyages by the end of the fifteenth century, including those of Vasco da Gama, Ferdinand Magellan, Jacques Cartier, and Francis Drake, when expeditions were bold enough to stay at sea for several months. Sixteenth-century English sea captain Sir Richard Hawkins said that "in his twenty years at sea he could give account of 10,000 men consumed with scurvy." British Navy voyages over the next few centuries fared little better, with whole crews ravaged by the disease.

The long and ugly history of scurvy is particularly tragic because most of the suffering could have been avoided with knowledge available at the time. Although unfamiliar with vitamins, Arctic and European traditional cultures knew that scurvy could be easily prevented, or quickly cured, by the consumption of raw food. Green plants and fruit are best, but large quantities of fresh meat, as long as it is raw or lightly cooked, contain enough vitamin C to fend off scurvy as well.

Scurvy is not necessarily a disease of starvation; it is instead one of the diseases that result from incomplete nutrition. We can suffer and die while eating sufficient quantities of food that contain insufficient nutrients. Deprived of vitamin A, for example, we develop night blindness; without vitamin B_1, we contract beriberi (thiamine deficiency marked by fatigue and weight loss); without vitamin C, we suffer from scurvy. Vitamin C is ascorbic acid, ascorbic meaning literally "anti-scurvy."

Plants and most animals synthesize it themselves, but primates cannot. Without vitamin C, we cannot produce collagen, an essential component of bones, cartilage, tendons, and other connective tissue. Collagen binds our wounds, but that binding is replaced continually throughout our lives. Thus, in advanced scurvy, old wounds long thought healed will painfully reappear, as if by dark magic.

A healthy individual has to go at least two or three months without vitamin C before showing symptoms of scurvy. Unfortunately, many people in the age of Antarctic exploration were malnourished at home as well.

Rapid European population growth had resulted in an urban, industrial society consuming a diet mainly of grains, sugar, and vegetable oils. Green vegetables, fruit, fresh meat, and animal organs could be expensive or hard to find. Sailors in particular tended to be poor and often "embarked with nutritional deficiencies."

That such deficiencies should still haunt Antarctic expeditions at the dawn of the twentieth century seems remarkable, considering that food had entered a new age of preserved and manufactured goods.

Americans were already treating themselves to Jell-O, jelly beans, and peanut-butter-and-jelly sandwiches when Raymond Priestley of the Northern Party noted wryly that, even in 1912, men of the heroic age "learned over again the lesson of nearly all polar exploration: It is not the winter cold but malnutrition and starvation that are the greatest enemies of explorers."

A survey of scurvy in the Antarctic, appropriately enough, requires telling the tales of two prominent Cooks: Captain James Cook and Dr. Frederick Cook.

In 1773–74, the great Captain Cook edged over the Antarctic Circle (66°33′ South) a few times with the vessels *Resolution* and *Adventure* in search of ice-clad southern lands.

He was the first to sail so far south and, more impressively, did not lose a single member of the *Resolution* crew to scurvy. (The *Adventure* lost a few, including its cook, described as a "dirty hinterland man, natural prey," before the captain adjusted that ship's diet.) At a time when the disease was as common as sunburn in the British Royal Navy, when ships arrived in distant ports with half-dead crews, Cook's success was remarkable.

He succeeded in part because the British Admiralty had ordered him to carry out an experiment. The scientific thinking in Europe from 1700 to 1770 had actually increased the occurrence of scurvy, as new hypotheses distracted physicians from the timeworn observation that the absence of fresh food created malnourished men. Cook's voyages, on the other hand, would test the effectiveness of alleged antiscorbutics such as sauerkraut, salted cabbage, "rob" of citrus (orange and lemon syrup), wort of malt (a fermented drink of sprouted barley), portable soup (dried animal offal), saloup (a medicinal drink of plant roots), carrot marmalade, soda water, and mustard.

Though he kept most of his men alive, Cook's experiment provided no clear results. He had carried too many possible cures and applied them without controls. Although Cook knew firsthand the antiscorbutic value of fresh greens, fresh fruit, and sauerkraut, he also praised the curative power of sugar, fresh water, and good hygiene. Nevertheless, through Cook's experiment and the eventual advocacy of an influential naval physician, Sir Gilbert Blane, the inclusion of lemon juice on navy vessels became mandatory from 1796 onward, and cases of scurvy were significantly reduced.

By the mid-1800s, however, citrus had been erroneously

discredited. The navy bureaucracy, seeking efficiencies, replaced fresh lemon juice with a distilled and bottled concentrate. No one knew about vitamins, of course, nor did they know that the heat of distillation and a chemical reaction with copper pots and tubing destroyed much of the juice's vitamin C. Then, when the navy replaced Mediterranean lemons with West Indian limes, which had only two-thirds the vitamin C, scurvy returned to the high seas. The 1875 Nares Expedition to the Arctic, for example, was forced to return early to Britain after sixty cases of, and four deaths from, the disease.

More than a century after Captain Cook's Antarctic voyage, scurvy was still a problem in the British Navy, and medical science was still confused about the solution.

ʃ two great cooks Ƴ

Twenty years later, in 1897–99, Adrien de Gerlache sailed the *Belgica* into Antarctica's ice-filled waters. This first major scientific expedition of the heroic age was staffed by a young, polyglot crew from Belgium, Norway, Romania, Poland, and the United States, including Louis Michotte — the lousy cook we met in Chapter 2 — and two future giants of polar exploration: Roald Amundsen, eventual winner of the race to the South Pole, and Dr. Frederick Cook, future false claimant to the North Pole.

Despite the ignominy that would haunt him ten years thereafter, at the time of the *Belgica* journey Cook was perhaps the greatest nonnative practitioner of polar medicine. He would become the savior of the *Belgica* crew. From an earlier

Arctic expedition with Robert Peary, Cook had learned beyond doubt that a diet of fresh food prevented scurvy. Cook spent fourteen months with the Inuit of northern Greenland and made careful observations of dietary and other adaptations to polar life. His hosts thrived on a diet of mostly raw or lightly cooked meat and fish, having little access to fruit and green leafy vegetables.

Dr. Cook, 1894 (L) and 1898 (R)

Other Westerners had made this observation, certainly, but Cook's genius was his twofold conclusion that the dread disease resulted from a dietary deficiency and that cooking food could make it deficient: "Scurvy is in the shadow line between tinned food and raw meat. In the process of cooking and preserving, something vital to our lives is in part destroyed." This knowledge put him in the vanguard of nutritional medicine, but hardly anyone noticed.

In Antarctic waters, the *Belgica* crew expected to retreat north before winter set in, but Gerlache pushed the ship too deep into the ice. Soon it was trapped. They carried only four sets of cold-weather clothing for eighteen men, and perhaps a year's worth of food. The ice could keep them for two years or more. In the darkness of an unplanned winter, the atmosphere of perilous uncertainty gave way to frustration, panic, anger, and lunacy. Depression was common among the crew, and two sailors went insane. One of them never recovered. Even the ship's cat turned strange and died.

What little antiscorbutic food they had was exhausted early, and the crew was left with Michotte's ineffective canned food. Frederick Cook noted that the men's digestive systems responded with constipation ("gastric inertia") to the tinned stuff, most of which tasted not like food with natural fiber, but like "laboratory mixes in cans . . . hashes under various catchy names; sausage stuffs in deceptive forms, meat and fishballs said to contain cream, mysterious soups, and all the latest inventions in condensed foods."

Scurvy symptoms soon appeared. Thus Cook, with support from the young Roald Amundsen, recommended to Gerlache that everyone on board eat fresh penguin and seal meat daily.

The commander took offense. The British Navy put its faith in lime juice, he said, and who knows more about scurvy than the navy? Moreover, Gerlache had sampled the animals, badly prepared by Michotte, and found them so disgusting that he tried to ban them from the *Belgica*. Even Cook compared the taste of Michotte's penguin to "a piece of beef, odiferous cod fish, and a canvas-backed duck roasted together in a pot, with blood and cod-liver oil for sauce."

The desperately ill magnetics expert Emile Danco refused to eat this strange new flesh. He died as a result, his body sent through a hard-won hole in the ice to the bottom of the ocean. In his position as doctor to the expedition, Cook was by late winter forced to prescribe the meat as medicine rather than food.

Those who obeyed first showed an immediate response: "I am not dead!" wrote Captain Georges Lecointe. "The coma into which I plunged yesterday did not even last very long. I came out of it, mechanically ate a piece of penguin meat and, a few hours later, I woke up feeling much stronger." Taking no chances, Lecointe ate penguin every day until the expedition left Antarctic waters.

Initially, Roald Amundsen had been ill with scurvy, but as he recovered under Cook's guidance, the Norwegian helped bring the *Belgica*'s crew back to life with the fresh meat he hunted: "Six seals with a layer of fat three inches thick appeared near the ship yesterday morning. Their fate requires no further explanation."

Amundsen seems to be the only one who actually liked the flavors of Antarctica. "Penguin meat tastes excellent," he wrote, "but you must ensure that all the fat is cut off the meat. It does not need to be treated with vinegar to make it taste good; you simply take the meat as it is and fry it in a pan with a knob of butter."

Some of it he ate raw. One emperor penguin, which can weigh ninety pounds, was enough to feed twenty-five men, but Amundsen preferred the tender meat of the fourteen-pound Adélie.

By the end of July, the crew was living mainly on penguin meat, with a marked improvement in their health. Gerlache was the last to consent, and thus the last to be cured, but subsequently offered rewards to the crew for bringing in penguins for the larder—one franc for living birds, fifty centimes for dead ones. This was easy money, as it turned out. The crew learned in their final months that they could summon both penguins and seals to the ship by simply playing a tune on a cornet.

While future heroic age expeditions paid little attention to Cook's success, Amundsen, at the time an unknown Norwegian second mate, would never forget. He went on to be the first explorer to sail the whole Northwest Passage, the first to reach the South Pole, and the first to reach both Poles, among many other achievements. Thanks in part to Cook's instruction, Amundsen's future expeditions to both Poles never suffered from scurvy, a claim very few early explorers could make.

In an ironic event that might have spelled the death of the expedition, Frederick Cook spent a frosty midwinter night alone, away from the ship, to observe the stars from his sleeping bag. His hair froze to the hood of his bag, but he avoided a worse fate.

On returning to the ship at dawn, he "learned that Lecointe, not knowing of my presence on the ice, had taken me for a seal, and was only waiting for better light to try his luck with the rifle."

This was perhaps the only moment in Antarctic history in which intended slaughter would have led to more scurvy.

the line between hunting and torture

After the *Belgica*, scurvy continued to haunt the heroic age, appearing in its full-blown form during nearly half of the era's expeditions. But scurvy-ridden or not, the men of the era had a relationship with wildlife that always turned ugly; someone had to die.

The carnage actually began in 1820, some eighty years before the heroes of exploration arrived, with the sealers and whalers who hunted sub-Antarctic waters for their oily prey. The same wildlife they slaughtered for profit was eaten at dinner in a makeshift survival cuisine. One mariner spoke of how delicious he found it: "Manna from heaven could not have seemed more delicious than lumps of seal or penguin meat made into a hash with a handful of oatmeal." Hunger, and the ever-present specter of scurvy, drove the men to make the shorelines "unsafe for any living thing."

Meat was just the start of the harvest. Blubber became fuel for stoves, for lamps, and, once they could stomach it, for men. Blood thickened the hoosh. Brains and organs, prized treats, were gleaned from the offal.

Like members of the terrestrial expeditions that followed, these mariners went as deep into the carcasses as their hunger demanded. An elephant-seal soup made by one shipwrecked crew, for example, was full of flippers, snotters (the nose), hearts, brains, skin, and sweetbreads (thymus gland and pancreas). The whole mass was boiled until gelatinous and then spiced with sea birds and their eggs. But it was their commercial slaughter that forever altered the Southern Ocean.

Well before the heroic age began, fur-seal populations were decimated and whales were on the way out. Less well known is that millions of penguins also fed the fires of the Industrial Revolution. In the 1820s, for example, hundreds of thousands of royal and king penguins on Macquarie Island were slaughtered for their oil. In a *single* year, three decades later, four hundred thousand Falkland Islands penguins were knocked on the head and rendered into 50,700 gallons (192,000 liters) of oil. Thus we learn at incalculable cost that one penguin is equal to one oily pint.

Despite their nobler purpose, the heroic age explorers and scientists who arrived decades later ended up just as begrimed by blood, fat, and smoke as the hunters had been. Photographs and narratives from every terrestrial expedition make it clear that the men were busy shooting, gutting, and flaying penguins and fat-rich seals to supply the kitchen or feed their sled dogs.

Carsten Borchgrevink's 1898–1900 *Southern Cross* expedition, with Julian's great-grandfather on board, had an Adélie colony on their doorstep at Cape Adare, which made it easy for the men to steal four thousand eggs and pack them in salt. The expedition's egg gatherers were its dog handlers, Ole Must and Persen Savio, two Sámi from northern Norway, who were more at home in the wild than the others and so thought little of herding a Weddell seal back to camp rather than butchering it away from the hut. They brought it in, as Borchgrevink noted, "just as peasants at home drive their cattle to market."

Likewise, seaman Leonhard Müller of Erich von Drygalski's 1901–3 *Gauss* expedition was seen "for all the world like the divine herdsman Eumaeus, rounding up his penguins for subsequent service in his beloved train-oil kettle in the boiler-room," where their fatty bodies burned with a bright flame. ("Train oil" is an old term for rendered blubber.) Seals too were boiled down, giving nineteen pounds (eight and a half kilos) of oil from twenty-two pounds (ten kilos) of blubber. At expedition's end, as the *Gauss* broke free of the ice, Drygalski noted a single emperor "waving its flippers as if in farewell."

Remains of penguins and seals drifted down into the cold waters from whence they came or were visible protruding from the filthy snow, "a clear sign that thirty-two men had lived here for a year."

Even more disturbing than this account is one by Roald Amundsen's Norwegian crew in 1912, when Japanese explorer Nobu Shirase visited with the *Kainan Maru*. A remarkable man, Shirase abstained from alcohol and tobacco and had long trained to inure himself to cold. In fact, he was unique in Antarctic exploration in that he apparently ate only cold food. Relations were cordial between the crews during the brief meeting, but the Norwegians were genuinely horrified at the Japanese sailors' treatment of wildlife. Coming from Nordic men who could gut a seal and flense a whale with their eyes closed, and from an expedition which at times treated their dogs like loaves of bread with legs, this criticism is notable.

There seems to be no racism in Lieutenant Thorvald Nilsen's account, aside from the impersonal description of people they could not understand: "They had put penguins into little boxes to take them alive to Japan! Round about the deck lay dead and half-dead skua gulls in heaps.

On the ice close to the vessel was a seal ripped open, with part of its entrails on the ice; but the seal was still alive." Nilsen and Kristian Prestrud asked the Japanese for a weapon to finish off the seal, but they apparently "only grinned and laughed."

Two other sailors drove a seal before them toward the ship, as men on Borchgrevink's and Drygalski's expeditions had done, but here they prodded the seal with long sharp poles, "quarrying" it out of cracks it exhaustedly fell into, laughing until eventually leaving it for dead. While moments of cruelty and a brutal pragmatism were commonplace during the era, Nilsen's account of the *Kainan Maru* ranks as perhaps the ugliest on record, because it crossed the line between hunting and torture.

⟨ compassion and carnage ⟩

Given this litany of cruelty, it is a minor relief to read Jean-Baptiste Charcot's account of his 1903–5 expedition aboard the *Français*. Charcot would fail to prevent scurvy from afflicting his crew, but he was noteworthy for his marked empathy for wildlife and his significant scientific and exploratory successes.

He was pragmatic—he imagined making shoes from penguin skins—but he found it "very painful to have to kill these fine and gentle beasts." Charcot was inconsistent in his sensitivity, though.

On one day, he might poetically transfer his guilt to a seal corpse hanging from the *Français*'s rigging, "silhouetted against the grey mist, like a criminal swinging from a gibbet," but on another he might mention offhandedly that seal pups provided very tender meat.

In a truly heartbreaking anecdote, he recounted that two of his scientific staff killed a female seal, only to contend with the arrival of the male seal "weeping" over her body and rubbing against her. Finally, unable to move him, they shot him too.

As for penguins, the French crew thought the meat compared well in texture and taste to mule. Charcot regretted harvesting penguin eggs, but they were a boon to the crew's health after the long winter. By early summer, the men were living on eggs almost exclusively, collecting over eight thousand "without counting those swallowed by the crew on the spot."

Charcot consoled the surviving adults with gramophone concerts. Some Adélies, in what Charcot noted as ample proof of their intelligence, sought his protection from the dogs: "Two of them, pursued . . . came to seek refuge between my legs, and certain of being in a place of safety, turned round to face their enemy. They only left me when the dogs had returned on board." Being the poetic sort, he imagined the tales penguins in years hence would tell of the strange tall creatures who came among them, "sometimes beneficent, sometimes hostile," and of their four-legged companions, the "fierce, cruel, devilish hairy monsters with long tails, red tongues, and teeth which tore flesh and brought death."

What Charcot had trouble imagining was the link between fresh food and scurvy. On this first expedition, one of Rozo's sample menus from April (early winter) of 1904 shows that only three meals per week included fresh portions of *phoque* (seal) or *pingouin*, though there was plenty of vitamin-deficient tinned meat and vegetables. Charcot's dislike of hunting may have deprived his French crews of vitamin C, since by midwinter the men exhibited various signs of nutritional deficiency, including lethargy, exhaustion, and depression.

Five years later, Charcot returned on his second Antarctic expedition, this time aboard the *Pourquois-Pas?* And again, Charcot and many of his men (including the cook, Modaine) suffered from scurvy during the winter. This time, they sought a cure in fresh meat, exercise, and antiscorbutics such as sauerkraut, tomatoes, dried vegetables, fruit jam, and lime juice. Two of the French scientists grew vitamin-C-rich hyacinths, watercress, and onions under a ship's skylight.

But Charcot was still tangled up in conflicting theories of scurvy, writing that their diet was good enough "to save us from the scurvy that attacked the expeditions of old" but insufficient against "what one may call modern scurvy—or, more strictly speaking, preserved-food sickness."

It wasn't the fresh meat that helped, he thought, but eating less tinned meat. For all of his empathy, Charcot had not trusted the answer to the scurvy question found in the traditional wisdom of the Arctic and explained more recently in Frederick Cook's work aboard the *Belgica*. Still, Charcot lost none of his men to illness and should be remembered for his moments of compassion in a place that had seen little of it.

On one occasion, Charcot discussed a day spent with a Weddell seal pup, watching it play with its mother, its "fine large eyes full of astonishment and roguery. . . . I drew close and took the little one in my arms. It was delighted, showing no fear, but acting just like a baby, and when I put the soft little body back on the ice again it came crawling up to me, rubbing up against my legs and asking for fresh caresses."

Like Charcot, Robert Falcon Scott, leader of the 1901–4 *Discovery* expedition, disliked butchering the tame wildlife. He also had an aversion to the sight of blood, and a horror of the taste of blubber. It was "an abomination both in taste and smell," and even a morsel left in to fry with seal steak was enough to make him lose his appetite.

The *Discovery* crew did initially eat *some* wild foods. A dish of seal kidneys and liver was a favorite breakfast. Lunches alternated between seal meat and canned meat, while dinner tended to be leftovers from lunch. But their diet was largely composed of refined or processed foods and the modicum of seal meat was insufficient for their nutritional needs, in part because the meat was probably overcooked.

Discovery cook Charles Clarke's "toothsome" cakes may have been tasty, but they would no more prevent scurvy than would Scott's sniffing tin cans for spoilage, or what he called "the virus of the bacterium of decay." Their refined diet bore its black fruit the next summer as sledging teams came trudging back with spongy gums and discolored limbs.

Robert Scott's own ideas on scurvy were shaped by his head surgeon, Dr. Reginald Koettlitz, one of just three men on the expedition with polar experience. Confused by the failure of lime juice in the navy and by the success of germ theory in explaining infection, Koettlitz was convinced that there was no such thing as an antiscorbutic. He was confident that scurvy was instead a disease caused by bacteria.

To his credit, Scott took practical steps after the outbreak. Aside from the fluffing of beds and cleaning of the ship (based on hygiene theory) and wondering in his journals about the source of the contamination, Scott consented to butchering as many seals as were necessary to serve their meat daily to the crew as a replacement for tinned meat. At this news, "there were not a few downcast faces," Scott wrote in his journal. But within a fortnight, he said, "I do not think there is a man who would go back to tinned meat." Their bodies recognized good food. Soon the men took turns waiting at a seal's breathing hole on the ice with a barbed harpoon.

As the expedition began its second winter, 116 seals were stored frozen in a snow trench and 551 skuas were hung from the *Discovery's* rigging. Scott deplored the lack of penguins in their menu (only at the end of the expedition did they find a nearby colony) but made do for carnivorous variety at lunch with frozen New Zealand mutton on Sunday, skua on Tuesday, and seal heart or seal steak on most other days. Kidneys were used for pies, and livers were added to two breakfasts a week, but the sweetbreads—thymus and pancreas—apparently never got farther than the mouth of cook Charles Clarke. Thursday, the only day they ate tinned rather than fresh meat, became known as Scurvy Day.

"I have come to the conclusion that life in the Antarctic Regions can be very pleasant," Scott wrote at the end of the *Discovery* expedition, after a final meal of penguin liver and seal kidneys. That he would die eight years later in a miserable, malnourished, starving return from the South Pole speaks not just to the length of time he would be away from the antiscorbutic abundance of the coast, but also to the abiding confusion about the nature of the disease.

it paid for its cheek with its life

It's not clear whether Scott had learned his lesson. His 1910–12 *Terra Nova* expedition ate plenty of wildlife while at the Cape Evans hut, built just a few miles south of the Adélie penguin colony at Cape Royds. Each man consumed one to two pounds of seal and penguin meat per day. The men sought variety in these meals, but Tryggve Gran noted that some experiments did not fare well: "Seal is splendid fried in butter, but fried in penguin fat, as it was tonight, it is dreadful." And as Frederick Cook could have pointed out a decade earlier, if the meat was overcooked, its nutritional benefit would have been dreadful too.

During the first winter, as they prepared for the next summer's assault on the South Pole, surgeon Edward Atkinson gave a lecture on scurvy. The lecture was one of many given during the winter meant to entertain or inform. For readers now it sounds like both, a medical equivalent to the story of the blind men and the elephant. Rather than describing the mysterious disease in its entirety, Atkinson focused on isolated symptoms—alkalinity of urine and acidity of blood—and an odd list of possible causes: tainted food, damp, cold, overexertion, bad air, bad light, "and the possibility of [bacterial] infection in epidemic form." Atkinson admitted fresh vegetables cured scurvy, but despite the experience of recent polar expeditions, he "was doubtful of fresh meat." The notion that medical science was building slowly and logically toward the best possible answers was undercut by what information it had chosen to ignore.

By March of 1912, Scott and his companions were dead in a tent on the Ross Ice Shelf, the possible causes ranging from too little food to too few snowshoes for their Manchurian ponies. Slight improvements in weather, planning, or skiing technique might have saved them.

Did they suffer from scurvy? No one knows for sure. Certainly, they starved. Apsley Cherry-Garrard, a member of the *Terra Nova* expedition, wrote years afterward, "I feel more and more that a ration free of, or seriously deficient in, vitamins played a leading part in this tragedy." Cherry-Garrard had stood over the glassy bodies of his friends when their tent was discovered seven months after their deaths and heard the ice in Scott's arm break as his diary — with its beautiful writing that glorified British heroism against impossible odds — was extracted. That heroism, as nutritional chemist Robert Feeney (author of *Polar Journeys: The Role of Food and Nutrition in Early Exploration*) puts it, "could not compensate for the poor knowledge of human nutrition at the time."

An odd and somehow symbolic event occurred during the saddened *Terra Nova* expedition's second winter. On a stormy April night, many weeks after Scott's party was given up as lost, a banging on the hut door startled Tryggve Gran. Gran suddenly had the wild notion that Scott had risen from the dead: "I rushed out of the hut into the blizzard. Something loomed up and I ran towards it. Ugh! A big emperor penguin was paying us a visit. It paid for its cheek with its life." The strangeness of an emperor knocking at the door seems, in Gran's grief, to have been ignored.

Meanwhile, as Roald Amundsen and his Norwegian team on the 1911–12 *Fram* expedition prepared to race toward the South Pole ahead of Scott, they knew no more than the British about the existence of vitamins or the dietary mechanisms of scurvy. But Amundsen's firsthand experience from both polar regions had taught him how to prevent and cure it. After his time with Frederick Cook in the *Belgica*, Amundsen spent nearly two years among the Netsilik Inuit in the Canadian Arctic and stayed healthy eating as they ate. Like Cook, he then put his hard-won Arctic knowledge to good use in the Antarctic.

He brought plenty of preserved Norwegian cloudberries and whortleberries, known antiscorbutics. And as a Native-trained polar explorer, he sought blood: "Scurvy, the worst enemy of Polar expeditions, must be kept off at all costs, and to achieve this it was my intention to use fresh meat every day." Two hundred fifty seals were shot, most of them soon after the *Fram*'s arrival. Penguins were rare visitors ("tourists," Lieutenant Kristian Prestrud called them) because they nest on rocky shores, rather than in the snows of the Ross Ice Shelf. But as Amundsen and his men built the hut at Framheim, an emperor "gave exactly the impression of having come up simply to pay us its respects. We were sorry to repay its attention so poorly, but such is the way of the world. With a final bow it ended its days in the frying pan." Just one year later, with a final Antarctic bow, Amundsen sailed in all good health from Framheim to report to the world his victorious arrival at the South Pole.

Coincidentally, four years before Amundsen sailed from Norway to Antarctica, the first clinical trials to establish scurvy as a dietary deficiency had taken place just a few fjords away. For the previous decade, Norwegian sailors had been suffering from beriberi because the government altered its bread ration from traditional hard rye made with yeast to soft white stuff that was deficient in vitamin B_1. The cause wasn't known at the time, but Norwegian researchers Axel Holst and Alfred Frolich systematically deprived their test subjects of normal diets until they died, and then examined the corpses. Their victims were small, cheap, fuzzy, and available, having become a popular children's pet: guinea pigs. (This is how guinea pigs became synonymous with test subjects.) The researchers had fortunately chosen animals that share with primates the inability to synthesize their own vitamin C. Guinea pigs fed grains without vegetables died differently from those starved on a complete diet, the former showing the classic scurvy symptoms of loose teeth, bad gums, and hemorrhaging limbs. Although the researchers had been studying beriberi, they had created scurvy in the guinea pigs. Oddly, there's no evidence that Amundsen knew about Holst and Frølich's revolutionary study, but through his hard-won polar experience he had solved the problem nonetheless.

ʃ I'm going out to kill the dinner Y

If some explorers (like the Norwegians) planned their food well and thrived, while others (like the British) planned less well and suffered the nutritional consequences, there were also some whose menus were fine but who suffered anyway. That's the risk of trying to inhabit a frozen continent that crushes ships and hopes. The heroic age solution to tragedy, as always, was the necessary relationship with wildlife: more slaughter to prevent more scurvy. An astonishing example is the two-year chronicle of Otto Nordenskjöld and the 1901–4 Swedish Antarctic Expedition.

Though far less known, the tale rivals Shackleton's *Endurance* saga for drama and Victor Campbell's Northern Party epic for stark survival. It began like so many Antarctic voyages with a ship (named the *Antarctic*), its crew, and a small winterover party. A year later, the ship was sunk by the ice and the expedition divided into three separate, desperate tales of penguin-fed survival. That all men but one survived the second unplanned winter is remarkable. How they were reunited seems a miracle.

We'll call these three stories Nordenskjöld's tale, the Hope Bay saga, and Larsen's account. Let's start with Nordenskjöld.

In their first Antarctic summer, Nordenskjöld and the *Antarctic*'s captain, Carl Larsen, sailed with the entire party as it made geographical discoveries around the Antarctic Peninsula, correcting old maps and discovering new coastline. As the summer ended, Larsen landed Nordenskjöld and five companions on Snow Hill Island to build a hut and spend a winter exploring and making scientific observations. Then Larsen, his crew, and the scientists still aboard the *Antarctic* retreated safely northward to South America for the winter to chart and study South Georgia and Tierra del Fuego.

Nordenskjöld and his men celebrated their first night with a civilized glass of Swedish punch, not dreaming that they would be hunkered down like castaways for nearly two years. Gustav Åkerlund cooked, but in that first winter they "scarcely tasted fresh meat." Instead, according to Nordenskjöld, they never grew tired of their generous portions of tinned meat, tinned soup, blood pudding, lobscouse (a kind of stew), porridge, potatoes, herring, and the like, and apparently never lacked for nutrition, as he gave no hint of malnourishment.

There was enough food, and they did not ration it. But "the day came," he later wrote, "when we repented of this free-handedness."

As the next summer passed, Nordenskjöld and his men made ready to depart, expecting the return of the *Antarctic* but noting anxiously that the ice around Snow Hill remained stubbornly in place. Then, by mid-February, when a powerful storm and cold snap heralded another winter, a second year proved inevitable. They began to hunt in earnest, if sadly, for what became a larder of four hundred penguins, thirty seals, and a pile of skuas. In a compassionate echo of Jean-Baptiste Charcot, Nordenskjöld said that only "bitter need could compel us to this horrible slaughter ... here, where the creatures have not yet learned to fear man." Penguins in particular made him feel guilty, because "in these deserted tracts, [they] come to be considered almost as good comrades and friends."

Seal blubber became a replacement fuel for the stove. Skuas tasted fine with applesauce, something like an old, tough grouse. Penguin meat was roasted or fried with or without butter, but the men liked it best boiled with pea soup. They found the menu boring, but it quickly grew worse. They had taken the unnecessary precaution of salting much of their penguin meat when freezing would have been easier and tastier. The salted birds were "as hard and tough as leather," mourned Nordenskjöld, but by September they were served at every meal.

They still had ship's biscuit twice a day, but after they ran out of baking powder it seemed they would have no more fresh bread, until they ingeniously cultivated a new source of leavening—yeast from rotten potatoes. It caused turmoil in their guts but tasted fine. Fresh vegetables were a dream, other than a lost pea that grew in Nordenskjöld's bed. It had "not only thrown out roots two or three inches in length, but was also provided with a long stalk and small undeveloped leaves."

Regretting their spendthrift diet in the first winter, they worried about the possibility of a *third* winter, and so consumed only tiny amounts of the most pleasant items, such as milk and coffee.

Nordenskjöld noted the importance of slaughter even in their dream life: "One of us fancied he had gone back to his schoolbench, in order to learn how to flay miniature seals which were of a size just suitable for use in instructing a class." Sigmund Freud later commented on this story in *The Interpretation of Dreams*. He thought such dreams were "infantile" and characteristic of "adults who are transferred into the midst of unfamiliar conditions," but perhaps missed the point that the dreamer was simply practicing survival skills in his sleep.

Not long after their third summer began, Nordenskjöld and Ole Jonassen had finished a meal of pemmican and coffee on a sledging journey when they spied a trio of penguins approaching over the sea ice. Miraculously, the penguins turned out to be men, the first they had seen in twenty months. The arrivals were unrecognizable under wooden snow goggles and a thick coat of greasy blubber soot that matted their skin and wretched clothes.

Jonassen quietly suggested that a revolver might be necessary. "My powers of guessing fail me when I endeavour to imagine to what race of men these creatures belong," mused Nordenskjöld.

But the creatures were their *Antarctic* comrades Gunnar Andersson, Samuel Duse, and Toralf Grunden, the long-suffering inhabitants of a tiny stone hut at Hope Bay, where unbeknownst to Nordenskjöld they had been landed by the ship nine and a half months earlier.

When the *Antarctic* failed to pick them up, the trio had begun one of the more difficult winters in Antarctic history. As the reunited men all sat down to coffee and hoosh made of Hope Bay homemade pemmican — fried seal meat and seal blubber — Nordenskjöld recoiled from the dish and marveled at their tale: the Hope Bay saga.

At the end of December 1902, Captain Larsen had dropped Andersson, Duse, and Grunden off at Hope Bay with a small depot of food and instructed them to travel to Snow Hill Island with the bad news that the *Antarctic* was unable to reach them through the ice. The trio was supposed to bring Nordenskjöld and his men back to Hope Bay for pickup, but halfway along the two-hundred-mile journey to Snow Hill, they were stopped by open water.

They turned around and were back on the beach at Hope Bay by mid-January. As they waited for the *Antarctic*, they built a stone hut just in case the ship failed to return. They tried but failed to chink the six-foot-high walls with wet snow, but built a tight roof with a sledge, some planks, and a battered tarpaulin.

Although they pitched their tent inside this tiny structure for added warmth, it rarely got above freezing inside. Their only luxury was the hut's carpet of penguin skins, which they swept clean with the wing of a giant petrel.

The ship never came. As they settled in to an unknown fate, the Hope Bay men took turns cooking on the blubber stove, with only enough fuel by late winter to cook two meals a day. Their frying pan was a large flat tin with a nail and piece of wood for a handle.

To fend off scurvy and supplement their small supply of tinned food, dry vegetables, and bread, they slaughtered seven hundred penguins, twenty-one seals, and twenty fish ("indescribable dainties" caught with a homemade hook and line dropped through cracks in the ice). "I'm going out to kill the dinner," the cook of the day said cheerfully.

They suffered a chronic hunger for carbohydrates. Rare treats of porridge, though made goopy by mold and boiled in a mix of snow and seawater, tasted better than anything they remembered fondly from Sweden. Just as tasty was their *dänga*, a traditional dish of bread crumbs softened in brackish water and then fried in seal fat. They celebrated Sundays and birthdays with a shot of gin, "glorious beyond description," according to Andersson.

Every meal ended with a Swedish civility—formal gratitude for the cook's effort—a "Thank you" followed by a "Don't mention it." Grunden sang Norwegian chanteys, while stories, jokes, and conversation were conjured up against what Andersson called "the desert of intellectual nothingness" and "the dark might of isolation and of extreme distress."

They had no books to read, only food labels. And while they never washed hands or faces, they did once or twice wash their feet in their soup plates.

Somehow winter ended, and as summer began, they fought their way through storms toward Snow Hill again. In that wondrous moment of reunion at the place now called Cape Well-met, when Nordenskjöld imagined he was seeing tall penguins, Andersson, Duse, and Grunden thought they were seeing seals walking upright. But a trembling suspicion overtook Andersson: "A delirious eagerness seizes us. A field-glass is pulled out. *'It's men! It's men!'* we shout."

Now nine men were at the Snow Hill hut, happy in their diminished loneliness but haunted by the fate of Larsen and the *Antarctic*. If the ship had sunk, who would rescue them? On the eighth of November, less than a month after the Hope Bay trio appeared at Snow Hill, Gösta Bodman and cook

Gustav Åkerlund of Nordenskjöld's party were traveling to nearby Seymour Island to collect seal blood for blood pancakes, as well as the season's first penguin eggs.

They were awoken, as if in a dream, by two clean, well-dressed Argentine ship's officers from the *Uruguay*, a rescue vessel sent south to discover the fate of the missing Swedes. When the four men walked into Nordenskjöld's camp a short while later, the expedition leader's heart swelled with both joy and sorrow, for while the Argentines brought salvation, they could tell him nothing of the *Antarctic*'s fate. And then, late that same night, the dogs barked. Bodman stepped outside, only to be stunned by another miracle. "*Larsen!* Larsen is here!!" he shouted, and out came Nordenskjöld to find his friend Larsen with five comrades, safe and sound, nearly two years after their separation. "No pen can describe the boundless joy of this first moment," wrote Nordenskjöld. "I could feel nothing but joy when I saw amongst us these men, on whom I had only a few minutes before been thinking with feelings of the greatest despondency."

Larsen gave them an account of his own party's survival. After the *Antarctic* had dropped off the Hope Bay trio, it was caught and pinched by relentless sea ice. Larsen gave the order to abandon ship. They were twenty men, as alone in the world of shifting sea ice as the *Endurance* crew would be a decade later. They set off for Paulet Island, twenty-five miles distant, dragging boats, fuel, gear, more than a ton of provisions, and the ship's cats. They spent two weeks trudging, hacking through pressure ridges, and ferrying loads by boat from ice floe to ice floe. As the ice shifted around them, possessions and supplies floated away on broken floes.

Their first meal on Paulet was memorable not just because

they were safe on dry land, but because it was the last time for eight months they would eat tinned meat, put sugar in their coffee, or eat freely of biscuits and butter.

They immediately harvested Adélie penguins from the late-season remnants of a vast colony, which botanist Carl Skottsberg called "a poultry yard worth having." To stay healthy and well-fed, they hoped to put up at least three thousand carcasses, but as winter approached, the colony emptied into the sea, and the men secured only eleven hundred.

The Adélies understood the hunters' intentions, and escaped across the snow, "throwing themselves on their bellies and kicking themselves forward at a most astonishing rate." The Swedes built a stone hut, thirty-four by twenty-two feet square, roofed with sails and thirty seal skins, and tall enough to stand in only under the ridge. Some of the twenty men, unwilling to sleep on bare stones, laid penguin skins down and kept them there even after they began to rot. Winter weather soon "assumed despotic power," trapping them in the hut for days with nothing to do. Cook Axel Andersson had plenty to do, and did his job admirably in a crude kitchen (just a small, drafty annex to their hut), "day in and day out, during the long severe winter on Paulet Island in biting cold, half choked by the nauseous smoke from the blubber," according to Skottsberg. Once, a fierce storm hurled the cook's roof out to sea. All the water for Andersson's soups and drinks came from a lake turned greenish-yellow by the guano of thousands of penguins nesting upslope.

The strong guano flavoring meant merely that the men could not taste the difference between Andersson's coffee, tea, or Sunday cocoa. "But," reflected Skottsberg, "we do not attach importance to trifles." What was important was that they drank the hardworking cook's liquids boiling hot to warm their souls.

Meals consisted of penguin and more penguin, with occasional seal and fish. Blubber became palatable, and blubber smoke filled the hut. Their only decent meal was an Easter feast of sea birds fried in margarine and rice porridge, an object of prolonged fantasy. At night, dreams came from a menu of two items, rescue and food, the same topics that occupied them by day.

During the winter, seaman Ole Wennersgaard suffered a prolonged heart condition, moaning through his sleepless nights. Skottsberg recorded that when "Death, the one guest who could reach us," found Wennersgaard, his corpse could not be buried on the frozen shore. So he was stuffed into his sleeping bag and, like their penguin meat, buried in a snowdrift until the spring thaw. Eight months after arrival on Paulet, Captain Larsen and five others, including cook Axel Andersson, risked their lives to row through ice-filled waters. Their three goals were to discover the fate of the three men they'd abandoned at Hope Bay, to reach Nordenskjöld at Snow Hill, and to somehow let the world know they were alive. And just as Larsen accomplished all three by reaching Snow Hill and the *Uruguay*, the remaining shipwrecked crew (with their sole surviving cat) at Paulet ransacked the newly laid eggs of the Adélie colony. "Oh, how we revel!" wrote Skottsberg. "Fried eggs, boiled eggs, raw eggs, eggs in soup, in coffee, in tea: I am a temperate man and never ate more than a score in one day, but I know of a sailor who ate three dozen in the same time."

Fearing another year in isolation, they gathered six

thousand eggs. This added a tragic twist to their great joy just days later, when Skottsberg woke to a magical sound, the *Uruguay*'s steam whistle: "I thump at the sleepers beside me: 'Can't you hear it is the boat—*the boat*—the boat!' 'a boat! hurrah!' ... the shouts are so deafening that the penguins awake and join in the cries."

It's worth noting that Carl Skottsberg knew how cruel and indulgent their enormous harvest of penguin eggs sounded as he wrote about it, and tried to preempt any criticism: "How many of my readers know what it means to lie in cold, and darkness, and hunger, week after week?" He might well have written "month after month," and that their voracious harvest of the "poultry yard" simply expressed their desire to live. And if we give these carnivorous men their due, then we have to admit that, for better or worse, their destruction of wildlife was inseparable from the human trait that sent them south: the desire to know, to travel beyond the horizon of our ignorance, even if it means leaving behind the world of compassion to get there.

Roast Penguin

Penguin breasts
Butter
Beef suet
Dried onions
Flour
Gravy granules
Salt and pepper to taste

Season the penguin breasts well with salt and pepper
and dip each piece in melted butter. Roll in flour
and fry in beef suet to seal the meat, turning once.

When each side is crisp, place in baking tray and pour
over the fat from the frying pan.

Sprinkle with dried onion and cook in the oven on
medium heat until tender. For the gravy — stir a
teaspoon of flour into the cooking fat then add a
spoonful of gravy granules and sufficient water or stock
to thicken

Meat and Melted Snow   4

My decade as an Antarctican followed a path outward into the hinterlands. As the years passed, I was determined to spend fewer workaday hours amid the trucks, warehouses, and cargo yards of McMurdo, the United States' massive research and logistics facility, and more time getting paid to camp in the icy and impossibly beautiful emptiness. McMurdo sits like an industrial wart on the pale skin of an ice-covered continent larger than the U.S. and Mexico combined. But it has a view of an inhuman paradise, and that's where I wanted to be.

The seasonal sea ice at McMurdo's front door and the permanent ice shelf at the back door are white tablecloths covering the dark and frigid waters of the Ross Sea. Wind-driven snow and a hard light play across them in a polar dance set to a song of hypothermia.

Beyond, the Transantarctic Mountains are filled to their ears with glacial ice, with stark peaks of bare and barren stone emerging like the heads of drowning swimmers. And beyond the mountains, the ultimate blankness of the true Antarctic landscape, a featureless plateau of snow-dressed solid ice as deep as an ocean and larger than Australia. No trees, bushes, flowers, grasses, or terrestrial animals. No culture or society, no religion or faith, and no history but Earth history.

The story of Antarctica before the heroic age is the rafting of a continent across magma, the tides of climates across eons, and the evolution of wildlife along its coasts.

Year by year, I succeeded in moving outward into these icescapes, doing field work I'll discuss in later chapters, which culminated in my season on the Odell Glacier with Julian.

The more I saw and experienced, whether flying by helicopter or LC-130 across crevassed glaciers or staring through a tent flap at the undulating sastrugi (hard waves of snow) of the polar plateau, the more I wanted to see. Antarctica gave me a front-row seat to the nature behind nature—the play of physics behind biology—and made me feel like I was camped out on the Moon looking back at Earth. I loved it.

Such desire was, until several decades ago, a death wish. Antarctica supports little life beyond a few species on the coast, some lichens in the mountains, and, in the interior, only microbes blown in on the jet stream to sleep for millennia amid ice crystals. The severe cold is antibiotic. Away from its coast, the continent offers nothing to exploratory humans but cold air to breathe and hard snow to melt.

In the windy, subzero conditions of interior Antarctica, considerable energy is spent simply keeping body temperature within normal range. Humans are better adapted to heat than to cold, and our physiological responses to cold range from ineffective to counterproductive. Shivering, for example, warms us only slightly.

The constriction of blood vessels close to the skin— intended to reduce heat loss—makes frostbite more likely, while creating a layer of insulation "less than that provided by wearing a typical business suit," according to one analysis.

Many expedition members shivered all night in their inadequate sleeping bags, burning calories in addition to those expended in the extreme daily effort of skiing, dogsledding, or manhauling.

A body consuming an inadequate diet will quickly begin to convert all fat reserves, and then, in the self-imposed starvation that is polar travel, the body will feed on its own muscle mass. As a body's fat and muscle mass deteriorate, shivering requires more energy and produces less heat. Over time, if sufficient calories are not found, the body will sacrifice any tissue it can to maintain the nervous system and the heart; the stomach will atrophy, while organs fail, and the victim descends from fatigue to apathy to death.

All of which reminds us that early travel into Antarctica required a level of planning and austerity unsurpassed in exploration until humans ventured into space. When the men of the heroic age left their huts to explore the hinterlands, they left behind the last vestiges of ordinary life. No stockpiled crates of food, no fresh meat squawking outside the door, no communication beyond voices in the wind. Sustenance was limited to what they could bring, and they could not bring much, because, paradoxically, the less food weight they carried, the farther they could go. Up to a point. Robert Scott, who in his race to the Pole would lay his life down in the gap between calories needed and calories provided, expressed the dilemma elegantly: "The issue is clear enough: one desires to provide a man each day with just sufficient food to keep up his strength, and not an ounce beyond."

Antarctic sledging was by its nature a profound exercise in logistics and risk management. A balance had to be struck between sledging goals and the realities of starvation, dehydration, and deprivation, and success depended on an austerity that matched the emptiness of the terrain. Sledging food had to be complete but also simple, concentrated, dehydrated, compressed, calculated, and packed tightly.

Most expeditions brought pemmican, the ancestor of today's Clif Bars and other high-performance nutritional supplements. Pemmican is a perfect lightweight endurance food made of dried lean meat and fat, used by Native Americans for millennia. Antarctic explorers supplemented it with a carbohydrate, usually biscuits, and often some modicum of sugar, caffeine, and dairy fat. Fuel to melt snow and heat the hoosh was critical, but heavy. Everything was calculated in volume and weight and accumulated only up to the thin line between ambition and death.

kitchen innovations

Pemmican was not the only culinary innovation that made Antarctic sledging possible. Every Antarctic traveler, from the first canvas-and-leather manhaulers to today's satellite-linked adventurers, owes a debt of gratitude to two Scandinavians: Frans Wilhelm Linqvist and Fridtjof Nansen, whose inventions revolutionized camp cookery. Nineteenth-century stoves were essentially lamps, using wicks to draw fuel upward toward a lazy, sooty flame. In 1892, Linqvist designed the Primus stove, which has been the basis for nearly every small camping stove since. The small Primus burner sat directly above its kerosene tank, connected by a narrow tube. The tank was pressurized with a small pump integrated into its side, providing a clean blowtorch-like flame. The flame then heated a loop in the fuel tube to maintain pressure throughout cooking. Borchgrevink's

Southern Cross expedition in 1899 was the first to use the Primus stove on the southern continent. For reasons of doubt or enthusiasm, they brought fifty-three of them.

Nansen had tested the Linqvist design on his monumental 1893–96 *Fram* expedition to the Arctic. His success did much to promote the Primus but, more importantly, he also designed and built a companion device for it soon known as the Nansen cooker. The lightweight aluminum invention was an ingenious reimagining of the relationship between pot and stove.

Typically, heat rises from a burner to the bottom of a pot, then escapes up and around it. Sledging journeys could little afford such waste of heat (and fuel). The Nansen design trapped that heat and forced it back down again, between an additional ring-shaped snow-melting pot and an external wall. A large lid fit tightly over all. Thus each unit of heat was utilized to warm the entire hoosh pot *and* melt snow for tea or cocoa. The savings in fuel weight more than made up for the combined twenty-five-pound heft of the stove and cooker together.

Still, converting handfuls of snow into a large pot of boiling hoosh for several men took half an hour, often longer. It required nearly as much heat to melt the snow as it did to bring water to a boil, and so the colder the snow, the longer the wait for the meal. Consuming the hoosh, however, took no time at all. Accounts of sledging meals spend more time describing the premeal wait and the post-meal hunger than the meal itself. "In less time than it has taken me to write this the food is finished," mourned Ernest Shackleton.

Which is why, several years after these technical inventions by Nansen and Linqvist, Shackleton introduced an equally important psychological innovation, one that attempted to soothe the irrational thoughts of hungry sledgers who were each convinced they had received less food than their companions. When the hoosh pot came to a boil, someone had to "whack out" the food, dispensing an equally inadequate portion into each man's mug. Robert Scott reported that, on his *Discovery* expedition, Shackleton's "noble game" of Shut-Eye made the apportionment blind by requiring that one man turn his back to the mugs into which the cook had equitably poured out the hoosh.

The cook pointed to each mug in turn and asked "Whose?" and "he of the averted head," as Scott put it, would name the owner. Despite the obvious fairness of Shut-Eye, Shackleton noted on his *Nimrod* expedition that hunger made them feel "a distinct grievance if one man manages to make his hoosh last longer than the rest of us." (Although Shackleton is given credit for inventing Shut-Eye, its origin may be much older; there is a nearly identical Inuit communal food-sharing custom.)

And finally, in Antarctic trail cuisine, utensils were also subject to extreme minimalism. A man needed only his spoon, a word almost as melodious as hoosh. Shackleton wrote of spoons as "indispensable possessions," as important as dentures to an old man. Forks, according to Jean-Baptiste Charcot, were "rejected as quite useless and . . . replaced by fingers, which were considered a great improvement."

Charcot also had a special camping utensil, which said much about the nature of Antarctic cuisine; he used a "carefully preserved piece of wood which was used to stir the soup, to scour the bottom of the saucepan, and to remove snow from the soles of our footwear."

the equivalent of toast

Cold, poor nutrition, and hunger challenged a sledger's body, but there was another, equally dangerous threat: Every man who dared the Antarctic interior was severely dehydrated, largely because Antarctic air is the atmospheric equivalent of toast. Antarctica is the driest continent, a great polar desert where every breath exhaled carries moisture from the lungs that cannot be replaced except by drinking melted snow or ice.

Fuel was extremely limited, however, and explorers could only rehydrate at meals. Eating snow or ice provides relief, but a human burns more energy in melting and warming it to body temperature than the drink provides. Sledgers did not often carry water containers, which were too heavy and too quickly frozen. Two or three hooshes per day—with cocoa, coffee, or tea—had to do. Ironically, this chronic dehydration occurred as the men marched over the largest mass of frozen water on Earth.

Severe dehydration causes a wide range of problems, starting with a loss of energy that can diminish a person's work output by nearly half. Chronic dehydration leads to less efficient digestion, joint and muscle problems, constipation, confusion, delirium, and liver or kidney damage.

The effects of dehydration are intensified at altitude and when the body is so starved that it has begun to consume vital tissues. Worse, when food is scarce, water is increasingly necessary to help extract fat reserves, so the more dehydrated these sledgers became, the less able they were to make full use of their diminishing body fat.

Though long acknowledged as part of Antarctic life, dehydration has rarely been discussed in terms of the success or failure of sledging journeys. Antarctic chronicler Roland Huntford told me that in his view, "dehydration is the critical deficiency, but has been neglected by most commentators." Amundsen knew this, Huntford believes, and provided "more than enough fuel to provide all the water that was necessary," whereas he thinks that "Scott and his men clearly suffered from chronic dehydration."

It's an open question how many miles these Pole seekers and other sledgers lost due to dehydration-related exhaustion, or what role their chronic thirst might have played in poor absorption of nutrients from the hoosh. Quantity of food was their first concern, followed by its quality and variety. Melting snow for water was merely the burdensome task en route to the hoosh. Day after sledging day, as they marched deeper into the bone-dry interior, they came increasingly to resemble their pemmican.

objects of greatest desire

"Contrary to what you may think, people liked pemmican," wrote Robert Feeney in *Polar Journeys*. "They had to. They lived on it for months." Most of us would gag on the stuff, a dense brick of protein melded with fat. Unless we were *truly* hungry, that is, hungry from burning so many calories that our bodies began to sniff unconsciously for the richest energy sources.

Like a grizzly bear emerging from hibernation looking for winter-killed carcasses, someone working long hours in the polar environment develops a starvation sensitivity to calorie-rich foods. Fats such as butter or oils became particularly attractive, though whatever sledgers were most lacking in their diet became the object of greatest desire.

European polar experience agreed with Native wisdom: Pemmican was the best food for the job. Arctic explorer Robert Peary made it clear: "Pemmican is the most satisfying food I know of. Many times I have reached camp feeling as if I could eat my own weight, and the one half-pound ration of pemmican has seemed painfully small. But by the time I had finished I would not have gone out of the igloo for the finest spread New York could furnish." Not all of Peary's fellow Arctic travelers were so sanguine about the taste, though: "Time reconciles it to the palate," said Alexander Mackenzie, first European to traverse North America, while explorer Gino Watkins mused that pemmican "kept the body twitching but not the soul."

Traditional pemmican was composed of lean wild meat — bison, venison, and the like — cut into thin strips, dried over coals or in the sun, pounded and shredded, then mixed with melted marrow fat and berries into a block of perfect food: meat for protein, fat for energy, and berries as antiscorbutic flavor. In the high plains of North America, Native Americans packed pemmican into bags of uncured bison skin sealed with fat. As the bags dried and shrank — like ancestors of the Ziploc — the food was as good as vacuum-sealed and could last for years. When it came time to eat, the pemmican might be consumed directly or made into a stew with whatever wild vegetables were at hand. (The Cree called this *rubaboo*, a word as fun for the tongue as hoosh.) Fur traders and other European explorers bought pemmican in huge quantities, and for many years it was the most important trade item after furs. It figured largely in a power struggle in the wilds of Canada called the Pemmican War.

By the time it reached the hoosh pots of Antarctica, pemmican had been transformed into a European industrial product. Rather than a handmade amalgam of wild meats and fat, it had become a canned factory food made of a fifty-fifty mix of beef protein and beef lard. No antiscorbutics were included. Unlike the traditional version, the new pemmican was not waterless, which, in addition to the tin can, made it heavy.

Perhaps the best pemmican of the period belonged to Roald Amundsen on his Pole journey. It was wrapped in foil, rather than canned, and designed by Amundsen along the lines of the Norwegian Army's emergency ration. It contained oatmeal and dried vegetables for better flavor, complete digestion, and prevention of malnutrition. This seems to be the only pemmican of the age that at least partly reflected the traditional Native American recipe. A few dried vegetables may not be much of an antiscorbutic, and Amundsen was so fast in his assault on the Pole that he had little chance to develop scurvy. Still, it is notable that throughout the heroic age no one else thought to improve the pemmican with some vegetable matter.

Pemmican was survival food, but biscuits were the most beloved of the sledger's holy trinity: protein, fat, and carbohydrates. Biscuits were crunchy reminders of a civilized home. Carbohydrates seemed to account for most food dreams, with tantalizing breads and cakes waiting just beyond the dreamer's reach. Here again, Amundsen seems to have planned his trail cuisine well. Rather than calling for the empty nutrition of white pastry flour and baking soda, the Norwegian recipe utilized whole-meal flour, oats, and yeast, which provided more of the necessary B-vitamin complex.

While biscuit recipes varied, the pleasure of eating something akin to bread did not. In all expeditions, biscuits were eaten by themselves, broken into the hoosh for a thicker, porridge-like meal, or both. For the *Nimrod* expedition, Shackleton dished out a pound per man per sledging day. "I eat all my lunch biscuit, but keep a bit from dinner to eat in the bag so as to induce sleep," wrote Shackleton. "The smaller the quantity of biscuits grows the more delicious they taste." The Norwegians were no less affectionate; they "positively caress the biscuits before they eat them," said Amundsen.

ʃ peaches and syrup ʃ

No one, not even Amundsen, knew what the ideal balance between fat, protein, and carbohydrates should be for Antarctic expedition food. Scientific consensus at the time held that significant protein was required to replace muscle mass depleted by the caloric demands of polar travel. But recent science suggests that fat and carbohydrates should make up the bulk of a polar ration, because fat provides a better, denser energy source than protein, while carbs can protect muscles from being converted to energy.

The brutal Winter Journey of 1911, a tale told by Apsley Cherry-Garrard in *The Worst Journey in the World*, was meant to be a quick scientific mission from Robert Scott's base at Cape Evans to procure emperor penguin eggs at Cape Crozier sixty-seven miles away (penguins were thought to be primitive links between dinosaurs and birds), but the journey was also a dietary experiment in preparation for the next summer's Pole journey. Scott had asked the trio to strip down their menu to just pemmican, biscuit, and butter, and that each try a high dose of either fat, protein, or carbohydrate.

Edward Wilson started high on fat (eight ounces butter, twelve ounces pemmican, twelve ounces biscuit per day), while Henry "Birdie" Bowers went for protein (sixteen ounces pemmican, sixteen ounces biscuit). This left poor, skinny Cherry-Garrard (known as "Cherry"), at the coldest time of the year in the coldest landscape on Earth, with twenty ounces biscuit and just twelve ounces pemmican.

Little did they know that conditions on this trial run would be far more demanding than on Scott's Pole journey the next summer. Cherry, Wilson, and Bowers left Cape Evans in the dark, five days after Midwinter's Day. No one had ever attempted such a journey. It was a death march that somehow did not end in death. Pain was constant, comfort unimaginable. They were always frostbitten, with large frost blisters repeatedly swelling up on their fingertips. Their sledge harness and clothing froze solid, once locking Cherry's head into a skyward-looking position during a four-hour march. Sweat turned to ice, which then crackled off and piled up in their clothes.

Sleeping bags were an icy hell. Not only did the men have to fight inch by inch to fit into the frozen bags, cramping up as they went, but they could not get warm overnight: "Things are getting pretty bad," Cherry wrote, "when you get frost-bitten in your bag."

Darkness ruled, with only four hours of dim light per day, hardly enough to see their footprints. Temperatures as low as –77.5°F made the snow seem like sand under their two fully loaded sledges. To glide, a sledge requires the melting by friction of the ice crystals underneath its runners, impossible at such low temperatures.

Much of their travel became relay work, as they hauled one sledge some distance over what Cherry described as the "soft, powdered, arrowrooty snow," then returned for the other, lit by one small candle.

Thus they trudged three miles for every mile advanced. On one typical day, they traveled a mere one and a half miles "by the utmost labour."

The ruined trio of Wilson, Bowers, and Cherry-Gerrard immediately after the Winter Journey, 1911

Under usual Antarctic conditions, these men prided themselves on getting a boil going for the morning hoosh in twenty minutes. Here, in the dark, it took them four hours from wake-up to harness. Cooking took much longer because melting and boiling times are determined by the temperature of the snow. Matches frosted up and would not light. Fingertips burned with the cold agony of handling food bags or cooking gear.

The job of cook was so hateful that rather than make it a weekly burden they swapped day by day. Cherry noted that it was difficult even "to splinter bits off the butter."

They had enough food. The problem was that their dietary experiment made eating unpleasant. Wilson could not eat all of his butter, nor could Bowers finish his pemmican. After his pile of biscuits, poor Cherry was still hungry, afflicted with heartburn, and more subject to frostbite. His body desperately wanted fat. Before giving in, Cherry experimented with more biscuit (twenty-four ounces total), but to no avail. He and Wilson swapped so they came out even: twelve ounces pemmican, sixteen ounces biscuit, and four ounces butter per day. "This is an extremely good ration," Cherry wrote. "We certainly could not have faced the conditions without." It would be the ration for the Pole party the next summer too, except that there would not be enough of it.

Nineteen days later—averaging a mere three and a half miles per day—they arrived at Cape Crozier as damaged men, but somehow life got worse. They found only a few emperor penguins, and Wilson was nearly blinded by a blob of burning penguin fat. Hurricane-force winds hurled their tent away, leaving them as dead men in sleeping bags buried under a snowdrift. "Such extremity of suffering cannot be measured," Cherry wrote, but "madness or death may give relief." For days, they communicated occasionally by shouting, to see if each was still alive. They did not eat. Pinches of snow served as a drink. Cherry lay in his bag thinking of what pleasures he had missed in his life: "The road to Hell may be paved with good intentions: the road to Heaven is paved with lost opportunities. I wanted those years over again. And I wanted peaches and syrup — badly."

As the storm eased, they rolled their ground cloth over themselves and made a hoosh. "The smell of it," Cherry wrote, "was better than anything on earth." After the storm, hoping against hope, they looked around in the dark until, miraculously, Bowers found the tent. It should have been miles away, buried under drifts. Not knowing what to say about such grace, they literally said nothing.

Starting the march home immediately, they slept as they walked. Meals took at least an hour, all hands pitching in. By the end, all of Cherry's teeth were dead, the roots split by the cold. They stumbled, grateful and nearly dead, into the hut at Cape Evans, where their friends, shocked at the destruction deep cold had wreaked, cut their frozen clothes off and fed them bread and jam and cocoa.

the whole grocer's shop

Variety in meals was never much of an option on the trail, other than the flavor imparted from an unclean pot (pemmican in your cocoa, for example). On long trips, sledgers had room for little else but the basics. For the hoosh, they could vary the ratio of pemmican and biscuit, or the amount of water in the pot, but they had their sledging rations, a few celebratory delicacies perhaps, and that was it. Hoosh and go, hoosh and sleep, hoosh and go, hoosh and sleep, ad nauseam.

Sometimes one man's experiment was another man's mistake. On the *Nimrod* journey to the south magnetic pole, an absurd argument broke out. "Mackay detected an unusual flavor in the hoosh, and cross-questioned Mawson severely on the subject," explained Edgeworth David, the third member of the team. "Mawson admitted a lump of sugar. Mackay was thereupon roused to a high pitch of indignation, and stated that this awful state of affairs was the result of going out sledging with 'two foreigners.'" Mackay was Scottish, the other two Australian, at a time when the difference was mainly in the quality of one's tan.

Dried milk powder, butter, or cheese might be added in moderate amounts to provide extra fat. Oatmeal was an alternative carbohydrate. Small measures of sugar and chocolate provided instant energy and sweetened a meal. Tea, coffee, and cocoa flavored what liquid heat the Nansen cooker provided.

Amundsen was an exception here too, having learned from the Netsilik to avoid stimulants like coffee and tea while sledging. The Norwegian Pole party grew weary of cocoa, however, and upon their triumphant arrival at Framheim, they asked for coffee: "After ninety-nine days of cocoa that coffee was delicious," wrote Helmer Hanssen. "There would have been a funeral in Framheim if we had been offered cocoa."

Scott in his *Discovery* account dismissed the idea that variety in hooshes was important, though his notion of simplicity was less than austere. His sledging rations included biscuit, pemmican, a bacon and pea-flour soup base, oatmeal, dried milk, cheese, chocolate, cocoa, sugar, tea, onion powder, salt, and pepper.

He had the right idea—packing, unpacking, and preparing meals should be as simple as possible—but

Antarctica required an asceticism that British expeditions had not yet mastered.

A few years later, Shackleton introduced a slimmer *Nimrod* trail-food menu: "Our cuisine was not very varied," he wrote, "but a voracious appetite has no nice discernment and requires no sauce to make the meal palatable; indeed, all one wants is more."

That said, he still brought for his attempt on the Pole twice as many items (biscuit, pemmican, chocolate, tea, cocoa, sugar, cheese, oatmeal) as Amundsen brought several years later (biscuit, pemmican, chocolate, and dried milk). Amundsen's trail lunches were truly austere: three or four biscuits, with some snow to quench their thirst.

Lieutenant Kristian Prestrud stated the Norwegian opinion plainly enough: "The bill of fare was identically the same every day, perhaps a fault in the eyes of many; variety of diet is supposed to be the thing. Hang variety, say I; appetite is what matters."

Amundsen added his deeper sarcasm: "I have never considered it necessary to take a whole grocer's shop with me when sledging . . . a rich and varied menu is for people who have no work to do."

Yet in the final days of Robert Scott's life, while working harder than any human should to return from the Pole, he blamed his downfall, in part, on a culinary experiment. "Like an ass I mixed a small spoonful of curry powder with my melted pemmican—it gave me violent indigestion. I lay awake and in pain all night; woke and felt done on the march." His right foot froze and he was too miserable to notice. It never thawed again.

⟨ math and aftermath ⟩

The death of Scott and the Pole party, however, resulted from far more than a spoonful of curry powder. There was no single cause, as far as anyone knows, but there was a litany of possibilities.

Much of it has to do with food and math: calories, quantity, and logistics. The extraordinary trial of traveling through the icy emptiness of Antarctica requires extraordinary calculation.

There is perhaps no place on Earth that better demonstrates the cause-and-effect of food math and fatal aftermath, and no better Antarctic example than the "race to the Pole" between Scott and Amundsen.

Tensions were high. Amundsen, a seasoned Arctic explorer, had arrived unannounced in the Antarctic with one goal: to beat Scott to the Pole and lay claim for Norway to the last great challenge of terrestrial exploration.

Scott's expedition championed a broad scientific program as well, but for personal, professional, and patriotic reasons, the journey to the Pole was an essential quest. How much his fateful logistical decisions were shaped by the competition with Amundsen is an open question.

The math and aftermath began with their rations. Perhaps, as Amundsen said, a hard worker prefers a simple menu, but there must be enough energy in his meals to sustain him

Just as an Antarctic explorer could eat plenty of food but die of scurvy, he could eat a substantial diet without replenishing the energy lost each day trying to keep warm, working hard in heavy clothes, battling extreme weather, and breathing the thin air at high elevation. Hunger, in this climate, is followed closely by hypothermia.

Roald Amundsen in fur and skins, circa 1920

One estimate suggests that, at –40°F, half of what someone

eats is utilized by the body just to maintain its proper core temperature. According to another study, at –30°F, men expend up to one thousand calories simply to warm and humidify the air they breathe.

It's thought that an average of 6,500 calories would have been necessary for the hardest days of Antarctic manhauling, an ordeal estimated to require more energy per day than competing in the Tour de France.

Amundsen and Scott both issued rations of approximately thirty-four ounces for their Pole journeys, or about 4,500 calories. But the two teams were not deriving similar benefits from their meals.

For one thing, the Norwegians burned less energy dogsledding than the British did manhauling (though the Brits did initially rely somewhat on ponies, dogs, and machines), and had more vitamin B in their biscuits. Both parties killed their beasts of burden (Scott's ponies and Amundsen's dogs) midtrip and ate their fresh meat, but Amundsen had also cached seal meat with its additional vitamin C.

On his return, Amundsen was able to increase his team's rations to 5,000 calories per day, probably more than needed, while harsher weather during Scott's late-summer return deprived his team more quickly of energy and nutrients. The caloric deficit between the British team's needs and what their rations provided is estimated to be about 2,000 calories per day. The men would each have lost more than three pounds per week. Scott himself probably lost about 40 percent of his body weight before he died. And in the end, Amundsen was on the trail for only three months, while Scott died after five.

The other crucial Antarctic math concerned depots, the

carefully quantified piles of food and fuel placed at strategic distances along the route through the Antarctic void. Because the men could not carry all the food and fuel they needed to travel hundreds of miles, the expeditions were organized along an umbilical trail of supplies. Many trips and enormous effort were required to lay these depots so that the Pole parties could leapfrog into the unknown.

The depot math was complicated. The power of men, dogs, ponies, and machines required to move the Pole parties south and then back to the coast was weighed against how much food and fuel was necessary to feed that power.

Much work was done by the *Terra Nova* and *Fram* expeditions in the early months of 1911, just after arrival in the Antarctic.

Scott's doomed group at the South Pole, January 1912

Amundsen, seven men, and dozens of dogs established

three depots, sixty miles apart, at 80°, 81°, and 82° South latitude, depositing more than three tons of material. Thirteen hundred pounds of it were placed at 82°, only 480 miles from the Pole. Amundsen's first trip, to 80° and back, took just a week. Meanwhile, Scott's teams—thirteen men, eight Manchurian ponies, and twenty-six dogs—placed two depots, one a bit past 78° and the other, One Ton Depot, halfway between 79° and 80°. Establishing One Ton took twenty-four days. More crucially, One Ton was intended for 80° South, thirty miles to the south, but the ponies were inadequate for the task.

The failure to place the depot farther south would have dire consequences. The following summer, the depot-laying was completed as both expeditions moved deeper into the interior. They brought more food and fuel from the hut, then spread out the previous summer's depots into several smaller ones closer to the Pole.

Amundsen had intended to lead a party of eight, but because of expedition strife he reduced the Pole party to five. This meant he had a surplus of food in his depots, and thus a substantial margin of safety.

His five-man party established seven more depots at regular, attainable intervals, including one called the Butcher's Shop Depot, where, as planned, they killed and butchered twenty-four of their forty-two dogs.

A few weeks later, they reached "the goal of our desires," as Olav Bjaaland (a national ski champion) put it, planting their Norwegian flag in the blank space that is the Pole before celebrating with a full meal of seal steaks, biscuit, pemmican, and chocolate.

The celebration was otherwise stoic—these were

professional polar explorers, after all—but the Viking raid against British ambition had been a success.

On their return from the Pole, each depot was easily reached and surpluses in quantity, energy, and nutrition were fully enjoyed. The seal meat stored in some depots as treatment for potential scurvy "was a pleasant distraction in our menu, nothing more."

The Norwegians and their surviving dogs actually *gained* weight on the return journey. They arrived "hale and hearty" at Framheim three months after departure.

The success, Amundsen was quite adamant to point out, resulted from "the most careful planning, sound judgment, and infinite patience in working out minute details."

The British had departed with careful, minutely orchestrated plans as well, however convoluted. Sixteen men, ten ponies, two motorized sledges (a third had been lost through the ice when unloaded from the ship), and twenty-three dogs worked to establish eight more depots at intervals en route to the Pole. In theory, each depot held one week's rations and fuel for each returning man—not just for the Pole party but also for each supporting party, which turned back northward at different times after dropping off their loads.

Some of the men, early on, had their doubts about Scott's math and transportation choices. Cecil Meares, Scott's dog handler, and Titus Oates "both damned the motor. 3 motors at £1,000 each, 19 ponies at £5 each, 32 dogs at 30 shillings each. If Scott fails to get to the Pole, he jolly well deserves it." At the foot of the Beardmore Glacier, at what they called Shambles Camp, the last five of their ten ponies were shot and cut up for food.

Some writers on this story have faulted Scott's decision to

add Birdie Bowers at the last minute to the final Pole party, in part because their rations were established for four men, not five. Famed polar adventurer Ranulph Fiennes has argued to the contrary that rations were not reduced, but rather simply redivided between the Pole party and their final support party, leaving in theory ample food for Scott's planned return. This doesn't account, however, for other difficulties of adding the fifth man, among them less tent space and increased cooking time.

They reached the Pole, but found it marked by Amundsen's extra tent and a Norwegian flag. Scott's diary tells the tale: "The Pole. Yes, but under very different circumstances from those expected. . . . Great God! this is an awful place. . . ." To have labored so only to arrive second, he wrote, was crushing. "Now for the run home and a desperate struggle. I wonder if we can do it."

They could not. Scott's men turned dispiritedly homeward and struggled to cover the long gaps between depots, in part because of slow sledging conditions and unprecedented weather.

Decades of weather data have since shown that the intense cold and severe blizzards experienced by the returning Pole party were unusual. As on the Winter Journey, their sledges would not glide easily across the colder snow. Scott described it as "800 miles of solid dragging."

They starved as they walked, their bodies weak and cold. Edgar "Taff" Evans died first, then Titus Oates; both had wounds that would not heal, perhaps because of nutritional deficiencies and severe dehydration. Exactly what they suffered from is impossible to know, as their bodies were never recovered and because some of the symptoms of deficiency diseases, starvation, and dehydration blend into each other as they grow more acute.

The torment of body and mind must have been terrible. After nearly five months and the expenditure of up to a million calories each, Scott, Wilson, and Bowers died at the end of March 1912, three weeks after Amundsen had broadcast his victory from Australia to the world.

That this aftermath was due in part to the expedition's early math seems clear. Their bodies lay eleven miles to the south of One Ton Depot, but nineteen miles north of where that depot was meant to be laid.

transport management

In the tradition of nineteenth-century European colonial journeys to remote areas of Africa, Asia, and the Arctic, some heroic-age expeditions brought beasts of burden to Antarctica that in hard times became meat for the hoosh. Ponies and dogs hauled and then became fodder. Douglas Mawson, leader of the Secret Society of Unconventional Cooks, reasoned that "in an enterprise where human life is always at stake, it is only fair to put forward the consideration that the dogs represent a reserve of food in cases of extreme emergency." Few things are as efficient on a life-or-death journey as the ability to eat your transportation.

Mostly this was a British affair. Of eighteen heroic-age expeditions, fifteen brought beasts of burden, but only six (four British, one Australian, and one Norwegian) converted them into food. Scott's 1901 *Discovery* expedition fed dogs to dogs as provisions dwindled. Shackleton's 1907 *Nimrod* expedition slaughtered its worn-out Siberian ponies and cached their meat in the depots they had helped to build. Shackleton was careful to eat this fresh, heavy meat before the lightweight, concentrated pemmican they could carry farther. Sometimes they chewed raw cubes of it as they walked. In Shackleton's shadow, Scott's 1911 *Terra Nova* expedition used the same ill-suited ponies as transport.

As the first five were shot along the trail, each made four or five meals for the dog teams. Scott reported that his men enjoyed the change too: "Tonight we had a sort of stew fry of pemmican and horseflesh and voted it the best hoosh we had ever had on a sledge journey."

What was unthinkable in normal life became normal on the ice. "One point which struck us all," Shackleton wrote later, "was how man's attitude towards food alters as he goes South.

At the beginning, a man might have been something of an epicure, but we found that before he got very far even raw horse-meat tasted very good."

Best of all, he said, was blood from a butchered pony frozen into an icy mass in the snow, which was then boiled to thicken the hoosh. Socks, Shackleton's last pony, fell into a crevasse just hours before he was due to be shot and cut up for food.

Shackleton later posited that "the loss of Socks, which represented so many pounds of meat," might have cost them the Pole.

The name most associated with eating domesticated animals in Antarctica is Roald Amundsen, whose slaughter of twenty-four healthy dogs just before claiming victory at the Pole is infamous. Amundsen's Butcher's Shop, like Scott's

Shambles Camp, marked not just the end of these animals' lives but also the place where carcasses were dressed for consumption. "Great masses of beautiful fresh, red meat, with quantities of the most tempting fat, lay spread over the snow," wrote Amundsen, a hungry Norwegian epicure for whom the dogs' corpses recalled "memories of dishes on which the cutlets were elegantly arranged side by side, with paper frills on the bones, and a neat pile of *petit pois* in the middle."

January 16, 1909: Mackay, David and Mawson become the first humans to reach the South Magnetic Pole

The story here is neither of epicurean savagery nor even of human hunger, but of transport management. Amundsen, the most professional and shrewd of polar explorers, created a calculus of weights carried and weights consumed for every day of the roundtrip journey to the Pole. He related this to the pulling power of a dog—how many pounds on the sledge each dog could haul. As food and fuel were consumed, weight on the sledge diminished, and at a certain point that lost weight would equal a dog's pulling power and the dog became superfluous.

Amundsen then figured "the average weight of edible flesh of a dog and its food value when eaten by the others. By these calculations," he wrote, "I was able to lay out a schedule of dates upon which dog after dog would be converted from motive power into food."

In this analysis, some dogs were killed so others could live comfortably on the trail. After twenty-four dogs were killed at the Butcher's Shop, and after the Norwegians had been to the Pole, six more were slaughtered, one at a time, allowing the surviving dogs to actually gain weight on the return journey. The open question is how many more dogs might Amundsen have brought home safely had he not stuck to his calculation so firmly.

Though Amundsen shows real affection for individual dogs throughout the story, he was a man on a mission. The animals were slaves to his cause, and so completely did Amundsen believe in that cause that he could write casually of their destruction: "I must admit that [the cutlets] would have lost nothing by being a little more tender, but one must not expect too much of a dog." In fact, Amundsen expected everything of them, and he got it.

hungry hells

In challenging the Antarctic, sometimes even the best-laid plans simply weren't enough. In these early journeys, careful provisioning and high-calorie pemmican were thin defenses, and poor planning was no defense at all. Hoosh was the warm line between life and death, which meant that men were always a few meals away from becoming icy artifacts buried by drifting snow. A single catastrophe could upend, or end, lives.

There are no better illustrations of this than the survival tales of Douglas Mawson's 1912 Far Eastern Party and Aeneas Mackintosh's 1914 Ross Sea Party. Both stories are about traveling impossible distances on starvation rations. They are about willpower despite vitamin deficiencies, and they are about loyalty amid death. Coincidentally, both groups were delivered unto and rescued from their Antarctic tragedies by the same ship, the *Aurora*.

On December 14, a sunny day of 21°F, Mawson and his companions, Xavier Mertz and Belgrave Ninnis, were traveling east over glacial highlands, paralleling the coast. They were one of six teams that sledged out from their hut at Cape Denison in early November to explore different areas of the unmapped region. The teams had spent the winter together in the hut as jovial Unconventional Cooks, but now the serious work had begun.

Mertz led by ski while Mawson followed, sitting on his sledge and studying his charts as the dogs pulled. Ninnis came last, walking briskly beside his sledge. Mawson looked up as Mertz suddenly stopped, looking behind them at a gaping hole in the empty trail. Ninnis, the sledge, and their six strongest dogs had disappeared into a crevasse. With them went the tent, all dog food, mugs and spoons, and all but about ten days of rations. Ninnis's death was the only loss of a human to a crevasse in the heroic age and represented a death sentence for Mertz and Mawson. As they kneeled and gazed with disbelief into Ninnis's deep blue grave, only a dying dog, part of the tent, and a two weeks' supply of food were visible on a shelf one hundred fifty feet down, all beyond the reach of their ropes. Mawson had deliberately assigned the best dogs and the most valuable provisions to what he considered the safest sledge.

He assumed that he and Mertz, traveling ahead, had taken the greatest risk. But Ninnis had *walked* onto the snow bridge, his feet punching through where skis and sledge had spread the weight.

Their grief for a friend with whom they had wandered "a lonely blizzard-ridden land in hunger, want, and weariness," as Mawson put it, was matched by their fear of "the future which loomed up sinister before us." They were 316 miles from the hut with little human food, no dog food, and six near-useless dogs—George, Johnson, Mary, Ginger, Pavlova, and Haldane.

All but essential weight was discarded. No depots had been laid, so what little they carried was all they had. Their first meal consisted of an ugly broth made from boiling food bags to be thrown away, while the dogs were fed worn-out mitts, boots, and rawhide straps. From then on, the dogs ate only each other.

On their first grief-stricken, desperate day homeward, they covered twenty-seven miles in a reckless dash, plunging across crevasses with what Mawson called "a tense heart and a grim sense of unreality." Mertz configured a tent out of the old tent cover and used sledge runners and skis for poles. It barely fit the two men. Mugs were made from biscuit tins, and spoons were carved from the sledge frame.

They tried to forget about food as much as possible, ate no

lunch, and didn't even stop to melt snow to stave off dehydration. Poor "stringy" George and "disreputable" Johnson were the first dogs to be slaughtered, but the latter was so rancid that in subsequent days Mawson and Mertz would define their day's luck by how much Johnson they pulled from the bag of mixed dog meat.

Things got worse as they agreed to mete out their meager food allowance according to how many miles they made in a day. Stormed-in days in the cramped tent were a hungry, claustrophobic hell. Mary tottered and fell. Haldane, too emaciated for his harness, followed suit, but not before nearly falling into a crevasse. "Fortunately," Mawson wrote, "I was just able to grab a fold of his skin at the same instant, otherwise many days' rations would have been lost."

Confined by weather to the tent, the men struck on an idea: Boil the dog carcasses for hours so that even the gristle, sinews, and paws turned into a jelly. This work made better use of the bones, extracted the marrow fat, saved them time for future meals, and lightened their fuel load. Mawson sanguinely described "a delicious soup made from some of Pavlova's bones cracked open with the spade."

To ease the stress of dividing their starvation rations fairly, he and Mertz relied on the tradition of Shut-Eye at each meal. The cook of the day turned his back, and in response to the other's question—"Whose?"—said either "yours" or "mine," even when dividing the skull of a beloved dog. By the time Ginger—their final dog—fell to the knife, Mawson and Mertz were on a diet of about fourteen ounces a day, less than half their usual thirty-four-ounce ration, most of it worn-out dog meat of little nutritional benefit.

Food dreams haunted them. Hopes for their survival on a

miserable Christmas were toasted with dog soup. Only the dogs' livers were easy to chew, but as Mawson wrote, "trouble of a new order was brewing."

Mertz fell apart, physically and mentally. Mawson first realized the seriousness of his friend's disorder when Mertz "lost appreciation of the biscuit."

This, surely, was madness. Neither Mawson nor Mertz showed clear signs of scurvy, though they were obviously starved and malnourished. But they could not explain the shedding of skin and hair. Mawson even shed the soles of his feet. Both suffered severe abdominal pains and Mertz's behavior grew erratic, eventually leading to a complete breakdown of body and mind. Marches of one or two miles were all he could do, then nothing at all. Mawson tended to Mertz, all the while begging him to keep walking as hopes of survival slipped away.

Decades later, an analysis of their symptoms and Mertz's sudden decline suggested a condition known as hypervitaminosis A. Toxic levels of vitamin A bioaccumulate in the livers of many polar marine creatures (like seals), and in dog livers if they are fed those creatures, as the vitamin produced by marine algae passes up the food chain. One hundred grams of these livers would poison an adult human, and the two men ate six livers between them.

It's possible that Mertz ate more than half, accepting Mawson's offer to share. In a strange frenzy near the end, Mertz bit off the frozen tip of his own finger. Dysentery and raving fits characterized his last hours in his sleeping bag, before he died next to an exhausted, grieving, sleepless Mawson.

Polar transport: Food pulled toward the South Pole by more food

In a heartbreaking bit of understatement, Mawson wondered "if there was ever to be a day without some special disappointment." He cut the sledge in half and dumped absolutely everything unnecessary for survival. His raw feet hurt so much while crossing the bare ice of the Mertz Glacier that he chose to walk *along* the soft surface of bridged crevasses, tempting fate as only a miserable man can. He did later fall into a crevasse, dangling by rope from the sled, which had not broken through. Mawson at first gave himself up for dead, but after several attempts, and then one final heroic push of adrenalin, he hauled himself up by the rope. He was motivated not by love or patriotism, but by a single culinary regret, "that after having stinted myself so assiduously in order to save food, I should pass on now to eternity without the satisfaction of what remained."

He questioned whether it was better to live or die. On one hand, he could continue to starve and move forward with little hope, or he could "enjoy life for a few days, sleeping and eating my fill." Whether tenacious or masochistic, he went on, and by the time he was down to twenty small pieces of dog meat, half a pound of raisins, and a few ounces of chocolate, with blizzards burying his tent up to the peak, he finally had his day without disappointment.

On January 29, he stumbled onto a cairn left just that morning by a search party. He attacked the food bag cached within it, scattering its contents on the ground. The search party had turned back to the hut, and Mawson followed, knowing he could be there in two difficult days. He reached Aladdin's Cave, an excavated hideaway and depot in the glacier five miles away from the hut, and feasted again. Three oranges and a pineapple were proof that the *Aurora* had arrived from Australia. But when Mawson turned to finish the last five miles, a shrieking blizzard blew in and lasted an entire week.

At storm's end, as Mawson limped within sight of the hut, he could see the *Aurora* leaving Antarctica for the year. Perhaps it was just as well, for despite the care of the men who had volunteered to stay behind, Mawson took months to recover his wits and health. Sailing home immediately through difficult waters might have killed him. Ten months later, the *Aurora* appeared again to bring him home.

In the following austral summer, the *Aurora* again slipped through ice-filled waters to deliver another ill-fated team to its trial by ice. Aeneas Mackintosh and the Ross Sea Party, full of hope and vigor, took up residence in Robert Scott's old hut at Cape Evans, unaware that their plans (and bodies) would fare only slightly better against the Antarctic austerity than Scott's dead Pole party. The men were the lesser-known half of Shackleton's famed *Endurance* expedition, which was simultaneously entering the Weddell Sea on the far side of Antarctica, intending to make landfall and prepare for Shackleton and a small team to make an 1,800-mile crossing of the continent via the Pole.

The purpose of the Ross Sea Party was to lay depots from Ross Island halfway to the Pole, thus providing supplies for Shackleton in the last weeks of his crossing. Fate had other things in mind for both parties. About ten weeks after the *Endurance* felt the fatal pinch of the Weddell Sea ice, the *Aurora* was ripped from its winter moorings at Cape Evans by a storm. Pinned within a giant raft of ice, the ship drifted north through the depths of winter and wouldn't return to Cape Evans for nineteen months. The marooned Ross Sea Party had a problem: The *Aurora* had taken with it nearly all the trail rations meant for Shackleton's depots. Those marooned had "none of their own fuel, clothes, or stores," wrote survivor R. W. Richards, yet had fifteen hundred miles of sledging ahead of them. They scavenged leftovers from Cape Evans where, luckily, some things were plentiful.

The flooring in a passageway, for example, was built with full cases of jam. Richards recorded that "general stores, flour and the like, we estimated to be sufficient for 10 men for two years."

Had they known that Shackleton would not touch the continent, they could have averted enormous suffering and tragedy. But one-eyed Aeneas Mackintosh and his men believed that Shackleton's fate lay in their hands. Come hell or hypothermia, they would lay depots to 83°30' South, at the foot of the Beardmore Glacier, even if it meant laying themselves down in the process.

Ten men and four surviving dogs—Oscar, Con, Gunner, and Towser—were all that remained, after the loss of the ship, to fulfill the party's obligation to Shackleton. One man, too ill to sledge, stayed the summer at the hut. The other nine began dragging loads with the dogs in early October, but progress in soft snow was excruciatingly slow and one of their three Primus stoves (unreliable leftovers from Scott's expedition) was soon beyond repair. With no means to make hoosh and hundreds of miles yet to travel, three men had to turn back to Cape Evans. Of the remaining six, divided into two groups of three, two already showed symptoms of scurvy. Mackintosh and Reverend Arnold Patrick Spencer-Smith were easily fatigued, and Spencer-Smith's legs were painfully swollen. What the party had cobbled together for trail rations were insufficient in quantity and deficient in nutrition.

Ernest Joyce and R. W. Richards realized how crucial the dogs were for their survival, and so began feeding them a hot hoosh of dog pemmican, biscuits, and a little seal meat every third night. It was a wise investment. Before the team reached the final depot at 83°30' South, the Reverend Spencer-Smith collapsed and had to be left alone in a tent with some food while the others hurried to finish the job. They returned days later to Spencer-Smith, whose legs were black from ankle to hip.

Their journey north was a fight against time and the progress of the disease. Dogs and men pulled as a single team. Joyce led in harness at the end of a twenty-five-foot rope, with Mackintosh, Spencer-Smith, Wild, Oscar, Gunner, Con, and Towser harnessed in along the rope. Richards and Hayward pulled on separate ropes from either side.

As the scurvy progressed, Spencer-Smith was laid on the sledge in his sleeping bag while Mackintosh tottered alongside. "I am afraid that one of us will give in," wrote Joyce about those who could still pull. "If so, the whole party will go under."

Their legs were so stiff with black swelling that the men did not dare bend them at night because they might not be able to straighten them upon waking. Before falling asleep, they strapped pieces of bamboo to the back of their knees to keep them straight.

They all forged northward until reaching the depot at 80° South on February 11. On the eighteenth, with three days of rations on hand, a blizzard of hurricane-force winds began to rage, burying their tents in snow. It lasted twelve days. The men quickly went on half-rations, then reduced again to a half-cup of pemmican and one biscuit per day. Like Robert Scott's ill-fated party four years earlier, they were starving and pinned down by blinding weather just ten miles from the Bluff depot.

After six days, they packed up, resigned to disaster. But Mackintosh collapsed and it was decided to leave him behind with Wild and Spencer-Smith while Joyce, Hayward, and Richards made a final attempt to reach the Bluff depot. That they made it four days later is a miracle.

The blizzard had not let up, they were out of food and pathetically weak, and they could not clearly measure distance or direction in the whiteout. They traveled at a quarter of a mile per hour.

In the end, Richards said, they owed everything to "the massive Oscar," who "just lowered his great head and pulled. . . . It may not be an exaggeration to say that he alone gave that little extra strength that enabled us finally to make the depot."

It took them three days to reach the invalids again. Wild actually stumbled out of the tent in harness to help them come in. "I cannot even recall it without a lump in the throat," wrote Richards. Like Oscar, he said, Wild was "a great chap . . . on whom one could rely to the end."

Mackintosh crawled out of the tent, while Spencer-Smith was still delirious in his sleeping bag. All together again, they limped slowly toward Hut Point. With just forty miles to go, Joyce wrote in his diary that Spencer-Smith was nearly dead and Hayward was in a walking coma, with "gums swollen and turning black, joints of legs swollen and black, feet can hardly bear any pressure on them."

Of the three invalids, Mackintosh was well enough to be left alone in a tent while the other two were dragged on toward the fresh seal meat at Hut Point.

It was too late to save the Reverend Spencer-Smith. They woke to find ice on his eyelashes and beard, only two days from salvation. They pushed on to the hut, where Richards saw sleeping seals and "had the strongest desire to rush to one of those animals and cut its throat and drink the blood that I knew would hose from its neck. Extraordinary! I had this instinctive and compelling feeling in me that this is what my scurvy-stricken system needed. It was almost overpowering."

Three days later, Joyce and Richards set off with the dogs and a supply of seal meat to rescue Mackintosh. By the time they brought him safely back to Hut Point, the Ross Sea Party had been out almost two hundred days, far more than any previous expedition, and it had been fifteen months since they had changed their clothing or taken a bath.

Things got worse.

They would spend months in the small, dank, cold hut at Hut Point, little better than a small filthy shed. "I never recollect Hut Point without a touch of mental distress," wrote Richards. "We lived the life of troglodytes." Return to the relative comfort of Cape Evans, thirteen miles away, was impossible until the sea ice thickened. Frustratingly, it often formed but then broke up again in the blizzards. On May 8, two months after being nursed back to health, Mackintosh and Hayward decided they would make a break for it. Joyce pointed to an oncoming southerly blizzard, but the still-frail pair headed out with a bag of cold seal meat for sustenance. They were never seen again.

Not until July 15, four months after the end of sledging, did the others cross. Six months later, Captain J. K. Davis and the *Aurora* carried Shackleton—fresh from the rescue of his men on Elephant Island—into McMurdo Sound to pick up this last sledging party of the heroic age. Davis recorded what they found: "Smoke-bleared eyes looked out from grey, haggard faces; their hair was matted and uncut; their beards were impregnated with soot and grease. . . . Their speech was jerky, semi-hysterical and at times almost unintelligible, their eyes had a strained and harassed look."

Five years later, as the heroic age closed around the wake of the northbound *Quest* expedition in 1922, Ernest Shackleton, Robert Scott, Aeneas Mackintosh, and William Bruce lay dead, their remains all consigned to the Antarctic. Shackleton lay in the soil of South Georgia, Scott in the ice of the Ross Ice Shelf, and Mackintosh in the waters of McMurdo Sound. Bruce died in Scotland, but his ashes were brought south at his bequest. Amundsen, Filchner, Gerlache, Nordenskjöld, Drygalski, and Charcot continued in the life of scientific adventure, though never again in the South. Lesser-known scientists and sailors slipped back into normal life, rare emissaries from a continent still so little known as to be indescribable to those around them.

Of expedition leaders, only Douglas Mawson returned to the ice, remaining afterward as an adviser to the Australian Antarctic program, adapting his hard-won wisdom about math and aftermath to the modern age.

All the efforts to travel inland into the inhuman Antarctic emptiness had made history, but at a terrible cost. Humans were simply not yet equipped for Antarctic life. Historian Stephen Pyne has written that these expeditions were anachronistic, romantic quests staging the last dramas of old-fashioned Earth exploration. A new age of science and technology had dawned but had not reached Antarctica.

The Ross Sea Party is a beautiful, tragic chronicle, but R. W. Richards knew even at the time that their journey would mark "the end of a definite era in polar transport, the era of heavy, slogging manhauling, with its slow progression and long absences from all sources of fresh food."

While heroic-age Antarctic explorers had been fighting scurvy, smitch, and starvation, a revolution in food production in the modern world had long been under way. By 1899, the year the *Belgica* returned home, factory food made up 20 percent of all U.S. industrial production.

By 1904, when Robert Scott ended his first expedition, hot dogs and ice cream cones were introduced at the St. Louis World's Fair. Eight years later, when snow gathered around Scott and his men in their sleeping bags, tea bags and instant coffee had taken America by storm.

Near the end of the heroic age, as the *Endurance* crew bolted from their makeshift hut on Elephant Island for the *Yelcho*, Americans at home marveled at pop-up toasters. And in 1922, while Shackleton was laid in his grave on South Georgia, well-off workers in the United States showed off their electric refrigerators to neighbors still stuck using iceboxes.

It would take another generation before these innovations (and many more) reached the ice to set the stage for the modern Antarctic life that Julian and I would eventually enter, a world in which calculations about life in the hinterlands were rooted more in abundance than in deprivation.

The starving wolf: Richard Byrd at Advance Base in 1934

"When cooking Penguin, I have an awful feeling inside of me that I am cooking little men who are just that little too curious and stupid."
–Gerald T. Cutland, *Fit for a FID, or How to Keep a Fat Explorer in Prime Condition*

How to Keep a Fat Explorer in Prime Condition 5

One of the great ironies of Antarctic life is that it requires a great deal of noise and complexity to live in all that silence and simplicity. Our industrial supply lines stretch all the way back to the warm world we've left behind. Ships, planes, helicopters, tracked vehicles, and snowmobiles bring us deeper into the desolation from which we connect back northward by radio, phone, and satellite.

The world you know is one filled with machines. Antarctica, however, is a distant world *reached* by machines. It is a continent that has known only the modern phase of our technology-obsessed species. By the time I arrived, it was easy enough to be "camping for cash" on a lunar ice sheet with little qualification other than a desire to be there and a tolerance for hard work in cold places.

I've sat in a tent on the East Antarctic ice cap with a glass of chilled whisky in one hand and a satellite phone in the other, flown cheerfully in a variety of planes and helicopters over ice that starved or killed the men of the heroic age, and watched a parka-clad researcher in a bulldozer-dug ice cave scrolling through images of 5,000-year-old ice crystals on her desktop computer. My relationship with Antarctic silence was a far cry from the brutal realities of early exploration and its small groups of pitifully outfitted men overwhelmed by cold, wind, and distance from home. I could (and did) toast their memory with my glass of whisky, but I felt more like a stranger than a member of their clan.

It's no surprise, then, that the history of Antarctic food loses some of its drama after the heroic age. Scurvy, for example, was banished. No more would sledgers limp back to Hut Point with black legs and swollen gums. The twentieth-century forces sending these new mechanized expeditions south were simply too wealthy and too well-informed. In 1929, the Nobel Prize in Physiology or Medicine was awarded for work on vitamins, and then in 1937, more Nobel Prizes were given out specifically for the isolation of vitamin C from lemon juice and for the synthesis of vitamin C. The vitamin was suddenly cheap and available in the marketplace, and thus a permanent part of Antarctic exploration. Food preservation improved dramatically. Better fruit extracts were devised, while canned and frozen vegetables retained more of their nutritional value. Meanwhile, with larger modern ships, more fresh and frozen meat survived the trip south.

This new era of exploration, sometimes called the "mechanical age," marked the arrival of machines that transformed access both to the continent and to the heart of the Antarctic. Steel icebreakers plowed through sea ice, bringing tracked vehicles to forge new trails across the ice caps and shortwave radios to connect them to base camps and the world they left behind. Aircraft opened up the last remaining regions of the continent. Antarctic logistics were finally reaching a level of sophistication that matched that of the modern science they were meant to support.

Behind these expensive mechanized expeditions were greater political forces with greater national ambitions. Polar historian Roland Huntford summed it up nicely: "Polar exploration was moving into the domain of the coming superpowers, for they had the resources and vitality for the complex scientific enterprises whose day had dawned." Although private expeditions still characterized the early mechanical age, after the Second World War, Antarctic exploration became part of larger national science missions. Expedition populations were larger, as scientific teams added new disciplines and specialists were required to maintain aircraft, vehicles, and generators. Dog handlers sat down to lunch with pilots, mechanics, glaciologists, and geophysicists.

Accordingly, cuisine in the new base camps began to more closely resemble the menu at home. The new expeditions brought products from suppliers like the British company Crosse and Blackwell, who in an advertisement titled "With Mawson to the Antarctic," explained that "science has shown us how to select foods of definite dietetic value."

Crosse and Blackwell offered everything from potted meats to chutneys to calves' feet jelly, all "prepared in spotless kitchens" and therefore perfect for expedition leaders and "a million careful housewives, too."

Larger kitchens and larger piles of more diverse supplies increased a cook's latitude, but still, the result that hit the table was only as good as the man who prepared it. The principles of Antarctic cuisine still held: limited options in *what* to eat, and no options for *where* to eat. Antarcticans and their cooks were stuck with each other, through dishes as familiar as hamburgers and as strange as grilled seal brains.

Antarctic wild foods were still on the menu, but for variety rather than economy or culinary extremity. As for trail food, pemmican continued to set the standard.

The Native American concept could not be improved upon, even if the modern recipe was unrecognizable. And though the term *hoosh* persisted into the mechanical age, it began to take on an historical air.

Dogs were still essential for hinterland travel, but they shared the trail with machines. The classic hassles on a sledging journey of untangling and feeding animals were matched by the equally difficult hassles of vehicle repair. Long hours were put into preparing aircraft or Weasels (small tracked vehicles) for leaving camp, and longer hours were put into repairing these machines once they failed en route or limped back to camp with fatigued metal parts for which spares had to be manufactured or improvised. Fingers were frozen onto bolts, carburetors, tracks, and wrenches.

Of the new machines, planes were by far the most important, used to survey vast territory and to transport food, gear, and personnel far above difficult terrain. From 1928 onward, after Sir Hubert Wilkins of the Wilkins-Hearst Expedition flew over the ice for the first time, no Antarctic expedition arrived without aircraft.

The promise of Antarctic aviation, expressed by Wilkins as a "tremendous sensation of power and freedom," spoke of liberation not just from gravity but from all the dangers of Antarctic surface travel.

For the first time, explorers could blithely survey the ice as they did the rest of Earth. The amount of food necessary for each mile of travel became negligible, notwithstanding the emergency rations tucked away in the plane for a not unlikely crash. In these first few years of the new era, planes brought human eyes to nearly every part of a coastline that had eluded ship-bound explorers for 150 years.

But it was the wildly popular American, Commander Richard E. Byrd, who made Antarctic aviation famous.

♪ encore, janitor, sugar 🐧

Commander Byrd was not only the first big player in the age of machines but also the first American expedition leader to set foot on the continent. Only on this 1928–30 expedition did the United States become a player in Antarctic geopolitics.

Byrd's base, jingoistically named Little America, was placed at the Bay of Whales near the location of Amundsen's Framheim (long lost under wind-blown snow). Little America housed sixty-three men in its construction phase and forty-two for the winter, far larger than any previous Antarctic wintering party.

One man who didn't make the cut for winter was cook Sydney Greason (a fine surname for a mess-hall cook), allegedly for excessive drinking. Greason shot back: "I never in my life saw such a bunch of double-crossers."

Perhaps it didn't help that he was not a Mason, the secret society to which Byrd and at least ten others in the wintering party belonged, including replacement cook George "Gummy" Tennant.

In the spirit of so many eccentric heroic-age cooks, Tennant was an itinerant, toothless teetotaler, red-bearded and so sloppy that when someone cleaned up in his absence, they found rotten pieces of meat lodged throughout the kitchen.

Nonetheless, second-in-command Laurence Gould knew that cooking for so many men under Antarctic conditions was no picnic: "

It would have been difficult to have found anyone anywhere who would have done as much work as George did and have done it with such good humor."

Since he didn't drink, Tennant's good humor didn't come from Little America's numerous barrels of "medicinal" alcohol. Though Prohibition was the law in the United States, Little America was hardly a dry town. The alcohol became notionally medicinal when mixed with handfuls of an antiscorbutic lemon powder, the result being a sort of alcoholic marmalade they called Blowtorch. Parties grew raucous, particularly during a disruptive three-week midwinter drinking binge. Byrd was no slouch with the bottle, having dressed up for an end-of-winter party as a "perfect dollar waterfront whore" while a football game destroyed the mess hall.

American-style breakfast arrived with Little Antarctica. Tennant laid out canned fruit, oatmeal cakes, molasses, and occasionally ham and eggs. With no official lunch, men stopped by the mess hall to make sandwiches from Tennant's fresh bread, often with canned sardines or salmon and cheese. Dinners were soup, either canned or homemade with leftovers; meat, including beef, mutton, seal, penguin, skua, or even whale; dried or canned vegetables; and pie or custard. Tennant also made a fine meal of crabeater seal cooked in tomato sauce with onions and breadcrumbs.

Their two tons of whale meat came from whaling vessels hired to tow their ship through the ice and had been cured by hanging it over the ships' toxic funnel smoke. "The men liked their whale meat best cut thin and fried or chopped and rolled with onions into meatballs," wrote Byrd. "It tasted like hamburger or, when cold, like lamb."

Some men, he said, "regarded penguin as a delicacy. . . . It is a very dark, rich and gamey meat and tasted like nothing that we have in civilization."

They had to rely a bit more on local meat than planned. Their Antarctic-born puppies were allowed to roam free until the night they raided the expedition's frozen meat storage, devouring most of the special cuts of turkey, chicken, and veal.

Nearly every decision Byrd made when planning the expedition relied on the wisdom of Roald Amundsen. The two men corresponded often until Amundsen died unexpectedly in the Arctic just six months before Byrd landed at the Bay of Whales. "Byrd had sat at Amundsen's feet," Roland Huntford wrote, and "adopted his principles." The siting of Little America, the route Byrd would follow through the mountains to the Pole, the use of dogs, the emphasis on aircraft for future Antarctic travel, proper nutrition, and attention to detail were hallmarks of the great Norwegian explorer that Byrd took to heart.

Despite the links to Antarctic tradition, it was technology that most distinguished Byrd's expedition from its predecessors. For the first time, electricity fired up power tools and lit up an Antarctic base against the polar darkness. And the American public grew to love Byrd's dramatic Morse code broadcasts to the *New York Times*, particularly when describing his momentous first flight over the South Pole.

Byrd's team flew on Thanksgiving Day, 1929, less than a month after Wilkins's pioneering Antarctic flight. Rather than eating turkey, they were flying the *Floyd Bennett*, a Ford trimotor with a seventy-foot wingspan, sixteen hundred miles to the Pole and back.

Initially, Byrd planned on merging old and new Antarctica by including dogs on the flight. That way, the crew could sledge home if forced down. But there was no room for the animals after two 125-pound bags of emergency rations were stuffed into the plane to feed the men if they crashed in the Transantarctic Mountains.

On its ascent of the Liv Glacier, the plane could not power over the last wind-scoured peak blocking their path, and it was Byrd's food that made them too heavy. Pilot Bernt Balchen shouted for them to dump it out the Ford's door. One bag went, but when the pilot looked at the mountain wall approaching the windshield, he shouted, "Dump more!" Perhaps it was best that Byrd didn't bring the dogs.

Meanwhile, Laurence Gould and the other five men of the dog-sledging geological party were listening in while camped on the Ross Ice Shelf. They provided weather updates and stood ready to rescue the Pole party if necessary.

But Byrd had created a secret code for radio transmissions with Little America, which he had not shared with Gould. The geological party heard sequences like "encore, janitor, frenchman, onalaska," and increasingly as the plane worked its way south, the word "sugar," which they correctly surmised meant "South Pole." Byrd, they knew, had circled the blank spot on the ice cap where Amundsen's tent lay buried under windblown snow.

While Byrd, Balchen, and the others flew home in the *Floyd Bennett* at over one hundred miles per hour to celebrate their sweet success with a turkey dinner and some Blowtorch, Gould, his dogs, and his men were straining through deep snow toward a summer of pioneering geological discoveries in the Queen Maud Range of the Transantarctics.

The *Floyd Bennett* did in four hours what took them four dog-killing weeks.

At the nostalgic climax of the summer, as Gould related in his book, *Cold*, he and his men found a stone cairn laid by Amundsen on Mount Betty at the foot of the Axel Heiberg Glacier. They found in it a full can of kerosene, some matches, and a tin with a note outlining his success at the Pole. Gould took the note for posterity and each man pocketed a small stone from the cairn, but they otherwise left the monument intact. One man, at least, had hoped for more. "Gee," said the ravenous Freddy Crockett, "he didn't leave any grub!"

Like the heroic-age Norwegians they honored, these mechanical-age scientists had their own dog-killing logistics. When they planned the eleven-week, 1,525-mile trip, they had three options: bring three thousand more pounds of dog food, receive supplies via airplane, or shoot some dogs to feed the others.

But the sledges were already overburdened, and Byrd refused to risk aircraft for the purpose. By the time the last pistol shot rang out, only twenty-one of their original forty-six dogs remained. "The dogs become pawns in a game," wrote Gould, "and the fittest survive the longest."

In *Cold*, Gould meditated on this awful experience, but like Amundsen, prioritized his mission: "We had to shut our eyes to sentiment or write the word failure as the end of all our efforts and careful planning.

After all . . . there is little difference between the sacrifice of dogs for such necessity as faced us and the sacrifice of such animals as sheep and cattle for food." Not for the first or last time, the hunger for scientific discovery in the Antarctic was conflated with real hunger.

ʃ the wolf starved Υ

Admiral Byrd, who had been promoted immediately by Congress after his famed South Pole flight, returned to Antarctica several more times.

In 1934, on his second trip south, he was back at the Bay of Whales at the renamed Little America II.

"If I had created anything tangible and unique in life," Byrd soliloquized, "it was this sprawling, smoke-spewing, half-buried city called Little America." His new, larger winter crew of fifty-six men ate their first meal in the old base with supplies left there four years earlier. "On the stove were cooking pans full of frozen food. . . . A fire was made in the kitchen stove, the food was warmed, and found to be as good as the day we left, four years ago," said Byrd. Piles of seal, whale, and beef left frozen in the tunnels were also ready to eat.

Aside from the familiar planes, radios, phones, and lights, they had electric grinders for meat and coffee in the galley and even an electric milking machine for their three dairy cows. These cows, the first in Antarctica, produced forty quarts of milk per day until production diminished to a trickle (which, according to expedition reporter Charles Murphy, "barely moistened the morning cereal") because Iceberg the bull refused his duty.

This second expedition also finally proved the viability of mechanical ground transportation in Antarctic travel. Major journeys of several hundred miles were undertaken with machines as the primary transport from Little America II into West Antarctica.

Cook Al Carbone, a loud, iconoclastic marine, moderated

mess-hall debates between dog drivers and tractor drivers (or as he named them, the dog catchers and the limousine explorers). This was not just banter during meals. The tradition of sledging under dog power was giving way to machines that could, barring mechanical failures, power through storms, deep cold, and even darkness while carrying far more weight at greater speeds. On one occasion, wrote Murphy, the tractors passed a party of "half-frozen dog drivers [who] were trying to spoon the evening hoosh past their chattering teeth. The *beep-beep-beep* of a tractor horn suddenly smote the Barrier silence." The "bloated daredevils," as one dog sledger called them, "were lolling on cushioned seats, chewing gum and eating chocolate like so many millionaires on a tour. Stop? Hell, those fellows went by with their noses stuck up in the air as if they were passing a family of peasants having a humble dinner in their miserable hovel!"

The Great Carbone, as Byrd called him, bunked next to his kitchen in the new mess hall, which at fifteen-by-thirty feet was large enough to serve as a general workshop. By day, men assembled trail rations, packed parachutes, and worked on sledges that dripped seal blood onto the dining tables, while three nights a week during the winter, the mess hall also became the expedition's movie theater. Carbone's bunk lay next to the soup-stained movie screen and occasionally he reached up in vain for a bottle of booze being handed from one character to another. Murphy recorded that on bad days, Carbone's volatility inspired him to quit, "knowing full well he had come to the one place where a man could neither resign nor be fired."

Other dramas played out in the kitchen. "Little America

reached its emotional zenith promptly at 6:15 every morning," wrote Murphy, "when the sleepy and shivering messmen, reporting for duty in the galley, found the fire out, the snow melter frozen hard, the dish water all used up, and the sink stacked high with dirty dishes flipped there by the midnight diners."

In what was the central drama of the expedition, Admiral Byrd created a hermitage for himself—what he called a "meteorological vigil"—at the Bolling Advance Weather Station, a nine-by-thirteen-foot hut 123 miles south of Little America buried in the snows of the Ross Ice Shelf. Advance Base, as it was known, was Antarctica's first inland station. No one had ever wintered alone in the Antarctic, but aside from some weather data and a quirky, philosophizing memoir—*Alone*—little was derived from the useless and nearly fatal disaster.

"I had gone there looking for peace and enlightenment, thinking that they might in some way enrich my life," Byrd wrote. "I had also gone armed with the justification of a scientific mission. Now I saw both for what they really were: the first as a delusion, the second as a dead-end street."

It was at once the foolish act of a flamboyant man and a remarkable inquiry into the essential Antarctic problem of how mind and body fare when placed alone against the cold emptiness.

In Byrd's case, the answer was—not so well. He was a forty-six-year-old Virginian born to old wealth and privilege, a self-described "city-dweller used to servants."

He settled into Advance Base with about 2,500 pounds of food stored in an adjoining tunnel (with a pit toilet carved into the far end) but knew nothing about food preparation.

"Thank heaven," he said, "there was no lack of can openers."

Cooking for himself at Advance Base began as a desperate matter before becoming much worse. Having dined at "a thousand banquets," he imagined lobster thermidor and "squabs perched on triangles of toast," but ate burned flapjacks instead.

He knew to butter the pan, but seems not to have considered its cooking temperature. He cleaned the pan with a chisel, until finally asking advice from his radiomen at Little America. They didn't know, but wouldn't trust Carbone either, so they sent a message to the chef at the Waldorf in New York City, who suggested that Byrd butter the pan. So the admiral shrugged and continued to clean it with a chisel.

Breakfasts were tea and a whole-wheat biscuit, while lunch "was habitually an out-of-the-can affair" and dinners were "a daily fiasco." Byrd's mealtime manners became, as he said, "atrocious." He ate mostly with his fingers, dining as a solitary man does — and as Epicurus long ago noted — like a wolf.

Soon enough, though, the wolf starved. Byrd was poisoned by carbon monoxide from his stove and generator, and managed only two healthy months before collapsing. (Even in that good period, he nearly died twice while above the hut in the winter darkness, once while lost and the other when his trap door froze shut.) Advance Base temperatures were always cold, so Byrd needed the stove for heat but suffered from its fumes. Depressed, enervated, nauseated, moaning, and afraid, Byrd lay in his bunk for weeks, but for a long time betrayed nothing to Little America in his daily radio link.

He struggled to keep down what little food or sips of water

he could stomach. As the weeks passed, half-emptied cans of frozen vegetables littered the room. Byrd lost fifty-five pounds on a diet of about 1,200 calories a day, probably a third of what he needed: "Though the mere thought of food is revolting, I force myself to eat a mouthful at a time."

This meant eating dehydrated lima beans and turnip greens, canned tomatoes, biscuits, cereal with powdered milk, rice, and on good days a chunk of seal meat. All of it he chewed "to the point of dissolution," for ease of swallowing. Quite a bit of it he vomited onto the floor, where it froze.

The men at Little America were alarmed enough by Byrd's radio calls that they decided he needed saving. In the fairy-tale ending Byrd constructed for *Alone*, he relates the hearty greeting he offered his rescuers, after dragging his "emaciated, hollow-cheeked, weak and haggard" body up to the surface: "Hello, fellows. Come on below. I have a bowl of hot soup waiting for you."

These three men—Poulter, Demas, and Waite—had just completed the first winter journey since Cherry-Garrard, Bowers, and Wilson stumbled home as frozen zombies from Cape Crozier in 1911. That they sallied forth in machines made it no less heroic.

It took them three attempts, fighting mechanical breakdowns and crevasses at terribly low temperatures, bouncing over hard sastrugi for 123 miles, and following the shaky beam of a searchlight improvised from a four-hundred-watt movie-projector bulb and a piece of aluminum stripped from a Primus stove. They certainly deserved a bowl of hot soup.

flying with pemmican

Wealthier than Byrd and even more indebted to Amundsen, Lincoln Ellsworth bought his ticket into the front lines of Antarctic exploration with the inherited wealth of his millionaire father. He had hardened himself on trudges through Canada and the Andes, but by the time he met Roald Amundsen in New York in 1924, he was focused on polar aviation. Amundsen had given up exploration and planned to retire quietly to a cabin in northern Alaska. Ellsworth put his money behind the famous Norwegian, and together they had two great adventures flying across the Arctic Ocean and North Pole, before Ellsworth went south to Antarctica. Byrd had already flown to the South Pole, so in 1933 Ellsworth sought instead to cross West Antarctica, from the Weddell Sea to the Ross Sea. It took him four attempts over three years.

The most idiosyncratic of Antarctic explorers, Ellsworth was a dogged collector of things and experiences, and in a sense he collected heroes as well: "I am frankly a hero-worshiper and always have been. Three great men have stood out before my eyes ... Theodore Roosevelt, Roald Amundsen, and the Western frontiersman Wyatt Earp." Of these he knew and loved Amundsen but was obsessed with Earp, whose wedding ring he wore.

On his Antarctic flight, he would carry Wyatt Earp's cartridge belt and holster, plus a Siberian squirrel-fur parka given to him by Amundsen, an 1849 ox shoe found in Death Valley, and a pound of Peruvian coca leaves, in case extraordinary endurance was required. Only the parka came in handy.

In early 1934, Ellsworth arrived with his ship *Wyatt Earp* at the Bay of Whales, just twelve miles away from Little America II, to make his first attempt.

He had Sir Hubert Wilkins with him as partner and adviser. (Wilkins was another polar oddball who, according to Ellsworth, always carried pemmican, even in New York.) Ellsworth brought supplies for two years, "twenty tons of the best of everything," except for a savory pemmican he grew to dislike. Not that he had much chance to eat it; the sea ice broke up under his plane, irreparably damaging skis and a wing. A mere four days after arrival, they went home.

Ten months later, Ellsworth made his second attempt, this time from Deception Island, but the plane's engine threw a rod, for which they had no spares. Ellsworth radioed the manufacturer for the parts and sent his ship north to Chile to pick them up. He stayed behind with four others to explore the island and eat wild foods. Adélie eggs, he wrote, "were not bad in omelets, but boiled—ye gods! Tough as rubber balls and fishy besides." Further attempts to fly, once the *Wyatt Earp* returned, failed as well. The expedition sailed north again.

Ellsworth succeeded in his third summer, flying 2,300 miles from Dundee Island in the Weddell Sea to the abandoned Little America. This time his pilot was Herbert Hollick-Kenyon, a fastidious Canadian with extensive Arctic experience. They carried 250 pounds of rations that provided 4,800 calories per day. These included pemmican, bacon, biscuits, oatmeal, chocolate, raisins, dried apricots, butter, powdered milk, and malted milk tablets. Thermos bottles of hot tea sustained them in flight.

They made four stops on their epic flight, either for bad

weather or to refuel. Problems quickly developed. By their first stop, the sextant was wonky and the radio broken. Crawling hungrily into the tent, Ellsworth knocked over their first hoosh of oatmeal and bacon. At their third stop, the Primus wouldn't hold its pressure and a blizzard pinned them down for a week.

During the storm, the plane filled up with snow, which in the tail section could only be delicately removed with a hoosh mug, one scoop at a time. Finally, they ran out of fuel sixteen miles from Little America.

They had to find the buried camp on foot, but with their sextant broken, direction was uncertain amid the endless white space. They ended up sledging over one hundred miles in a "confused, nightmarish" path, eventually arriving twenty-three days after departure. They had been out of touch since midway through the first day, and the world, expecting to hear updates from the *Wyatt Earp* by radio, assumed the worst.

In the ruins of Little America, while waiting for the ship, Hollick-Kenyon hunted through the icy rooms and corridors looking for food.

He found plenty of canned beef, but its excessive seasoning made Ellsworth "long for the old diet of oatmeal and bacon." Meanwhile, Ellsworth surprised Hollick-Kenyon with a celebratory bottle of Napoleon Brandy he had been carrying for three years. And then Ellsworth, the wealthiest polar explorer in history, found an old wad of gum stuck under his bunk and debated with himself for two days about whether Antarctica's natural refrigeration made it safe to chew.

ʃ seal of approval Ỵ

As Lincoln Ellsworth made his flight to Little America, John Rymill and his 1935–37 British Graham Land Expedition (BGLE) were listening intently to their wireless for whatever information Ellsworth could provide about the territory they were about to spend three years exploring. As it turned out, what little Ellsworth thought he saw from the air was wrong. It would be Rymill and his eight men who would slowly and methodically discover and map the true geography of the Antarctic Peninsula through a combination of aerial surveillance, aerial photography, and long sledging journeys.

The BGLE was by all accounts a remarkably successful private scientific expedition, despite having a relatively tiny budget (20,000 British pounds, equivalent to $2.4 million in U.S. dollars today). Their plane was equipped with skis and floats to land on snow and water, allowing them not only to survey the unknown peninsular region but also to lay depots for dogsled teams. Another innovation was their Northern Base hut in the Argentine Islands, which was the first two-story building in Antarctica. The downstairs served as workshop, dining room, and kitchen, heated by their Aga cook stove. Upstairs was a cozy bedroom with nine bunks, canvas chairs gathered around a stove, a table, and a bookcase: "When sitting in front of the stove after dinner with a good book," wrote Rymill in his expedition account *Southern Lights*, "it was easy to forget that one was in the Antarctic at all."

Not for long. On a low budget and a traditional meal plan, Rymill was eating local. Fortunately, seals were plentiful, both crabeater ("vastly superior in flavour and eating qualities") and Weddell, which were killed for dog food. Both dogs and men refused to eat the meat of the predatory leopard seal. Rymill's party ate some penguins, shags, skuas, and other seabirds, but they did so rarely, as "preparing them for the table involved too much trouble for the small quantity of meat gained."

While they did eat plenty of penguin eggs, storing over 1,200 in barrels of flour for later use, it was seal meat they craved. "The longer we lived on seal meat," noted Rymill, "the more we appreciated it as a staple food, for we found that even after two years we were still enjoying it."

Like the Unconventional Cooks of Douglas Mawson's expedition, BGLE members shared cooking responsibilities during winters in the hut. The cook of the week rose at 7:30, woke the crew at 7:50, and had breakfast on the table by 8:00. "Methods of calling vary with the cook," Rymill mused. "Some are so pleased with themselves for having got up early that they make a great deal of noise about it, while others are so quiet that if one wants to lie in bed for a while it requires very little concentration not to hear them at all." Breakfast consisted of oatmeal with milk and sugar, toast with margarine and jam, and tea. Two men cleaned up after the cook, while the others dried dishes, tended the fire, and swept the floor.

After breakfast, the cook of the week stoked the Aga and baked the daily bread, then set out a midmorning break of biscuits and cocoa. A typical lunch, at 1:00 p.m., might be thinly sliced seal meat and dehydrated vegetables in a thick brown gravy, baked for about twenty minutes. By 7:15 in the evening, the cook looked askance at all the clothing, gear, and other projects sitting where their dinner was about to be served and yelled, "Clear the table!" A typical dinner was roast seal, Yorkshire pudding, mashed potatoes, green peas, and a baked jam roll.

Rymill envied the famed Ross Sea expeditions of Scott, Shackleton, and Amundsen, because they had great sledging conditions at their doorstep throughout the year, whereas the men of the BGLE "were sitting on a miserable little island, the surrounding sea too thickly strewn with ice to the south to let us get through by ship or motor boat, but with the ice too broken to make sledging possible."

In the end, though, they made impressive travels over treacherous ice, often skidding from one loose floe to another, sometimes trotting knee-deep in slush for days at a time. While sledging, they were often greeted by curious Adélies. One, wrote Rymill, "came sliding right in amongst my dogs. Before he had time even to look surprised there wasn't a feather left." Another hapless Adélie approached dogs who had eaten only pemmican for a month. It took a few seconds before "some tail quills and the blood on the dogs' lips" were all that remained.

On one of their most important sledging journeys, Rymill and Dr. E. W. Bingham made the first crossing of the stormy, crevassed Antarctic Peninsula toward the Weddell Sea. They often lay wind-bound in the tent, sometimes for a week at a time, among crevasses on the high ridges. They fended off malnutrition with a daily dose of fish oil and an orange juice concentrate called "Califorange." Rymill cooked breakfast so that he could work up his daily survey maps in the evening while Bingham made dinner. Before dinner, Rymill and Bingham liked to lie down on their sleeping bags and muse about their options. "Not that there was much choice," he wrote, "but it is always pleasant when one is really hungry to anticipate a meal by talking about it, and after all we might have our pemmican broth thick, thin, or medium, according to how much pea flour or dried potato the cook put in."

Making detailed maps of this unknown coastline occasionally meant establishing a sledging base camp away from the hut from which they could head out daily to survey the region. For men hardened to constant travel, this was a luxury. "To go home to a camp already made, after a period of pitching one's camp daily," wrote A. Stephenson, "is like going to a house in civilization, hanging up one's hat and coat on the peg, and sitting down to a meal."

🐧 while they boil, we ferment 🐧

Like the BGLE, the 1947–48 Ronne Antarctic Research Expedition (RARE), under Finn Ronne, also accomplished much in terms of geographical exploration as its traverse teams mapped the last unknown coastline of Antarctica. But unlike the cozy, congenial Brits, the members of the RARE suffered from serious personal conflict from the time the ship left the docks in Texas. The crew was nearly as divided as Wilhelm Filchner's *Deutschland* expedition had been thirty-five years earlier. The expedition brought planes and other modern innovations, but nothing was as modern and unusual as the inclusion of two women. Before the RARE, only one woman had ever set foot on the continent, and none had spent the winter. To be clear, neither of the women were the cause of the conflict, but one of them would be honest enough to tell the tale.

Jennie Darlington, author of the unusually candid

expedition account, *My Antarctic Honeymoon*, had recently married Harry Darlington, Ronne's lead pilot and third-in-command. When Ronne invited his wife, Jackie, on the expedition as an exclusive human-interest story for the North American Newspaper Alliance (for which he received some much-needed funds), Jennie was included as female companionship. As it turned out, the tensions that developed between Finn and Harry divided the women as well. Though Jackie Ronne initially wrote dispatches for the *New York Times* about "The First Two Women in South Pole Land," Jennie's name was later left out of expedition news stories.

The first sign of trouble in what should have been a close-knit team was the looting of food as the ship headed south. Culinary delicacies went first. "It became competitive," explained Jennie Darlington. "When you wanted something you ate it quickly or got none, and this led to gorging." Ronne's angry statements and memos made no difference except to accelerate the thievery. And so began the expedition's undercurrent of contempt and suspicion.

Ronne admitted to "long-smoldering feuds, quite a few open quarrels, and a couple of cases of disciplinary action," but in a feeble defense proclaimed that there were "many times when things ran smoothly and everybody was friendly and helpful." In Darlington's candid book, we read only her side of the story, but her slings at Ronne echo others written about his leadership.

Even after the RARE took up residence at Stonington Island, the looters continued their thieving unabated. "When it was found that certain offenders could not be reformed, we gave up trying," wrote Darlington. "Our moral outlook changed from chastisement and anger against the looters to pride in outwitting them." She, Harry, and their allies invented the game of "loot the looter," stealing valuable foodstuffs, particularly chocolate, from the thieves' hiding places.

One expedition stalwart was cook Sigmund Gutenko, a twenty-year navy man and veteran of a few polar journeys. Darlington recorded that the cook made the RARE pemmican from an antiscorbutic recipe featuring "dehydrated beef grits, bacon grits, dehydrated liver powder, beef fat, bacon fat, whole-milk powder, green-pea meal, oatmeal, soybean grits, dehydrated celery, onions, tomatoes, dehydrated potato shreds, carrots, synthetic lemon-powder juice enriched with ascorbic acid (vitamin C), paprika, cayenne and black pepper, and salt."

Darlington provided the first feminine food review in Antarctic history: "With all due respect to Gutenko, whose labors in the pemmican mines were long and arduous, my own conclusion was that the twelve-ounce ration was something *Good Housekeeping* should not endorse without checking into."

Good Housekeeping was not available, but Gutenko did receive a comment on one of his meals from a British scientist from the nearby Base E, which was just one hundred yards away. He gave the cook and his diners some bad news: "For your information, gentlemen, I can tell you that the small fish you've just finished eating are the egg carriers for the millions of parasites found in the stomach of the Weddell seal." Gutenko kept eating, "parasites or no parasites."

Ronne's poor leadership not only incited in-house looting and quarreling, but also led to clashes with the Base E commander, arguing without basis that the island was

American rather than British territory. RARE members ignored the politics and sneaked over for British tea and rum, scones and conversation.

On one cheerful occasion, the Darlingtons dined with the more cohesive British community, eating pea soup, seal-meat pie, dehydrated potatoes, "hammyeggycheesytopside" (made with penguin eggs), and pies made with dehydrated fruit.

The most notable international squabble was a dispute over ownership of the two-hole outhouse located halfway between the bases. In a heated debate liberally spiced with jokes about "squatter's rights" and "the county seat" and "privy councils," it was the presence of the two American women that turned the tide. The British built their own privy. "If anybody had told me I would be a deciding factor in an international dispute over the only plumbing on the Antarctic continent," Darlington mused, "my reaction would have been to advise that person to see the nearest psychiatrist."

Though Ronne insisted the expedition be dry, an important part of the Darlington gang's nightly activities was the homemade liquor they called "schlaunch," a bucket mix of ethyl alcohol, water, liquor (gin, brandy, or rum, smuggled out of Punta Arenas, Chile, on the way south), and lemon extract. They looked out for the Ronne "revenuers" coming to break up their secret parties. They insisted that the drinking reduced tensions in the community. "While they boil," said one poetic drinker, "we ferment. Better to enjoy life than to be in torment."

Harry would have reason enough to drink, as a set of disputes with Ronne over safety protocols in the aviation program resulted in his demotion and a permanent schism with the leader. It was both a defining moment of the expedition and a symptom of its fault lines. Well into the winter, pro- and anti-Ronne factions were reduced to "bunkhouse bitching," with two groups sitting at different ends of their long dinner table. The scene at the table, lit by a dim bulb casting shadows over morose, bearded faces, sometimes resembled a "bad, blackened reproduction of The Last Supper."

Sometimes it was the food itself that caused the friction. Gutenko refused to cook seal meat, which some of the crew wanted but the cook thought only suitable for dogs. This exacerbated the usual expedition problem of dietary monotony. As a result, confessed Darlington, "the craving for what we called goodies leveled us to boarding school behavior patterns." She hoarded cornflakes, just about the only food in camp that wasn't fried.

She and the other schlaunchers drank furtively before dinner to improve their attitude before they cheerfully "descended on the dry diners at the long, darkened mess table ... with quips, clanks, and chuckles as they sat down to uninspired steak or the undefinable Gutenko goulash." Not surprisingly, the tensions only increased. Darlington described the dark psychology that accompanies an unhappy group during polar winter: "Without light, trapped in a dark hole of oaths, stale air, and monotonous diet, pettiness, irritability, and personality differences increased.... Touchiness became akin to godlessness. Invented rumors took priority over truth."

But nothing that occurred on the RARE was as strange as Jennie's secret announcement to Harry that she was pregnant. Late at night in their semiprivate room in the expedition bunkhouse, they whispered about the strange wonder of the first child conceived in Antarctica. At 3:00 a.m., they sat up to eat a celebratory meal of looted cornflakes and chocolate creams, washed down with scotch. They laughed quietly and dreamed of "crisp green artichokes smothered in hollandaise sauce, green salads, fruits, [and] ice-cold champagne."

The Darlingtons insisted on keeping the pregnancy private from Ronne but felt their friends who had stood by them through their difficult year should know. Without a word, then, as her friends sat around her in the Darlingtons' little room, Jennie dramatically dipped her hand into a looted pickle jar, pulled one out, and ate it. Confused, they watched her. Silently she reached for another, and another, until all at once they began laughing. They kept her secret, even as Jennie could barely fit herself into her mummy-style sleeping bag.

❨ winning international recognition ❩

Though they used machines to explore an unknown Antarctic region, the great novelty of the 1949–52 Norwegian-British-Swedish Antarctic Expedition (NBSAE), led by Norwegian John Giaever, was that it was Antarctica's first truly international expedition. Created by the three governments, it also included scientists from Canada and Australia. Although a few heroic-age expeditions had received funds or carried men from other countries, all went south under single flags, and most had nationalist goals.

The NBSAE would serve as a role model for the new age of cooperative international Antarctic science that continues to this day. Glaciologist Charles Swithinbank, who would remain active in Antarctic research for more than five decades, was at twenty-three the expedition's youngest member. He marveled at the meals the polyglot crew ate while the *Norsel* fought its way through Southern Ocean pack ice: seal liver and kidneys, breast of penguin with slices of bacon, braised whale steak with onions, whaleburgers, and grilled seal brains.

Then there was the feast on local offal: heart, tongue, and liver of seal served up with heart, kidneys, liver, and testicles of emperor penguin.

Maudheim, their base, was established on an ice shelf off the coast of Queen Maud Land. Three years' provisions for fifteen men were unloaded, but cook Scholberg Nilsen had second thoughts about living on floating ice. He chose to go home in the *Norsel*, replaced by the ship's young steward, John Snarby, though not until Mrs. Snarby, alone with their young son at home, agreed via telegram.

Giaever joked that, with this crew, it was easy for Snarby's cooking to win international recognition. Better yet, butter, cheese, and jam were always available, though all of the butter had turned rancid during the *Norsel*'s passage through tropical heat. Swithinbank wrote that "the choice was simple: eat rancid butter — or none at all for the next two years. I came to like the taste."

Culture did affect cuisine. The British did not consider lutefisk (whitefish steeped in lye) edible, while some of the Scandinavians refused to eat "worms" (spaghetti). The crew's two favorite meals, Norwegian fish balls and meatballs in gravy, came out of cans. Leader John Giaever confessed to boredom with their first winter's menu, suffering "a sort of culinary *weltschmerz*," a gastronomic blues.

Come summer, wildlife returned to Maudheim. Seals were

slaughtered for the dogs, while emperors died for the men. Teams left the base to explore the interior by dogsled and Weasel. To save time on the trail, Swithinbank kept cocoa warm by placing it on the Weasel's exhaust manifold as they traveled: "At other times the aroma of burning bread reminded me that my toast was done."

In their first journey to lay a depot almost two hundred miles away, three Weasels toted seven tons of food and gear and made it back in just eight days. (Had Robert Scott's motor sledges been half as effective, he might have won the race to the Pole. Amundsen's three dogsled teams were incredibly fast, but had only moved half a ton 160 miles in the same amount of time.) Dogs were essential to the summer science programs but were best used as a tool for light, efficient travel into the unknown. Machines did all the preliminary heavy work.

The NBSAE's pemmican was made by Bovril, supplier to the heroic age, but a new recipe included pork as well as beef in the usual fifty-fifty mix with fat. Swithinbank described its texture as like "very hard cheese." The men carried tins of delicacies but seldom bothered to eat them because of the hour or so it took to thaw them out.

Occasionally they experimented with the menu: from seal steaks with tinned cabbage to an attempt at *bacalhau* (salted dried cod) made with the dogs' dried stockfish ration. The latter was an ammonia-scented failure, because the fish had been repeatedly scent-marked by the huskies.

Upon arrival, the dogs had been so accustomed to drinking from buckets aboard the *Norsel* that when first staked out on Antarctic snow they grew desperate with thirst. One by one in their dehydrated fury, wrote Swithinbank, they accidentally "gnashed their teeth into the snow," realizing suddenly that there was unlimited water at their feet. On the trail, they had their own pemmican ration but preferred human feces. One man "rewarded his favourite dogs by defecating in front of them," wrote Swithinbank, who respected the bond between dog and driver but thought such a gift fraught with danger "from dogs seeking to ensure that their snack was steamingly fresh."

Back at Maudheim for the second winter, they had a new cook. John Snarby had returned home to wife and child. He was replaced by Bjarne Lorentzen, described by Giaever as a "cheerful, wizened little man" and a fine cook who had spent his life at sea. He introduced himself to his new boss, saying, "You don't need a big fellow to cook. Napoleon was a little chap too, and he didn't do badly."

Lorentzen surprised the crew by producing a lovely meal of skua gull *à la ptarmigan* in cream sauce, overcoming Giaever's opinion that "such inveterate carrion-eaters" weren't fit for human consumption. Giaever never determined if the quality of the meal was due to the attributes of the birds or of his new cook, but he knew "that quiet little Bjarne Lorentzen from Lodingen was a culinary artist. . . . I have never met his match or tasted such food in any polar region. The result of all this was an undignified excitement before every new meal and a tranquillizing distension afterwards — together with rapidly rising lines in the doctor's weight graphs." Likewise, Lorentzen later confided to Giaever that his year at Maudheim was the happiest of his life.

While out on the trail in their second summer, Swithinbank noticed that fresh bread frozen for a year retained its texture and taste. In the spirit of their multinational expedition, perhaps, he conceived a novel plan to help humanity; Antarctica should serve as a deep-freeze warehouse for the world's grain surplus. While the United Nations has yet to take him up on the idea, the NBSAE would soon make its contribution to a better world.

Through the sharing of meals at Maudheim and on the trail during two intense years, these men from five nations created an alternative to the flag-waving expeditions that characterized the first fifty years of Antarctic exploration. To that end, three men at the trail party's farthest south drank three toasts: The Australian physicist toasted the Norwegian king, the British glaciologist cheered the Swedish king, and the Norwegian polar expert raised his mug to the king of England.

hit it on the snout and cut its throat

"This is not, and does not pretend to be, a Cookery Book in the accepted sense of the term." Thus begins the mechanical age's greatest contribution to the story of Antarctic cuisine, Gerald T. Cutland's wonderful cookbook, *Fit for a FID: Or, How to Keep a Fat Explorer in Prime Condition*, a compilation of British Antarctic recipes from 1957. In this book, Antarctic cuisine reaches a sort of apotheosis: simple meals made with some flair and bloodlust by a capable, charismatic cook. Perhaps the most endearing aspect of Cutland's work is that you can almost smell that it was typed up—all fifty pages of it—at Base F in the Argentine Islands on an old typewriter while the tea was on the boil and dead cormorants hung outside the door in the clear, cold air.

Cutland was a FID, the nickname for members of the Falkland Islands Dependencies Survey, Britain's Antarctic agency from the end of World War II to 1962. Cutland wrote with humor and sympathy for his desperate local readership, creating hearty, simple recipes that his fellow travelers could follow: "It would grieve me no end if a FID went bald, or had to be carried out in a strait-jacket after struggling two years with my recipes and getting no results."

Gerald T. Cutland

It should be noted for posterity that Cutland modeled his work closely on a contemporary cookbook that a colleague had brought south: *Fit for a Bishop; or, How to Keep a Fat Priest in Prime Condition,* by Stephen Lister. In fact, there are at least a few instances of outright theft, like the line above about the Cookery Book.

His recipes are certainly his own, however, and very much Antarctic. Cutland's purpose was not to publish, but to write a practical, local guide for the amateur FID cooks who would each take their turn at the Base F stove.

With those realities in mind, tinned meats, once the bane of heroic-age meals, make up one of Cutland's largest chapters, with fifteen recipes ranging from Beef Steak and Kidney Pie to Cornish Pasties and Carbonnades Flamandes (cubed beef brisket fried in beef suet, covered in onions, mixed herbs, and a teaspoon of sugar, then marinated with beer in a casserole dish. Cutland praised canned food and scorned the notion that "because it is tinned we can only turn it out on to a plate and serve cold."

He conjured makeshift soups of tinned vegetables and meat leftovers. As for fish, which at home he only ate fresh, he designed recipes that were "quite delicious" and turned "what might be a crude meal into a delicacy."

Perhaps he was thinking of his Crayfish Thermidor or Creamy Fish Pie, or maybe the heavy comfort of some Imitation Scotch Woodcock, for which toast is buttered well and then slathered with sardine butter (a tin of sardines mashed with two ounces of butter, salt, and pepper), topped with more buttered toast, cut into sections, liberally drowned with a sauce made with two ounces of butter, two eggs, six tablespoons evaporated milk, two teaspoons parsley, salt and pepper, and served piping hot.

Even the desserts in *Fit for a FID* were kept simple and relevant for "the person with an interest in trying to produce something that is edible without causing him any undue worry about the job."

As an Antarctic pragmatist, Cutland suggested that a FID might beat the Mock Cream slowly and steadily with an old boot or a blubber hook. And though he recommended vanilla flavoring, he recalled one man who requested essence of seal blubber instead.

It is in the chapters on wild meats that *Fit for a FID* really shines. When Cutland arrived at the UK's Argentine Islands Station (originally the home of John Rymill's BGLE expedition), he was pleasantly surprised at what he found. God, Cutland asserted, was "very generous in respect of fresh meats to be found in this, the white desert of the South." And he was not shy about telling his readers how to acquire that meat: "The younger the seal the better, and the best way to do this is to hit it on the snout and then cut its throat."

Seal meat "can be made quite wholesome and very tasty," wrote Cutland, if prepared and cooked carefully: First, kill your seal as described above, so as not to damage its delicious brains; second, wash all traces of blood off the joints of seal (seawater is fine for this); third, remove every bit of blubber, as that fat is what gives seal its "characteristic strong smell"; fourth, hang your seal for a couple of days to cure it; fifth, if the seal is older, it requires blanching; and sixth, "a point always to remember in the cooking is at all times to use BEEF SUET as during the process of cooking the suet will permeate the meat and tends to give you a beefy-flavoured meat which will be appreciated by all." In other words, transform the seal into a cow.

Fit for a FID lists seven recipes for seal meat: Roast Seal, Roulades of Seal, Braised Seal, Casserole of Seal, Seal Meat

Hamburgers, Tournados of Seal, and Tournados of Seal Portugaise (served on a large "crouton of bread," covered with a tomato sauce, and garnished with tomatoes and peas).

It also delves deep into the organs, of course: Braised Seal Heart, Roast Seal Heart, Savoury Seal Heart, Fried Seal Liver, and Faggots (a mince of liver, bacon, onion, and herbs, with a thick slice of soaked bread, baked for an hour before being served with peas and sautéed potatoes).

Cutland reserved a special place in his heart—and book—for seal brains, "one of the delicacies and luxuries of the Antarctic." First, make sure the brains are fresh and free of blood clots: "If they are saturated with blood then throw them away as they are of no use." Wash them in cold water, soak them for an hour, changing the water a few times, then blanch them in water with vinegar, boiling slowly for fifteen minutes. His recipes are all very simple—Fried Seal Brains, Seal Brains au Gratin, Brain Fritters, Seal Brain Omelette, and Savoury Seal Brains on Toast—each using no more than a half dozen ingredients. The omelet, which serves six, was whipped up from two seal brains chopped into very small pieces, four penguin eggs, and some reconstituted egg, butter, salt, pepper, and mixed herbs. For fritters, "an excellent breakfast dish," Cutland mashed brains with a fork until they were soft and light, then mixed them into a batter with eggs, flour, melted butter, and some herbs. Tablespoons of the brain batter were dropped into boiling fat until each turned golden brown. Cutland was a real advocate for shags, otherwise known as cormorants. Shag species in the Antarctic are five-pound diving birds with a three-and-a-half-foot wingspan, a white breast, and a black back. If you have any around your hut but haven't tried them, he wrote, then you're "missing one of the luxuries of the Antarctic and my advice is that if you see any around, take a .22 rifle and knock a few off."

A shag is a meaty bird and served six FIDs, though some people on base were prejudiced against the bird's strong flavor. To fix that, Cutland said to simply hang it up for two weeks before preparing. Outside is best, "but where you hang it up is up to you — I couldn't care less."

Even so, he admitted, the shag's flavor is rather rich, "but anyone who is used to any game bird will appreciate the value and the delightful change in diet that this bird makes." Skin your shag rather than plucking it, blanch it to cook off the malodorous fat, and whenever the shag recipe calls for fat, "the best to use is BEEF SUET as this tends to enhance the flavour and is most certainly better for the making of the gravy." Options include Roast Shag, Shag Maryland, Spanish Paella with Shag, Casserole of Shag, Fricassee of Shag, Jugged Shag, and Savoury Hot Pot with Shag.

Perhaps it was the Jugged Shag that Cutland's friend Taffy Hughes drooled over in a scene described by the cook in his introduction. If so, the jointed bird was first browned in a pan with beef suet and bacon and then placed in a casserole dish, covered with gravy, dry onions, salt, pepper, a sachet of herbs, and two drops of oil of cloves stolen from the station medical kit. Cooked until tender, or about two to three hours, the shag received a final touch — two to four glasses of port wine stolen from the station's Christmas rations. Taffy's verdict: "Not only was it tender, it was succulent, a wing crumbled under his touch. . . . Well, to cut a long story short, 'Taffy' was soon up to his ears in this wonderful bird."

Penguins were a different matter, as Cutland was shy of them for two reasons: cuteness and flavor. In chapter 6 —

PENGUINS—he wrote, "This is going to be a fairly short chapter, and for several reasons; the main being that I do not like the stuff." This is a strange departure for Cutland, who was obviously not scared off by gamey flavor. Perhaps his reasoning was entirely emotional, for while he may advocate slicing seals' throats and picking off shags with a .22, he faltered when it came to our little well-dressed friends: "When cooking Penguin, I have an awful feeling inside of me that I am cooking little men who are just that little too curious and stupid." A penguin even walked into his kitchen one day, and for a moment Cutland thought it was nice of the chap to come to the kettle so fresh, but he didn't have the heart to kill it: "Even though I have cooked many I have always left that job to those who would eat it."

Penguin preparation is much like other Antarctic fare, but Cutland begins his instructions with a warning: "First of all most of you will know that they are very strong in smell and flavour. If you don't, you soon bloody well will when you start to cook one." If, after cutting out the breast meat and washing it, hanging it outside for a few days, washing it again, blanching it, and washing it one final time, it still reeks of penguin, his advice was to sling it out through the nearest window.

His penguin recipes are identical to those for seals and shags. Penguin breasts might be roasted, braised, fried, or sautéed; prepared as roulades, escallops, or tournados; or put into a casserole. His recipe for Savoury Penguin Breast says simply to "proceed as for Savoury Seal Heart, substituting Penguin Breast for the Heart."

And whatever you do, don't forget the BEEF SUET.

Savoury Seal Brains on Toast

1 prepared seal brain
3 reconstituted eggs
1 dessert spoon tomato sauce
3 ounces butter
Grated cheese, hot toast
Salt, pepper, and a little grated nutmeg

Chop the brains into very small pieces and mix together with eggs, tomato sauce, and nutmeg. Heat the butter in a saucepan, pour in the mixture and cook for a minute or two, stirring all the time.

Serve on hot buttered toast sprinkled with grated cheese.

Into the Deep Freeze   6

During my decade on the ice, I came to think of Antarctica as a second home. My whole life—work, friends, relationships, travel, reading, and writing—revolved around this place that had captured my imagination and pulled me away from family and familiar ground every year. But I also knew that Antarctica could never be my home because it's far too otherworldly to be anyone's home. Yes, a handful of children have briefly lived there (to anchor sovereignty claims by Chile and Argentina), and yes, some people live there comfortably for a few years at a time or (like me) spend long periods in the region every year for part of their lives. But in the end, we're all low-budget astronauts and cosmonauts, briefly visiting the livable Earth's edge while tethered to the warm world by supply chains of food and equipment.

Yet the feeling of home-away-from-home persists. I'm sure residents on the International Space Station feel the same attachment. Any place you earn your wage and fill your belly, day after strange and spectacular day, takes up residence in your heart. In McMurdo, I worked with friends under a 24-hour sun, laughed and shared stories around imported dining tables, and socialized with beer and snacks in dorms built over the previous half-century. Life at nearly every Antarctic base bears little resemblance to home life—no kids or elders, no apartments or restaurants—but it's an intense and meaningful life nonetheless.

Much of what makes it meaningful is the community. We're all there for the same purpose, and we've all self-motivated to leave the warm world to work in the icy hinterlands. I've never been in a community anywhere else that's half as interesting. A century after the heroic age, the ice is still inhabited by travelers, scientists, and misfits. On any given day, I might shovel snow alongside a yoga instructor, seismologist, and whitewater kayak guide, then share a meal with a musician, retired teacher, and meteorite hunter. I heard more good stories in an Antarctic week than I heard in a year back home.

One of the glories of Antarctica is the company you keep, whether at work or at table. It's as true for snow-shovelers like Julian and me as it is for international teams of climate scientists. It's been true since the hard-won manhauling days of Shackleton and Scott, and remained true after the world arrived to stay in the mid-1950s, the most consequential few years in Antarctic history and the origin story for the year-round Antarctic community I would come to love.

∫ for sure we were going to eat ⦗

About the time that Swanson produced the first TV dinner (turkey with dressing, green peas, and mashed potatoes), forty thousand scientists from sixty-seven nations were gearing up for the 1957–58 International Geophysical Year (IGY), a remarkable global scientific program focused on the geophysical study of Earth and its relation with space. In Antarctica, the IGY brought to an empty continent fifty-six scientific stations built by twelve nations. Scientific work in these new facilities led to major advances in the study of auroras, cosmic rays, geomagnetism, glaciology, gravity, ionospheric physics, meteorology, oceanography, biology, medicine, and more.

None of this would have been possible without advances in aviation, with U.S. military planes flying people, fresh food, and cargo directly from New Zealand to Antarctica, as they still do today.

Ice-scarred ships remained crucial to Antarctic logistics but were no longer the only means of reaching the continent. Soon large aircraft began to serve as regular transportation to and within the Antarctic.

A new pattern was established. "With favourable weather conditions and all regard for safety," David Burke noted in *Moments of Terror: The Story of Antarctic Aviation*, "it had been shown that aircraft could fly into Antarctica from the world beyond . . . by plane it was now a matter of 10 hours, not 10 days or 10 weeks away."

As Antarctic logistics grew more effective and we began to permanently occupy the ice, the rationale for expeditions had to evolve as well. No longer could crews pack their ships with pemmican and head south to look for new lands "on a vague quest of knowledge and adventure," wrote Laurence Gould. "Little as we know about the Antarctic, we yet know enough to realize that we can go looking for specific things." A deeper study of Antarctica required men to live there long-term, and fortunately the advances in science that led to detailed inquiry coevolved with the necessary logistical know-how.

The American effort to create an Antarctic home was run by the U.S. military and titled Operation Deep Freeze. In Deep Freeze I, which began in the pre-IGY summer of 1955–56 before the scientists arrived, the U.S. Navy was tasked with establishing two beachhead bases: McMurdo Station (initially named Williams Naval Air Operating Facility) next to Hut Point on Ross Island, and Little America V on the Ross Ice Shelf.

The Navy Seabees (from CB, Construction Battalion) worked hard through the summer to unload ships and build the nascent McMurdo, but it was two months before they could eat fresh baked bread in their new mess hall.

For the first time, Antarctica had refrigeration; fresh meat and produce bought in New Zealand could stay fresh, and frozen meat could thaw slowly and safely. Ice cream became a common Antarctic dessert.

As Dian Belanger relates in her excellent IGY history, *Deep Freeze*, modern American sailors had little interest in the ancient mystique of pemmican. When Sigmund Gutenko, veteran cook of the Byrd and Ronne expeditions, prepared nine thousand bars of 2,600-calorie pemmican, using twenty-six ingredients to make it palatable to this new Antarctic generation, his efforts were to no avail; one cook noted that "fixed as a stew, soup, or pie," it was still pemmican. One sailor tried to eat it while camping and called it "oh, God-awful." He begged the kitchen for cans of tuna instead.

Meanwhile, in the other Deep Freeze I operation at Little America V, unloading materials to build the base had been a disaster. Goods painstakingly differentiated in the United States were thrown willy-nilly around the base site, much of it soon buried under blowing snow and some never seen again. Not the food, however: "We always knew where the food was. For sure we were going to eat," said chief commissary man William McInvale.

Once settled in, Little America's seventy-three winterovers ate well and were happy with the open-fridge policy that allowed them to snack at will on leftovers and baked goods. Unlike other stations, there was ham and bacon to eat as well. That the pork products came from twenty-year-old stockpiles at Byrd's Little America III didn't bother them. Ironically, the other stations didn't bring pork because the navy had decided that it wouldn't keep safely in the Antarctic. Not for the last time, an Antarctic community would make practical decisions while management was busy making rules.

high-altitude cooking

Operation Deep Freeze II in 1956–57 was a much larger, broader, and more difficult logistical program. The archipelago of U.S. IGY bases was growing. It involved twelve ships and 3,400 men establishing five more bases. Three of these — Ellsworth, Hallett, and Wilkes — were scattered around the coastline of the continent. Little America V was the starting point for establishing Byrd Station in the middle of West Antarctica, and McMurdo served as a launch pad for the extraordinarily ambitious construction of a station at the South Pole.

To build Byrd Station, a "tractor train" (a convoy of tracked vehicles) had to travel 650 miles from Little America V to the blank spot at 80° South, 120° West in West Antarctica. This included crossing a seven-mile-wide band of major crevasses.

Planes were able to scout a safe route, but more than three dozen of these large slots would have to be dynamited by army specialists and then filled in with snow pushed by D-8 tractors.

The result was a tortuous path, flagged thoroughly to guide nervous tractor drivers through slots that could kill them as quickly as one had killed Belgrave Ninnis and his dog team back in 1912.

Men on the tractor train were forced to hot-bunk (taking turns sleeping in the same beds) as the caravan rumbled along around the clock. One exception was cook Ray Mishler, who earned his own bunk by making dinner, breakfast, and bag lunches simultaneously, twice a day, in a rough kitchen on a sled bumping across the sastrugi.

Mishler's stovetop had a rail built to hem in pots that wanted to bounce off the burners, but he was forced to give up part of the rail for a jerry-rigged repair of a D-8 engine's pushrod.

Two hours after arrival, Byrd construction began. In just six days, the station's buildings were up, the first of various incarnations that would serve the U.S. research community for nearly fifty years. Fifteen tons of food were flown in, but variety and quantities in that first winter weren't really up to navy standards.

Some men complained, while others joked about it. "We were low on brandy and hard liquor, the beer froze. But that's not hardship," geophysicist Charles Bentley told Dian Belanger. "We had plenty to eat, we had good food, we had a warm place to live, we didn't have to work very hard."

Chicken, rabbit, lobster, shrimp, and other choice meats all ran out quickly, along with condiments, canned tomatoes, and cheese. Mostly they had roast beef, stew beef, or hamburger.

Even so, winterover cook Robert Marsh managed to fatten up most of the men at Byrd, even on just two meals per day during the more indolent weeks of darkness.

Their only crisis was a lack of beer. According to one tragic tale, a sailor drank ten beers one early winter evening, right before discovering that he was on an allowance of ten beers *for the entire winter.*

The enduring dining room at Vostok Station in January 2000

Back in McMurdo, as the Deep Freeze II summer got under way, life was hectic and crowded. The base's population quickly rose to a nearly unmanageable 360 men. They slept everywhere, including in tents and the chapel, and ate in three crowded shifts, shoveling down typical American breakfasts — eggs, bacon, ham or sausages, fruit juices (or less often, fruit), and muffins or toast with plenty of butter — before making way for the next wave.

The navy increased their usual food rations by 30 percent to account for Antarctica's calorie-burning conditions. But none of these inconveniences would compare to the difficulties some of the young Seabees would face as they established a base at the South Pole.

The Seabees bound for the Pole looked forward to the challenge, not understanding that in all of human history only ten men had set foot there, staying only a few summer days, and that half of them had died of starvation, poor nutrition, frostbite, and exhaustion on the way back. Furthermore, no one knew the first thing about *living* at the South Pole. Nothing like it had been attempted.

Three of these Seabees got a taste of the history that preceded them when, while taking a dogsled training run from McMurdo to Cape Evans, they were caught by a storm and had to take shelter in Scott's 1910 *Terra Nova* hut. They broke in through a window to find an interior both sacred and spooky. This was the hut where Cherry-Garrard, Wilson, and Bowers had stumbled in from their brutal winter journey, the same hut where the devastated *Aurora* expedition had awaited rescue. The three newcomers waited out the storm, shivering amid the mess left by the *Aurora* men forty years earlier, including a dining table littered with frozen cocoa, crackers, and jam.

Ready or not, on November 19, 1956, they and the rest of the Seabee construction crew flew to the Pole on small ski-equipped R4Ds. They landed eight miles from the actual Pole, as close as the plane's crew could navigate on the wing. Dogs helped to pull gear those eight final miles but weren't of much use later on when machines that could haul tons of equipment arrived.

All but a pup named Bravo went back to McMurdo by summer's end. The men did not eat well during this construction phase, as the blond-bearded Ray "Sperocious" Spiers, their temporary cook, admitted he was more useful as a mechanic and barber. His daily dish of mashed potatoes was "thinnish, anemic, and tasteless," wrote scientific leader Paul Siple, mainly because Spiers didn't bother to read the instructions on the box. Meanwhile, important things were being mashed outside the new base as well.

The occupation of the South Pole required several large Air Force Globemaster aircraft to airdrop 730 tons of cargo. But "stream-ins," when airdrops plummeted deep into the snow because parachutes failed to open or disengaged in midair, haunted Pole construction. Sausages were squeezed out of their cans on impact, and a year's supply of tomato juice bloodied the snow.

These gastronomic losses weren't as depressing as the daily high-speed destruction of other key items: a tractor, the mechanic's toolbox, barrels of fuel, construction timbers, science equipment, and a bag of mail, to name a few. Sometimes, Siple said, it seemed as if half the airdrops in a day disappeared into the snow.

To be fair, the air force airdrop riggers handled hundreds of tons of loads in a short period of time, and most of their drops were successful.

Moreover, as recompense, they sent a few illicit gifts as the last loads reached the Pole: a sexy female mannequin; two boxes of fresh vegetables signed "Stolen, rigged and dropped by four of the most competent thieves of the First Aerial Port Sqdrn"; and forty-seven eggs, which came down packaged under an Easter-egg-colored parachute. Only one egg was cracked, and when winterover cook Chet Segers lifted it out of the carton, he found a note underneath: "This egg was cracked before we dropped it. [Signed] U.S. Air Force."

When construction ended, the first Pole winter crew of nine navy men, nine IGY science staff, and Bravo the dog replaced the Seabee construction crew, bringing with them the final tons of food and other cargo. What had been an abstract human concept—reaching 90° South—amid the emptiness of an ice cap larger than Australia was now a tiny Antarctic society huddled against the cold, linked by radio to other IGY bases and the world.

Of the community's eighteen winterers, only Paul Siple had Antarctic experience, while four others had spent time in the Arctic. Of the rest, some had only been in Antarctica for five days before flying to the Pole. Most were in their twenties; cook Chet Segers was thirty and Siple was forty-eight. Siple, a four-time winterover, would call it the "most pleasant and smoothest" experience he'd had during an Antarctic night. "Pleasant" is perhaps misleading, as the average temperature during the winter was –55°F, with a maximum cold of –102.1°F, shattering the previous world record from Siberia.

Segers and several other desperate men almost spent the winter without tobacco, until a last-minute summer flight brought their lung-choking relief. Until then, they had been scavenging cigarette butts from the trash, sometimes holding the smallest nub with needle-nose pliers.

In a frantic experiment reminiscent of Victor Campbell's Northern Party in their tobacco-deprived ice cave, Segers mixed coffee grounds and tea in his pipe but became sick after a few puffs.

The cook made the completed galley's first meal on January 2. Devoted to the job, Segers was, however, a trained navy butcher rather than a cook, and hadn't cooked for two and a half years before arriving at the Pole. Siple praised Segers's hard work, but as the sun spiraled down to the flat Antarctic horizon and their six-month winter night set in, Segers had things to learn about cooking in South Pole's difficult climate. The temperature dropped by three degrees per day.

It took Segers a week to thaw foods frozen at outside temperatures, and he had to use a pressure cooker to speed up cooking times slowed by altitude. The South Pole sits at 9,301 feet, but atmospheric pressure makes it feel like 10,000 feet; fluctuations in pressure can ratchet up the perceived altitude to almost 12,000 feet.

Segers's first loaves of bread turned to bricks in South Pole's near-zero humidity until he learned to protect them in plastic bags. But Segers could not understand why his cakes kept falling.

He finally radioed Pillsbury, the home of Betty Crocker, which he said sent one of their industrial food experts up in a plane to bake a cake at 10,000 feet. More likely, she stepped into a kitchen-equipped pressure chamber, which Pillsbury had purchased from the air force several years earlier to create formulas for high-altitude cake mixes. Her advice to Segers was to add more flour to reduce the effect of the baking powder.

Some stir resulted from this private exchange," Siple punned, because the navy was embarrassed that it "had simply failed to instruct Segers in the fine art of high-altitude cooking."

Segers also got occasional help from other staff with mess duty. Community members all took turns creating weekly menus, and even the station leaders—Siple and Navy Lieutenant Jack Tuck—pitched in to clean the kitchen and take out the garbage.

Segers usually did the dishes himself, he told Dian Belanger fifty years later, because he had "nowhere to go anyhow."

Grilled cheese and tomato soup made a popular lunch, while steaks, burgers, and roasts were usual dinners. Despite plentiful food, these first Polies lost weight, an anomaly among the IGY stations. No doubt this had to do with extra calories burned in the extreme cold.

For fresh water, the crew took turns digging a snow mine, because snow on the surface had been contaminated during construction. Luckily the mine doubled as a glaciology project. Eventually 270 feet long and 90 feet deep, the tunnel was dark and very cold but protected from the weather. A navy electrician ran a makeshift string of lights down the lengthening shaft.

Paul Siple estimated it cost a million dollars per man just to begin the first South Pole winter. Nearly all of that money was spent on logistics rather than science. The technique pioneered by Admiral Byrd of massive, expensive operations with lots of men to support a few scientists was the new Antarctic reality.

But all those millions of dollars could only put them at the Pole; once winter set in, no amount of wealth could have rescued them if things went badly. Out of reach of the rest of humanity, the possibilities for trouble at South Pole were endless.

They might as well have been on the Moon. Frostbitten faces and fingertips were commonplace. Frozen pulmonary and nasal capillaries made men cough up blood or drip it from their noses. Terrified that a midwinter fire would leave them injured and homeless in the coldest place on Earth, they first split food, fuel, and gear between the two halves of the station in case part of it was damaged in a blaze, and they eventually established a separate emergency shelter in case the whole place burned down.

Otherwise, this was no longer the South Pole of legend. One IGY scientist had arrived in tennis shoes, another in a Hawaiian shirt. Men sat around at the Pole drinking beer, though this was not without its difficulties; they found themselves cutting the tops off frozen beer cans and spooning out the slush.

The trappings of religion arrived too; Pole's four Catholics received permission from the Vatican to forego the Friday food rules since there was no way to properly determine when a Friday occurred while simultaneously living in all of Earth's time zones.

Whatever Amundsen and Scott might have thought about Vatican dispensations and beer slushies at the Pole, their names were formally attached to the station. U.S. authorities had admirably decided upon the un-American official name of Amundsen-Scott South Pole Station.

When telephones were set up for room-to-room calls around the base, Paul Siple felt civilization encroaching too much on the Antarctic silence he had relished for nearly three decades.

"Perhaps this was the price we had to pay," he wrote, "for no longer living on pemmican."

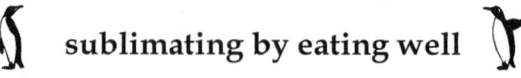 sublimating by eating well

In the Deep Freeze II community at Ellsworth Station, the price the young scientific staff had to pay for the privilege of doing pioneering Antarctic work was suffering under the leadership of Captain Finn Ronne. And the price was steep. Ronne had led the notoriously unhappy 1947 RARE expedition made (in)famous by Jennie Darlington's *My Antarctic Honeymoon*, and he was just as problematic at Ellsworth, once again turning camaraderie into confrontation and conflict. Though an experienced explorer and apparently likable at home, as a leader Ronne carried the unhappy combination of hubris, mercurial moods, and inflexible thinking.

Moreover, this was Ronne's fourth expedition in twenty years, and he had less interest in the IGY program than in furthering his legacy of geographical exploration. He refused to let the nine scientists begin work on their projects while the base was still under construction, changing his mind only when he learned that as a result, his station lagged behind the others in the IGY mission.

Though Ronne loathed the young, independent science crew—calling them at various times "sissies," "rotten eggs," or "immature juveniles"—he initially insisted that because the navy had ranked them as officers, they should eat with him and the other officers at a table waited upon by sailors. No other U.S. IGY base had an officers' table, instituting instead the nearly universal Antarctic ideal that in hardship everyone works and eats together.

Their companionship at Ronne's table didn't last long. The

leader was livid when he found an enlisted man reading a copy of *My Antarctic Honeymoon* he had borrowed from the scientists. Ronne soon "demoted" the science crew to eating cafeteria-style with the men, which of course they preferred. (Scientists and sailors drank together too, for unlike Byrd Station, which could offer only ten beers per man for the entire winter, Ellsworth had an alcoholic abundance. Each man could drink ten cans per day if he chose.)

Later, when Ronne tried to turn the enlisted men against the civilians, it was too late. "If he wants to 'divide and rule,'" seismologist John Behrendt wrote in his diary, "he should never have moved us in to mess with the men. When you get to know a man and eat with him every day, you are more apt to like him than dislike him."

Ronne managed to insult everyone at Ellsworth at some point, and even cheated at games. Soon no one chose to be his friend. It was a recipe for disaster, a possible *Caine Mutiny* (one of Ellsworth's most popular films). There were run-ins every day and long-simmering disputes throughout the year, particularly over the scientists' right to use the shortwave radio.

At other U.S. IGY stations, everyone helped in the galley. At Ellsworth, Ronne used mess duty as a punishment. He tried to order each of his scientists to do two-week full-day stints in the kitchen, including serving him at his officers' table, but without requiring his naval officers to do the same.

When they broke through Ronne's censorship of radio communications with IGY officials, the young scientists were vindicated and Ronne had to retract his threat of mess duty.

Some of them volunteered anyway, enjoying the work, and earned respect from the cook and baker, who—like Rob

Taylor and his gifts for Julian and me on the Odell—illicitly gave them fresh pies and loaves of bread to take on their fieldwork journeys. Ronne tried but failed to stop these gifts of food.

John Behrendt pointed out in *Innocents on the Ice*, his scrupulous memoir of the first winter at Ellsworth, that "although we had a much more difficult time during the winter in our interpersonal relations because of Ronne, we sublimated by eating well."

Many men gained twenty to thirty pounds. A navy psychological assessment team that came in to survey the damage at winter's end confirmed Behrendt's observation, documenting the excessive "oral needs" of the deprived community.

Behrendt and four colleagues escaped Ronne and formed their own small, sane society when they went on a scientific traverse the next summer, covering about 1,200 hard-won, crevassed miles. Often, they didn't know if they were eating breakfast or dinner as they worked under a 24-hour sun without obedience to the clock. Ellsworth's tight navy schedule and tighter rules were far behind them.

They worked feverishly, sometimes up to thirty-six hours at a stretch, and slept when it seemed best to sleep. They ate well. The meticulous Behrendt planned four months of meals, ranging from American cuisine (Spam, Minute Rice, Royal instant pudding, and Tastee Freez ice cream) to modern trail fare such as dehydrated steaks and dehydrated cheese. Meat, frozen (tenderloin strip steaks, ground beef, and stew) and canned (corned beef, bacon, and ham), made up the bulk of their large meals.

"We weren't vegetarians!" said Behrendt. Cans were

thawed over several days in the Sno-Cat or simply put into boiling water. Dishes were never cleaned, just scraped and left to freeze until the next meal.

Only the Meat Bar, a small military-issue block of pemmican-like substance, "paid slender homage to the historic days of sledging," as Dian Belanger put it. Behrendt wrote that Meat Bars were used occasionally to make hoosh, but he enjoyed eating them in their cold, solid form.

In another break from Antarctic tradition, when they all wanted the last piece of canned fruit, they did not select the winner via Shackleton's classic game of Shut-Eye. Instead, they played horsengoggle, a counting game similar to rock paper scissors.

Behrendt did most of the cooking, usually outside the vehicle and usually making it up as he went. One of his on-the-spot concoctions consisted of frozen burger, dehydrated cabbage, celery salt, dehydrated onion-soup mix, curry powder, Minute Rice, and half a pound of butter. The grease in their thick beards, in fact, came from the 288 pounds of butter they carried to ensure adequate fat consumption. But despite devouring 4,000 to 5,000 calories per day, their hard, cold work on the trail made these young men slough off the weight gained in psychological self-defense during the difficult Ellsworth winter.

∫ this is an apple ϒ

As Deep Freeze III began in the austral summer of 1957–58, the IGY was coming to an end. Around the continent, the hugely successful cooperative science done by twelve nations continued apace, even as navy and civilian crews changed over. Scientific discovery went on uninterrupted and life in Antarctica was characterized by a continuation of widespread, if sparse, semipermanent settlement. For the first time, people lived a slightly normal life in Antarctica.

On Ross Island, what would become a long-lasting friendship had formed between the residents of McMurdo and New Zealand's Scott Base, its new neighbor just two miles away. McMurdo had been built squarely on what New Zealand considered its territory, the Ross Dependency. (New Zealand is still quietly producing documents reaffirming this claim while working affably with its gargantuan occupier.)

In the IGY a deal was struck: The United States provided air and ship support to the small New Zealand program in exchange for the right to use the city of Christchurch as a base of operations. Little has changed during the intervening decades in what has been a model of cooperative Antarctic logistics and a daily reminder of the importance of community, whether sustained by a midday tea at Scott Base or an evening beer in MacTown.

Planes brought in fresh New Zealand fruit and vegetables to both bases. As a reminder for those who had forgotten about life on Earth, someone placed a shiny red object on the McMurdo galley piano with a sign reading, "This is an apple." Unlike the small dining room at Scott Base, typical of other Antarctic stations, McMurdo required a large cafeteria. Then, as now, the American program was far larger than any other.

At first, dining in McMurdo was a democratic affair. "In our main Antarctic base," Rear Admiral Dufek wrote proudly in 1959, "everyone lines up cafeteria-style and eats in the same mess hall, whether he be an admiral or a new recruit."

It would cost too much in labor and effort to build another, he wrote. But just one year later, McMurdo had exactly what he disdained: a split facility that separated officers (on the comfier "O side") from enlisted men (on the larger "E side"). McMurdo did not return to a single cafeteria until 2000, several years after I arrived.

Wildlife was scarcely on the menu in the McMurdo galley, which aimed to serve each man 4,000 American calories per day. Some of the crew occasionally cooked up seal steaks and liver intended for the dogs, but generally they showed little interest. If the navy could ship filet mignon to Antarctica, why should a sailor eat a greasy penguin?

Over at Scott Base, the men were the beneficiaries of donations from New Zealand food producers of snacks and other goodies, plus tons of raw meat, butter, and six hundred dozen eggs. The eggs froze once they reached the ice, of course, but were perfectly usable if brought in to thaw four hours before a meal. New Zealand Expedition leader Sir Edmund Hillary, of Mount Everest fame, made sure to promote those sponsors' wares in his account of the expedition, as leaders have always done. Sandy's Salted Peanuts, he said, "provided all the requirements in peanuts for Scott Base, and very popular indeed they proved to be." New Zealand cook Sel Bucknell stored the fresh meat from home in a nearby ice cave, but also experimented with the local wildlife, cooking seal and penguin recipes he'd acquired from the French Antarctic Expedition, until some men "had second thoughts after they knew what it was they had eaten."

Between meals at their cozy base, the New Zealanders held morning and afternoon teas, sitting down to chat over a hot drink and biscuits. Bucknell baked bread twice a week and had every Sunday off, replaced by an ever-changing roster of two mess cooks. Everyone, including Hillary, took his turn. One pair simply laid out sardines and chocolates for lunch "and dared offer pemmican for dinner," wrote Hillary, while others conjured "menus that would have graced any hotel in the world." Some of these rough-and-ready Kiwis showcased talent that, "in all probability, was well hidden from wives and sweethearts back in New Zealand." To ward off scurvy, the men dutifully drank a popular mix of rum and rosehip syrup.

The Kiwis paid further homage to their scurvy-fighting predecessors in a prewinter pilgrimage to Cape Crozier, where Hillary and his fellow searchers found totems of the heroic age abandoned by Apsley Cherry-Garrard, Edward Wilson, and Birdie Bowers more than forty years earlier on their horrific 1912 winter journey. Perfectly preserved amid the stones of a storm-wrecked shelter, they found emperor penguin carcasses, a Nansen sledge, Primus and blubber stoves, and tins of pemmican.

Hillary spent the Deep Freeze III summer leading his own astonishing journey, as he and his team trundled along with three little Ferguson farm tractors on a route they pioneered from Scott Base across the Ross Ice Shelf, then up the Skelton Glacier to East Antarctica. This amazing feat was their supporting role in the 1955–58 British Commonwealth Trans-Antarctic Expedition (CTAE), led by Sir Vivian "Bunny" Fuchs. Fuchs and the CTAE accomplished the old Antarctic dream, originally Wilhelm Filchner's and then Sir Ernest Shackleton's, of crossing the continent from the Weddell Sea to the Ross Sea.

As with Shackleton's *Endurance* and *Aurora* plan, the main party led by Fuchs began on the Weddell Sea side and proceeded via the Pole to Ross Island, in the latter half of the journey picking up the depots laid by Hillary.

The most remarkable part of the CTAE story is its beginning in 1956, when the eight unheralded men of Fuchs's advance party suffered a terrible first winter constructing their base on the Weddell Sea coast. Much of what they owned sank or blew out to sea.

They had just enough fuel to cook their meals through the winter, with none left over for heat. They were, as far as I know, the only men in modern Antarctic history to winter on the continent in unheated tents.

They took turns cooking, four days at a time, with the cook of the moment earning the privilege of living inside a twenty-one-by-nine-by-eight-foot Sno-Cat crate and drying his ice-encrusted sleeping bag while the others shivered in the tents. Temperatures sank to −63°F, low enough to freeze the whisky, gel their diesel fuel, and make potatoes rattle like rocks in their storage sacks. The menu grew tiresome, but one man upped the culinary ante by creating mint-flavored peas, with toothpaste as his secret ingredient.

Meanwhile, on the other side of the continent, Hillary and the Kiwis stopped every three hours, when they felt "too miserable to continue," and brewed up tea and cocoa. Hillary hated pemmican, one reason he lost twenty-eight pounds on the journey. He preferred his Hillary Hash, bacon slopped together with potato powder and dried onions. A "sumptuous" Christmas dinner included salmon fishcakes, tinned peaches thawed out over a Ferguson heater, cocoa, fruitcake, and a tot of brandy.

"We were soon," wrote Hillary, "in a slight haze of bonhomie and good cheer."

He laid his depots as planned, and then—rather than turning back to Scott Base—thought he might as well finish the job and scout a route to the Pole itself. That his underdog New Zealand team could arrive at the Pole first, beating Fuchs's British team with its bigger machines and greater ambitions, was the more obvious motivation. In a nice bit of understatement, this world-famous mountaineer later noted that playing "a supporting role was not my particular strength."

They inched along, he wrote, "over the snowfields of eternity," like three ants looking for the picnic on an endless white tablecloth. They arrived with just twenty gallons of fuel in reserve. The men were equally drained, because of the caloric gap between Hillary Hash and the pemmican they were supposed to eat. But the Americans fed them well before flying them home to Scott Base.

Fuchs arrived at the Pole a fortnight after Hillary, and then drove all the way to Scott Base, completing his historic journey along the route established by the Kiwis. In a tribute to British Antarctic history, Fuchs carried around his neck the watch Robert Scott wore on his doomed 1912 *Terra Nova* Expedition. The real homage, though, was to Amundsen, in that Fuchs fueled, maintained, and abandoned his machines one by one in a logistical calculation similar to Amundsen's sacrificial use of dogs.

Noel Barber, a British journalist covering the CTAE story, had his own experience of the heroic age when he bumped into famed Australian aviator Sir Hubert Wilkins, who in 1928 had been the first to fly over Antarctica.

Wilkins was visiting McMurdo and Scott Base for a brief tour but managed to take Barber to Robert Scott's 1912 *Terra Nova* hut at Cape Evans, where he had the audacity to break open a fifty-year-old food cache to make dinner for two. "I'll give you a meal you'll never forget," said Wilkins to Barber, who indeed called it "the strangest meal of my life." The excellent Stilton cheese crumbled, but the biscuits were crisp, the greengage jam "wonderful," and the tinned mutton was unchanged from the day it was plopped into the can.

They followed the meal with more biscuits and "the very same brand of Oxford marmalade I eat at home each morning," Barber noted, "and in just as good condition."

A navy pilot who shared his room with Wilkins in McMurdo was less enamored, and recorded three things about this celebrated explorer:

First, he was far too old to be in Antarctica, and indeed he died the following year; second, he claimed the honor of belonging to a unique interstellar cult, which chose from across the galaxy only a few worthy members, each of whom communicated telepathically "over the vastness of space"; and finally, Wilkins's feet absolutely reeked, because he refused to remove his socks until they fell apart. So much for the good old days.

Even the heroes had their doubts. Sir Charles Wright, half a century after the *Terra Nova* expedition, confessed in a radio interview how bad Clissold's food had been. He then reversed himself, saying "I shouldn't have said that. It will embarrass the cook and the expedition," of which Wright was the last surviving member.

☾ hair pie ☝

The Australians established three IGY communities, including the continent's first permanent base, Mawson Station, built a year earlier than McMurdo in 1954. Phillip Law, the head of the Australian program, was the man who grilled seal brains on Charles Swithinbank's 1949 voyage in the *Norsel*. Law was known for his wild foods and did not tolerate Australians who turned up their noses at "such items as roast penguin breast or fried seal's liver or crumbed brains." Such men, insinuated Law, were sissies.

Law showed more empathy in an article titled "Nutrition in the Antarctic," where he noted that digestive illnesses in his close-knit year-round crews were often rooted in social discord: "Indigestion, gall bladder trouble, appendicitis, neurotic stomach troubles—these are the principal ills of an Antarctic party" at odds with each other.

To build harmony among expedition members, Australian bases adopted the "slushy roster," a practice mandating egalitarianism. Everyone on station took a turn as slushy, assisting the cook for a week with dishes and food prep, and replacing him on Sunday. "It was an equaliser" between the "ordinary fellows" and the "boffins" (scientists), said one cook. That such rules and roles remained in place as team members arrived and left, year after year, showed that the era of Antarctic *employment* had begun.

While taking his turn as slushy, the doctor at Mawson Station in 1956 made a caramel sauce so thick and chewy that it sucked fillings out of teeth. They came out, he said, "like machine-gun bullets—you could hear them popping!" The next morning, the crew lined up outside his door, suspicious he had cooked up a plan to get some dentistry practice. In another tale of Australian Antarctic dentistry, Dr. Stefan Csordas, the station medical officer at the base on Macquarie Island, needed to carve three new teeth for his cook's denture but had no bone to work with. Until he looked to the Macquarie shoreline for inspiration, that is, where male elephant seals yawped at their harems. Csordas spent two weeks paring down the seal teeth to human size. The cook liked the elephant-seal teeth so much that he wore them even after returning to Australia, hoping perhaps to acquire his own harem.

Jim Morgan, another Macquarie cook in the IGY era, grew tired of a crew member who was obsessed with finding hair in his food. According to one of their companions, the complainer poked at each meal and when he found a hair he held it up and said, "Look, here's another short and curly!" So Morgan planned his revenge. He gathered up clippings from someone's haircut and stuffed them into one of the fruit pies he made for dessert one night. Everyone but the whiner was aware of what lay beneath his custard, and had a good laugh when hair fluffed out as he dug his spoon into the pie. There is no record of how the complainer responded, but "he was certainly cured of ever mentioning that he had found a hair in his tucker."

Estonian peasant food

The Soviet Antarctic program established Mirnyy (on the coast) and Vostok (deep inland) as their first permanent bases during the IGY. Several other permanent and seasonal facilities followed in the years afterward, as the USSR built the most widespread program on the continent.

Juhan Smuul, a noted Estonian writer under the USSR banner, penned an eccentric and patriotic book called *Antarctica Ahoy* that celebrated the Soviet IGY effort. Smuul traveled by ship during the second IGY summer to Mirnyy, where he embedded with the research community for two intense months.

Arriving in Mirnyy, Smuul sat down with Vvedensky, a journalist at the end of a year-long stint, to a private meal of cognac and some extraordinary salted pork fat. The pig had been brought as a piglet to Mirnyy, raised on scraps in a piggery distinguished "from all other piggeries in history" because he shared it with four penguins.

Smuul claimed that the effect on the eater of such penguin-influenced pork is that "the poet, willy-nilly, awakens in him." The gleaming salt crystals of the pork fat shone "snow-white, ice-cold." The prosaic layout of Mirnyy, filled with what he had described earlier as an ugly array of "flat boxes," took on a Van Gogh haze: "The snow was whiter, the path narrower and the arrangement of the houses more haphazard. The green aircraft had twice as many propellers as in the morning."

Smuul first flew into the Antarctic interior on a quick flight delivering fuel to a temporary camp built on the route to Vostok. On the way back to Mirnyy, a crewmember fired up an onboard gas cooker to make an in-flight lunch of potatoes and pork fat. The two of them sat down, "one on a crate, another on a suitcase, and each with his own fork and appetite," around a still-sizzling frying pan.

Above a continent he now knew to be "enormous, cold, cruel, lifeless, monotonous, sinister and yet beautiful," they ate a meal worthy of Estonian peasants, he said, the potatoes and pork fat cut into big lumps and nicely browned.

Mirnyy's mess hall, the Penguin Restaurant, didn't serve penguin, but the food was fine, with an abundance of meat, butter, powdered milk, sugar, and fruit. Smuul praised the Soviet cooks. "I am willing to bet," he said, "that cooks who have been with an Antarctic or Arctic expedition can redeem the position of any restaurant going bankrupt."

Smuul's real taste of Antarctica came with his second flight, this time to Komsomolskaya, a tiny four-person advance base on the route to the Pole of Inaccessibility (an imaginary point, calculated by geographers as the hardest place to reach in Antarctica). He spent a week at this one-building, four-room facility hunkered down at 11,220 feet. Pavel Sorokin was a better radioman than cook but was excellent at cajoling the men to eat, saying, "A man who eats sparingly is no good, is fickle and has no respect for the cook's work."

At first, Smuul suffered from altitude sickness, his labored breathing "like drinking from an empty cup," and from literary nightmares in a "turbid backwater of sleep haunted by grinning, sinister faces, by lines from *Fleurs du mal*, by ghosts from sunken ships." Soon the writer recovered and joined Sorokin in the kitchen peeling South African potatoes, each one "so white, smooth and polished that you sit back and admire it as though it were a happy phrase."

The poet, about to depart Mirnyy for home, acknowledged his own uselessness on the ice. He did not understand cosmic rays, geomagnetism, or seismology, and so communed with the dogs instead:

However poetic your soul, to whatever layers of the

atmosphere your feelings soar, if you have no technical education and no real understanding of technology the only thing you are good for in Antarctica is to pull sledges."

But the dogs of Mirnyy, like unpatriotic Soviet writers, were out of style. For the Soviets, as at other bases, the ice continent had become an abstract habitat made for man and machine. An American exchange scientist named Morton Rubin arrived in Mirnyy on the day Smuul departed, and later noted a horrifying fact in his diary: Of more than forty dogs on station, two were given to the Australians, twenty-one were kept at Mirnyy as a precaution, while the remainder were "thrown into the sea to drown." They don't work, he was told by way of explanation. They just eat.

Collaboration between cultures and communities was the secret to success in the IGY. "There was almost a magical quality about the I.G.Y. in the way it lowered international barriers and opened closed doors," wrote Gould. "There was a simplicity, a flexibility and freedom from political consideration hitherto unknown." Scientific data was created cooperatively and shared freely between all IGY programs. Soviet and U.S. programs exchanged scientists. "Here in the coldest place on earth," exulted Gould, "occurred the first thawing of the Cold War." Antarctica had become not merely a second home for researchers and support staff, but a home for a more peaceful future as well.

There were, of course, dissenters. "Do we want to spread the disease of communism even to the penguins?" asked Senator Thomas Dodd, an anti-Soviet Democrat from Connecticut trying in vain to convince penguin-loving members of Congress not to ratify the Antarctic Treaty. Luckily, Dodd failed. The treaty was, and still is, an enlightened document that set aside the ice continent for peaceful purposes. Signed in 1959 by twelve nations, including the USSR and the United States, the Antarctic Treaty owes everything to the ambitious, cooperative IGY era. It was, in fact, the first arms control agreement to appear during the Cold War. Senator Dodd may have been eventually appeased by the era of peace and international cooperation in Antarctica that resulted from the treaty, and he may even have appreciated that the penguins, long banished from the supper table, would end up neither dead nor Red.

Charlie Burton using the pressure cooker on Ranulph Fiennes' Transglobe Expedition, 1979-81

"Freshies were precious commodities, more valuable than money. If there had been five-dollar bills scattered over the snow with the oranges, I'm convinced the guys would still have gone for the fruit. I would have." —Jim Mastro, Antarctica: *A Year at the Bottom of the World*

"Food took the place of sex, anticipated with salivating eagerness and savored to the last lick." —Ranulph Fiennes, *Mind over Matter*

Prisoner-of-War Syndrome

7

I didn't worry about food as I planned for my first departure to Antarctica. Why would I? It was a job and an adventure; sustenance was an afterthought. And besides, I had been hired by a large corporate government contractor that had bought my plane tickets and would pay my salary, provide housing, and feed me. I knew I was reverting to the culinary vagaries of a cafeteria-fed life, as in college, but I was still a young man with a big appetite and low standards.

That there was a century-long Antarctic history of big appetites and low standards I did not yet understand, nor that those low standards were sometimes still far too high for what Antarctic cuisine could provide. I didn't know that even in the waning years of the twentieth century, after decades of modern outpost life fed by massive ships and frequent flights, Antarctica could still make me desperate for "freshies" — fruit and veggies still in their raw beauty, unsullied by canning, freezing, or processing. If an overeducated and underqualified poet could pack up and ship off to the ice, I figured, then why would there be a dearth of apples?

I would learn that sometimes a lack of freshies is simply about cargo priorities (people and equipment come first). Sometimes it's about the lack of intelligence and empathy of someone in a Denver office making culinary decisions for folks in an off-world outpost. But mostly, I would realize, it's because Antarctica is still in charge.

The technological advances that produced and sustained the IGY gave humanity a permanent foothold on the ice, but a foothold isn't the same thing as a comfortable existence. Through the period (1960s to the 1990s) between the IGY and my arrival, collaborative human endeavor and logistical advances improved the quality of life, but these advances all took place on a continent whose antibiotic realities cared little about our desire for salads and bananas. The planet's worst storms and deepest cold still played havoc with the best that modern civilization could throw at the continent. We had become (mostly) free to come and go between the ice and the warm world, but then as now, it didn't take much to make us prisoners of Antarctic realities.

Yet the International Geophysical Year had managed to transform Antarctica from a howling, empty wilderness into a howling, scantily settled wilderness. The ancient grind of wind seething over snow could still be heard over the racket of generators, diesel engines, and electric bread mixers, but it was no longer alone. Snowmobiles were introduced in 1960 and became the new dogs, strong enough to tow sledges but light enough on their tracks to cross most bridged crevasses. As long as a research party had enough food, fuel, and spare parts, these simple machines could take them everywhere they needed to go.

More importantly, ski-equipped LC-130 Hercules turboprop cargo planes (Hercs) revolutionized Antarctic logistics. No longer were airdrops and slow-moving tractor trains necessary to transfer freight. With the Herc, the United States had a workhorse plane that could carry large piles of cargo and land anywhere it was needed. For more than fifty years, Hercs have been supplying inland bases, seasonal camps, and roving deep-field parties with everything from Sno-Cats to oranges.

In this new era, men (and finally by the late 1970s, some women) lived for long stints at permanent bases, supporting or practicing science in the field. Little has changed since the early 1960s but the details.

Technologies and logistics are constantly updated, but since the IGY, Antarctic life has been a hybrid operation of humans and machines under the aegis of science. Antarctic cuisine, too, has become a menu of predictable sustenance, occasionally spiced with the kind of desperate or extraordinary meals that only prisoners can concoct.

𝄞 clubbers and plonk 𝄞

Although the Cold War was being waged elsewhere, on the ice a spirit of international cooperation remained intact. "In a sense," wrote David Burke in *Moments of Terror*, "the cold, white ice cap stripped ideologies of their stupidity in the struggle to study, live and survive." There were formal exchanges of scientists between the U.S. and Soviet programs and informal exchanges of fuel when needed. When difficulty struck, hospitality was extended between "enemies" without conditions.

On a Christmas Eve sometime in the 1960s, with bad weather preventing an American Herc from landing at either South Pole or McMurdo, the plane touched down at the USSR's Vostok Station, situated at the south geomagnetic pole (a theoretical point used to measure variation in the Earth's magnetic field). Elsewhere on Earth this might have been a diplomatic incident, but here it was an occasion to consume caviar, shashlik (marinated lamb kebabs), and vodka while talking "like long-lost cousins."

Likewise, in January of 1962, two Soviet aircraft landed at Mawson Station to wait out a storm. After tying the planes down, fourteen Russians and seven Australians crammed into a tiny hut, squashed together on bunks or sitting on each other's knees. Australian Mike Lucas described the scene: "

In this remote place, where the silence of the great rock mountains rising sheer from the surrounding ice is only broken by the audible swish of snow petrels as they dive and bank around the buttresses high above, there followed the most extraordinary party I have ever witnessed. . . .

The chicken was passed round, the 'plonk' and 'clubbers' uncorked, and much linking of arms, clinking of glasses and cries of 'friendship' ensued." This went on every night the Russians were trapped at Mawson. Russian dancing, singing, and vodka were met with Australian bush songs, Maori hakas, clubbers (homebrew), and plonk (cheap wine).

That same year, in a lonelier sort of collaboration, six Australians made a 1,780-mile round-trip scientific traverse from Wilkes on the coast up to Vostok and back. Expedition leader Bob Thomson imagined the voyage as a science fiction scene on a lifeless planet in which "dark, hairy, unkempt creatures . . . shambled among gaunt metal monsters."

The unkempt creatures quickly grew gaunt as well. Intense cold, weeks of whiteouts and blizzards, and constant mechanical breakdowns made travel excruciatingly slow. Worse, all their Christmas goodies—"succulent chickens, mouth-watering ducklings . . . [and] cans and cans of good

Aussie beer" — had fallen off a sledge and been lost.

Their luck improved when they reached a cold, hollow Vostok that the Russians had temporarily but suddenly abandoned a year earlier. The Australians found a dining table already set and a frying pan full of steak and onions on the stove. After 890 miles, the Australians were tired of canned food and pemmican. So one of the guys put on the Russian cook's apron hanging nearby, turned on the stove, and warmed up the steaks while the others sat down to await their first real meal in weeks.

ᛌ aerovodka and gristle ᛉ

The bonds formed between Cold War "enemies" extended far beyond the occasional diverted plane or wild party. One of the exchange scientists who spent a year on a Soviet base was glaciologist Charles Swithinbank. At Novolazarevskaya with the 1963–65 Ninth Soviet Antarctic Expedition, he lived a very different life than he was used to in England. As Swithinbank relates in *Vodka on Ice*, he learned while sailing south on a Soviet ship that his diet would be impoverished in both quality and variety. "Apart from feast days," he wrote bluntly, "the food was not good." Cabbage soup (borscht or *shchi*, depending on the type of cabbage), ragout, and compote ("an insipid rust-coloured liquid with a faint taste of boiled apples") became distressingly familiar. The quality of the beef was quite poor, all gristle and bone. Soviet cattle, he learned, fed on sparse grass.

Although the meat was poor, somehow the butter was excellent. So was the black bread. And those feast days really were exceptional. Swithinbank sobered up after a New Year's celebration full of black and red caviar, pickled herring, pickled mushrooms, sausage, crabmeat, and more. A May Day feast included roast chicken, crab salad, ham, salmon, smoked salmon and sturgeon caviar, apples, oranges, champagne, brandy, and orange juice spiked with "aerovodka," airplane de-icing fluid.

Drinking aerovodka wasn't restricted to holidays. Swithinbank noted a more frequent aviator's tradition at Molodezhnaya: "On landing back at base after a long flight, it was the duty of the navigator to drain a litre of fluid from the aircraft's de-icing system. Unlike some de-icing fluids, this was pure alcohol (ethanol). Once indoors, it was served to the aircrew and passengers." One observer of a similar USAP habit—drinking a rocket fuel known as JATO (jet-fuel assisted take-off)—equated the practice to that of "a warrior culture drinking blood."

At Novolazarevskaya, the dining room was the community's social center. One long table fit them all. Here Swithinbank spent his year of good company, good science, and terrible food. The cook, Ivan Maximovich Sharikov, had spent more than thirteen years in the polar regions as a weather observer. "The oldest, tallest, baldest, and humblest man" on staff, Ivan took on the cook's role at Novolazarevskaya when no weather job was available. For him, as for all Soviet Antarctic staff, the pay was irresistible, since he earned five times what he might make in Russia. Ivan was not much of a cook, though to be fair he had little to work with. Much of the better meat left by the previous year's crew had gone to rot. Ivan was stuck making borscht, *shchi*, fish soup with bones, boiled potatoes, and to Swithinbank's dismay, lots of ragout. Ivan's ragout, he wrote, consisted "of stewed gristle with chips of bone, generally served with macaroni. Aside from the gristle, fat, and bone, the amount of lean meat remaining could be held on a teaspoon."

Ivan at least made a reliable porridge to swallow with the bread and butter every morning. Occasional treats included caviar, sauerkraut, and cheese.

Cucumbers and tomatoes grew in window boxes, and ice cream was made from milk powder and freshly drifted snow. Each Russian expedition member also received a monthly five-hundred-gram chocolate ration. The married men saved it to bring back to their wives, whom they had left behind for a very long time.

After an end-of-year inventory revealed more than one hundred missing bottles of vodka, champagne, and eau de cologne from the liquor stock, Ivan the cook confessed. He had a habit of taking walks alone after dinner, but Swithinbank "had assumed that it was to get a breath of fresh air as an antidote to the heat of the kitchen." The eau de cologne was, for some Russians, an "esteemed substitute" when they ran out of vodka.

When Swithinbank at last returned to England, he had trouble adjusting to his old diet. Meat, fish, and cheese made him ill.

He eventually found a doctor with a good memory of World War II, who diagnosed him with prisoner-of-war syndrome.

After a year of high-carbohydrate meals garnished with stringy meat, Swithinbank's body could no longer absorb high-protein English food. "The solution," he wrote, "was simply to wean me slowly from the Russian diet."

part envy, part hunger

Antarctic cuisine has always made prisoners out of residents. The higher someone's culinary expectations were, the darker the prison they found. In 1982, when Jim Mastro arrived in McMurdo, he found that he had exchanged his healthy California diet for trays of bland, institutional slop issued from the navy galley. He came in on the first Winfly (winter fly-in) flight, the transition period in the U.S. program when about two hundred people arrive in McMurdo to help the skeleton crew of pale souls who've lasted the long winter prepare for the summer onslaught of another thousand people.

Most Winfly meals were a struggle. "Occasionally," Jim said, "one was bearable." He noticed that the five-compartment dining trays were the same as those issued in prisons. The cuisine didn't belie the similarity. Frozen and canned vegetables were overcooked, he wrote, "resulting in mush." Jim investigated a box of lobster tails and found they were packaged in 1969.

The menu offered a two-week rotation of meals heavy on meat, fat, and starch and sadly devoid of flavor, barring the occasional overdose of salt. But Jim understood the difficulties of the McMurdo kitchen: "To be fair, the cooks had just come out of a long winter, and they were burned out. Suddenly they had three times the number of people to cook for—with no additional staff."

Jim and other new arrivals were told to tread lightly around the winterovers, who varied in their ability to socialize. Nowhere was this clearer than in the galley, where the two groups circled each other as carefully as two predator species at an African water hole.

A more serious predation resulted from the gender imbalance. During Winfly, only fifteen of three hundred people in McMurdo were women. The women could risk socializing in this frontier community outfitted with several bars (and beer-stocked vending machines), or they could hide. Jim observed one new female employee surrounded by so many eager men buying her drinks at one of the bars that soon "ten or twelve cans of beer were lined up like an aluminum train on the bar next to her seat."

There was certainly more beer to be had than freshies. Each time a vegetable-laden flight arrived, Jim ate salad desperately until it ran out. There were also the rare special meals, like Mexican night, a respite "between the chicken yakisoba and fried rabbit." Otherwise, Jim had a choice: Either embrace the bland piles of meat, fat, and starch or turn to the only real flavor on the menu—sweets. "I ate way too many New Zealand ice cream cups," Jim wrote. "The baker, unfortunately for me, made exceptional donuts. Between the high-fat food and the abundant desserts, I sensed trouble."

By November, with summer in full swing and McMurdo's population approaching twelve hundred, the galley was crowded with sailors, electricians, snowmobile mechanics, heavy-equipment operators, research scientists and their graduate students, mountaineers, and bureaucrats. Long lines ran through the E-side into the hallway. Freshies were gone before latecomers could get a taste. Jim gained weight on sweets and prayed for another flight from Christchurch, all while preparing to spend the next winter in McMurdo.

During the last weeks of summer, Jim and the winterovers

joked about kicking out the tourists. Soon enough, in a clear case of being careful what you ask for, the streets were empty, the cold was colder, and the work harder. Sensory deprivation altered Jim's sleep patterns and distorted his dreams. It was his turn to struggle with normal social skills. Darkness dominated. Sounds—machines and wind—had not altered but felt lonelier. And food was "utterly tasteless," other than some extremely salty soups. A cook explained that the saltiness was intentional: "It's very dry down here, so we have to make the soups salty so people will drink more." Jim didn't have the heart to tell her that both her hypothesis and her soups were "complete hogwash."

The galley did provide odors more pleasant than the usual McMurdo taint of diesel fuel, but he nonetheless found the smells more industrial than life-giving: "Just like randomly mixing a bunch of different paints together will produce a muddy brown, the random blend of food smells in the galley produced a 'brown' odor."

Jim and his friends continued the Antarctic tradition of fantasizing about better food: "With the remains of a leathery steak and powdered mashed potatoes on our trays, we'd talk about what fresh food we missed the most." Jim imagined sitting down with a whole watermelon for himself, "scooping out spoonful after spoonful of the sweet, juicy meat. Or I'd describe the sensation of biting into a plump ripe peach and having the juice run down my chin."

On Midwinter's Day, McMurdo received an airdrop, a tradition from 1973 to 1995 in McMurdo and from 1981 to 1995 at South Pole. For the winterers, it was Christmas in June. A U.S. Air Force C-141 Starlifter from Christchurch streaked south under the light of a full moon to circle over frozen men and oil lamps marking a drop zone. The air force crew pushed out a hundred cardboard crates with small parachutes attached. The crates contained mail, freshies, and some important items ordered during the winter.

For Jim, there was one secret item he hoped the authorities in Christchurch had allowed through, but he wouldn't know until everything was found and inventoried. When the 141 came into view, his heart leapt, as he felt he "was witnessing the arrival of the first spaceship from Earth."

The boxes dropped, some plummeting—in an echo of the 1957 "stream-ins" at the Pole—because their parachutes never opened. "Freshies in those boxes," Jim mused out loud. "For sure." And he was right. Men chased oranges and pieces of broken watermelon already beginning to freeze. This was serious business: "Freshies were precious commodities, more valuable than money. If there had been five-dollar bills scattered over the snow with the oranges, I'm convinced the guys would still have gone for the fruit. I would have."

Perceptive friends in the United States had mailed him tortilla chips and lilac-scented soap while others sent candy and chocolate, which McMurdo provided every day. The brief bounty of freshies in the galley was a revelation, with the whole town, he said, "relishing every bite and laughing out loud at the sheer joy of it."

When Jim was called up to Cargo to pick up his secret package, his genius was an inspiration to the guys working there, who gave him a look that was "part admiration at my audacity, part humor, part envy, part hunger." They handed Jim six pizzas he had ordered from Spagalimi's Pizza Parlour in Christchurch.

"This," he wrote, "was real food, not the tedious, tasteless, repetitive McMurdo fare we'd grown to loathe. This was food with flavor. This was gold." He gave one to the Cargo guys to buy their secrecy, since he didn't want all of McMurdo hunting him down for a slice. With nine months of lousy food behind him, and another three to go, the pizzas were the best thing he'd ever eaten.

dreaming of lamb curry

Ask Rupert Summerson about his best Antarctic meal, and he's unlikely to choose lamb curry. In the early 1980s, Rupert worked two contracts doing fieldwork with the British Antarctic Survey (BAS). BAS trail cuisine was contained in uniform boxes of what they called "man food" — "a necessary distinction," he reminded me, "in the days of dog sledging." The man-food boxes fit like puzzle pieces onto the Nansen sled, and each contained a precise arrangement of tins and packets of food whose contents quickly became tedious.

Nearly twenty years later, Rupert could recite the litany: "a big tin of hard tack biscuits (which was later to be put to use as an oven, washing up bowl, washing machine and general purpose storage), tins of butter, tins of chocolate, tins of cheese, a jar or two of Marmite, a tin of bacon, which was highly prized . . . tins of porridge, tins or packets of sugar, tins of tea and drinking chocolate, tins or packets of potato powder and packets of dehydrated 'main meals.'" For main meals, they had a choice between beef stew, lamb stew, or lamb curry. But on a two-man journey near Rothera Station, Rupert and the researcher he was guiding ran into a problem.

Rupert looked inside his first man-food box and found

only lamb curry entrées. No worries, he thought, and opened another box. Lamb curry again. Every main meal in every box for three months of fieldwork was lamb curry.

Being the rugged sort, he and his researcher put up with it for some weeks before finally putting in a plaintive radio call to the base, requesting a plane to swing by and drop off some variety. "After the usual sorts of jocularity you would expect," Rupert told me, "along the lines of 'We used to *dream* of lamb curry' [from Monty Python's Four Yorkshiremen sketch], an aircraft was eventually diverted to bring some relief. Funnily enough I still like lamb curry."

In another desperate effort at culinary variety, Rupert switched from man food to dog food. One of his duties at Rothera was to shoot seals for the dogs, and watching the huskies slobber and growl over seal meat eventually made him, seventy-five years after the peak of the heroic age, curious about the taste. After consulting with the base chef, he cut slabs off both crabeater and Weddell seals, removed every trace of blubber, and cooked up the steaks. He thought the crabeater meat compared well with venison and other wild game. He sampled the liver as well but was leery of parasites and — remembering the cautionary tale of Mertz and Mawson in 1913 — vitamin A poisoning. Even another box full of lamb curry was better than that.

steaks on the garbage dump

After thirty years of occupation, there was a greater dilemma facing Antarcticans than culinary monotony. The environmental group Greenpeace arrived in the summer of 1986–87 to highlight it, in an expedition unlike any other in

Antarctic history. They built their own small year-round World Park Antarctica Base and conducted research, but their mission was more ethical and political than scientific.

For too long, Antarctic occupation had meant a thoughtless contamination of the most pristine place on Earth. Authorities in each program argued that they had no choice, that Antarctica made it too hard to act responsibly, and that isolated pollution on a massive continent didn't matter. None of that was true, though. Modern Antarctic programs were not such helpless prisoners of the harsh climate that they couldn't clean up after themselves; they were just lazy and more worried about conserving budgets than ecosystems. The Greenpeace crew was there to tell the world the ugly truth, because according to the Antarctic Treaty the empty continent belonged to everyone.

On the way south, they protested at France's Dumont d'Urville base, where colonies of penguins and other sea birds had been obliterated by dynamite in an attempt to build a runway. Then they built their tiny base on the beach of Cape Evans, next door to Robert Scott's *Terra Nova* expedition hut and just nine miles from the severe pollution at McMurdo Station and Scott Base.

For decades, the U.S. Navy put old vehicles, fuel drums, and other waste out on the ice to fall eventually to the ocean floor. A 1971 study of the base's effect on the McMurdo Sound seabed found that the ecology had been seriously impacted by the "rug of litter" made up of heavy equipment, fuel hoses, "honey buckets" of human waste, and thousands of beer cans, among other things. In some areas, beer cans outnumbered the sea floor's sponges.

McMurdo also created landfills along the shoreline of

Winter Quarters Bay and above town in an area known as Fortress Rocks. The seabed of Winter Quarters Bay was so polluted with chemicals, particularly PCBs (polychlorinated biphenyls), that it became (and remains) one of the most polluted bodies of water on the planet.

The Greenpeace strategy was a campaign of frequent visits to both stations, pulling stunts like unfurling banners and sampling McMurdo's pollution in front of the cameras before sending the images and test results back to the warm world. U.S. and New Zealand authorities described the activists as a bunch of troublemakers, but Greenpeace cook Irmi Mussack knew that those who dedicate their lives to fixing the human relationship with life on Earth must use the media as a loudspeaker. "We are just screaming the problem," she said.

Charles Swithinbank had already noted problems with food waste and disposal in 1960, when the sixteen-ounce steaks served at supper in the mess hall were far too large. The cooks refused to serve smaller portions, "so half of my steak ended up on the garbage dump — which was bulldozed into the sea." Now Greenpeace exposed another food-related disaster: the outpouring of excess nutrients into McMurdo Sound via a sewage outfall pipe. The huge nutrient-rich mound of outfall debris, known locally as "the corn pile" for its bright sprinkling of undigested corn, caused enduring damage in the slow-growing ecology of the sound's cold waters. The sewage also directly threatened local seal populations through the transmission of human intestinal pathogens.

U.S. authorities insisted that they agreed in principle with Greenpeace's goals. They acknowledged both their long history of polluting and the slow cleanup of their facilities.

And they pointed to the good work they'd done so far. Greenpeace biologist Gudrun Gaudian responded diplomatically: "McMurdo is said to have tidied up. . . . I think that's fantastic. I'm sure McMurdo would never admit it, but it's kind of like the mother coming in, and the children cleaning up before she arrives, so they don't get their hands smacked." But the photos and stories Greenpeace sent north ensured that U.S. and New Zealand hands were smacked hard in the court of world opinion.

Greenpeace occupied World Park Antarctica until 1992, a year after the U.S. and other Antarctic Treaty signatories agreed to the Madrid Protocol on Environmental Protection in 1991. The Madrid Protocol required signatories to "commit themselves to the comprehensive protection of the Antarctic environment and dependent and associated ecosystems and . . . to designate Antarctica as a natural reserve, devoted to peace and science." Greenpeace's activism had accelerated this shift. Their activism and negative publicity had also accelerated the U.S. cleanup. By the early 1990s, just before I arrived, the Fortress Rocks landfill and the shores of Winter Quarters Bay were partially cleaned before the remnants were hidden under new layers of gravel. All USAP waste, including material salvaged from the landfills, was sorted into recyclables and trash before being sent back to the United States for processing. But there was much, much more to do.

flat horizons, flat emotions, flat thoughts, and flat tastes

While the national research programs went about their business of science, logistics, and cleaning up their messes, a trickle of private expeditions arrived to test themselves against the inhuman Antarctic landscape.

They were led by adventurers who wanted to see the ice for themselves. As far as they were concerned, Antarctica was still an empty continent full of opportunities. Research traverses had crisscrossed regions of Antarctica no human had ever seen, but those were scientific journeys unconcerned with first ascents or individual accomplishment. These newcomers found, on incredibly difficult journeys, how Antarctica confines the body and challenges the mind.

No one challenged the Antarctic wilderness as fully as Will Steger's 1989–90 International Trans-Antarctica Expedition. The ITAE was a punishing polar adventure that lasted longer than the worst scurvy-ridden heroic age journeys, yet was as ecologically minded as the Greenpeace mission.

Six men from six nations, reiterating the international spirit behind the Antarctic Treaty and encouraging environmental protection of the continent, traveled 3,741 miles by dogsled along the longest possible transect of the continent.

It took more than seven months, beginning and ending in incredibly harsh near-winter conditions, including hurricane-force winds, temperatures below –60°F, and windchills far below –100°F.

This was the largest and most logistically complex private expedition since Fuchs and Hillary in 1956. Three dogsleds and six men required five tons of human food and fifteen tons of dog food, much of it laid out by airplane in fifteen depots across the continent. Each man was allowed some personal food items as comfort against the cold, like Steger's forty pounds of wild rice from northern Minnesota; seventy pounds of Russian bread made by the mother of Russian meteorologist Victor Boyarsky; bean sauce and jasmine oil for Chinese glaciologist Qin Dahe; and ramen, soy sauce, and seaweed for Japanese dog-handler Keizo Funatsu.

The team camped in three two-man tents. Each tent's kitchen consisted of a stove set on an empty dog-food box, with holes cut into the sides for stowing their trash. Tent pairings changed periodically to help with what Steger predicted would be their greatest challenge: remaining friends throughout seven months of physical and mental misery. One of his strategies was to break out a fresh, cheerful placemat and cloth napkins for each new companion.

Boyarsky, Steger's first tentmate, was a remarkable polar man who could ski ahead of the dog teams for twenty-six miles a day while navigating a straight line into whiteouts and blizzards. He also went out naked and barefoot every morning, regardless of the weather, to scrub himself with snow. But even polar men grow desperate for calories in the middle of Antarctica. After only a month on the trail, Steger described in *Crossing Antarctica* a meal he made to stave off their hunger: "Victor and I had a great multicourse meal of soup, toasted bread and a heavy-duty, high-octane concoction of meat poached in butter with a pound of cheese melted on as topping. We ate slowly, and I felt like a caveman as I ripped apart dripping, greasy meat with my fingers in the dim candlelight."

Seven months of oatmeal for breakfast was a trial, even when supplemented with granola or peanut butter. Lunch was spartan too: dried fruit and nuts, chocolate, granola bars, energy bars, or pilot biscuits.

Dinners gave some variety, though each was based on either egg noodles, rice, or dried potatoes. For protein and fat, their dinner rations included four ounces of butter, four ounces of sixty-forty pemmican (made with beef and pork with lard), six ounces each of dehydrated soup and cheese, and occasional treats of canned fish (tuna, sardines, or salmon).

As they reached each new depot—a four-by-four-foot box marked with a nine-foot-tall pole and flag—the team dived into it like hungry looters. They wanted sweets, dried chicken, brandy. Then the horse-trading began, the guys swapping the parts of their rations they disliked for those they craved. Boyarsky, Qin, and Jean-Louis Étienne wanted sardines, which Funatsu, Steger, and British dog-handler Geoff Somers traded for brown sugar and fruit-and-nut bars. Steger and Boyarsky had "a chicken in the bank," given to them by the Chinese base from which the expedition departed. The other two teams ate their chickens right away, and weeks later Victor and Will wondered what luxury they should trade for: perhaps more toilet paper.

The cold was so severe, Steger felt like crying after a few hours on the trail. He perfected a lunch routine that allowed him to eat without taking off his gloves. He softened everything—the energy bar, the nuts, and the chocolate—in a thermos cup of hot water. The group lunch was "hardly a social event," he wrote, as each man hunkered down with his calories.

With four months of traveling completed and the South Pole just a few days away, Steger was a victim of culinary monotony. "I can't bring myself to eat pemmican anymore," he lamented, eating eight ounces of cheese at every dinner instead. "I often wish," he said, "we could somehow get by without eating."

At least Boyarsky and Funatsu found excitement in the royal jelly donated in great quantities by the Chinese government. As an alleged aphrodisiac ("not very useful given the circumstances," mused Steger), they said it filled their dreams with women. Steger disagreed, saying, "The Indian girl on the Land O' Lakes butter package doesn't look any better."

They were all thrilled, though, to arrive at the Pole, where they would at least see some women. It was a destination in a destination-less land, a *thing* on the empty prison of the ice cap, and it was occupied by the first new people they would meet since the expedition began 138 days earlier. Considering the strangeness of the landscape, the billions of dollars invested in life at the Pole, and the excitement they felt, Boyarsky described it perfectly: It was, he said, "like visiting Disneyland, Las Vegas, and Mars simultaneously."

Unfortunately, their fantasy destination had a grim gatekeeper. While the men and women at the Pole greeted them with cheers, hugs, and pats on the head (for the dogs), the National Science Foundation (NSF) representative sternly reiterated what had become the USAP hard line on private expeditions: It would offer no support whatsoever. The NSF somehow calculated that if it appeared more generous, they (with the largest aviation program in Antarctica) would be forced to rescue any expedition that got into trouble or be accused of negligence if they did not. The expedition, Steger was told, was entitled to a cup of coffee and nothing else. Even though the expedition was self-sufficient, professional, and well-supplied, they weren't allowed a hot shower or hot food. This was a new and foolish Antarctic hardship. The landscape was punishing enough; a lack of hospitality was an insult. Qin and Boyarsky were astonished, and Steger ashamed, at the NSF's rudeness, since the Russian, Chinese, and Chilean programs had all been generous to the expedition. The NSF had forgotten the spirit of the IGY and Antarctic Treaty, and failed to recognize that this expedition represented that spirit. Tellingly, when Étienne took the NSF representative aside to say he understood that she was in a tough position, wedged between policy and reality, she began to cry.

Eight hundred miles and twenty-four days later, they received a proper reception at Vostok, where they were greeted like heroes. Their warm welcome was based in part on the success of the expedition; partly on the presence of their Russian compatriot, Boyarsky; and partly on the reality that no one ever visited Vostok. This run-down, no-frills base where, Steger wrote, "lumberjacks and dogsledders would feel right at home," felt much more like the end of the Earth. Here, where the thermometer had dropped in the winter of 1983 to a world-record −128.6°F, they were welcomed with open arms: "We engaged in a traditional Soviet toast of bread dipped in salt and vodka," Steger recounted, "then moved on to a table spread with red and black caviar, sturgeon, salami, sweetbreads, kiwis, cherries, apples and oranges," all washed down with champagne and vodka.

They had nine hundred miles to go but the journey was over a well-known supply trail to Mirnyy on the coast. It was grueling, with temperatures sinking to −50°F, but it was straightforward and downhill. Flat horizons, flat emotions, flat thoughts, and flat tastes were all that lay between each campsite and the finish line at Mirnyy. Food was misery: "I force down oatmeal in the morning just to have enough strength to travel," wrote Steger. "I eat lunch only to ensure that I have the strength to make it to camp. Dinner is dreary." Only his memories of the feast at Vostok and the prospect of a fruit salad once he left Antarctica kept him going.

∫ we are slowly starving 𝚼

Antarctica is no place, Sir Ranulph Fiennes has written, to escape "the nightmares loose in your skull." Fiennes knew well the prison he was describing. He had pioneered the era of modern private Antarctic adventures, leading the 1979–82 TransGlobe Expedition in a dangerous, cold, crevasse-haunted two-month crossing of the continent by snowmobile.

Before the crossing, Fiennes, his wife Ginny, Oliver Shepard, and Charlie Burton spent eight months in a small, half-buried camp built of reinforced cardboard. In the winter darkness, the camp shook badly under katabatic winds — cold air masses sliding off the ice cap — and Ginny lived on coffee for twenty-four-hour stretches as she ran the expedition's scientific program in her radio hut half a mile away.

Exhaustion led to hallucinations, especially in the wind-filled dark as she clung to the safety line between base and hut. Antarctica was prison enough, but Fiennes admitted that Ginny's auditory delusions of crying babies in the blizzards and "someone whispering incoherently from close behind her" made it downright spooky.

Fiennes returned to Antarctica in 1992–93 for an even more strenuous continental crossing. He and physician Mike

Stroud were attempting to be the first to ski from coast to coast without any resupply. Fiennes's book *Mind over Matter* is an honest account of the psychological difficulties inherent in suffering frostbite and starvation while skiing into the empty icescape day after day. Before them, he wrote, was "the greatest void on Earth . . . it yielded nothing at all upon which to fix my gaze and concentrate, nothing to take my mind off the festering broth of my thoughts."

Fiennes remembered reading in Reinhold Messner's *Antarctica: Both Heaven and Hell* of the author's imaginary encounters with women on the trail. Whereas most sledgers fantasized about food, Messner, the legendary mountaineer, conjured erotic fantasies while manhauling: "Time and again I encountered figures of women, living, obstinate, wanton women. I pictured them naked and sometimes as my partner." Fiennes tried to fantasize about sex instead of food, but to no avail. "Perhaps the English really are colder fish than others," he mused, or perhaps in his starvation he could only eroticize his next meal: "Food took the place of sex, anticipated with salivating eagerness and savored to the last lick."

Fiennes and Stroud ate large meals of complex carbohydrates for several months before leaving England and, once they reached the ice, ate rations packed with 5,200 calories per day, made up of 57 percent fat, 8.4 percent protein, and 34.6 percent carbohydrates.

This, it turned out, was nowhere near enough. Fiennes feared that as a much larger man he would break down first, like Edgar Evans in Scott's doomed Pole party, but he and Stroud suffered equally, each losing almost a *third* of their body weight.

Stroud, who did extensive physiological studies throughout the expedition, noted that Fiennes eventually lost forty-nine pounds and expended up to 10,000 calories per day, while he himself lost nearly forty-five pounds and burned up to 8,500 calories per day.

Stroud and Fiennes burned that much energy for two reasons. First, they left their starting point with sleds that weighed 485 pounds each, "a figure well beyond our worst nightmares," and more than double what Scott's team dragged to their deaths. Also, Fiennes and Stroud had to manhaul their loads from sea level up to 11,000 feet en route to the Pole. Once up at high altitude, they burned about 7,000 calories per day. That was the good news. The bad news was that because they were so far behind schedule, they had few available rest days and would have to cut their 5,200-calorie ration down to just 3,000 calories to have any hope of making it to Ross Island. Stroud wrote in his journal that this was impossible: "Our calorie *deficit* has been the equivalent of the total *input* of a normal person. It is exactly as though a normal person had eaten nothing, I repeat nothing, all this time. . . . We *are* slowly starving."

On the bright side, Stroud considered their starvation a godsend for his physiological research. Two surprising initial findings showed that while they consumed more muscle mass than expected, they also had "remarkably adapted [their] ability to absorb fat from the gut and move it as a fuel supply into the bloodstream." Not that there was much fuel supply; Fiennes wrote that Christmas lunch was "a bitterly cold affair sitting side-by-side and hunched against the wind to crunch two squares of chocolate and gulp down a pint of tepid glutinous soup." Their only Christmas surprise was a bout of diarrhea suffered in that bitter wind, caused by bacterial growth in their unwashed thermoses.

Fiennes debated the virtue of saving bits of food for the shortage they knew would befall them after the Pole. Stroud insisted they should eat full meals earlier to maintain strength and reduce sledge weight. They were already ravenous and jealous of each other's spoonfuls of stew. By the fifth week, after losing twenty pounds, Fiennes dropped the subject. They reached the Pole with little joy in their hearts and stayed only briefly. Near the end of their run, they had almost reached the Ross Ice Shelf but knew in their hearts they lacked the time and food to reach Scott Base.

They were still trying, and failing, to ration their chocolate portion throughout the day. "At every step my thoughts refused to concentrate on *anything* other than the chocolate in my pocket," wrote Fiennes. "Eventually, I decided to eat *all* the chocolate at once and at one sitting, so that the mental conflict would cease." Soon he was eating both bars within ten minutes of their morning start. Stroud ate two-thirds of his chocolate in the morning but grew hypoglycemic in the afternoon. "What life will be like in another few days or after further food reduction," he wrote, "I hate to think."

There was no further reduction. They called it quits when they hit the ice shelf, imagining the alternative: their starved and frozen bodies, like those of Robert Scott's Pole party, curled up in a tent somewhere short of Ross Island.

In 1999, Fiennes was the winning bidder at an unusual auction at Christie's in London. Up for bid was a legend—a broken sledging biscuit said to have been found in the tent with the emaciated bodies of Scott, Wilson, and Bowers. Why starving men ignored a biscuit that a hungry man would have wolfed down is an unanswered question. Perhaps they didn't. Fiennes later decided that the provenance of the biscuit was unclear even though it had been preserved by Scott's family through the twentieth century like a holy relic.

Fiennes's winning bid of roughly $6,700 speaks to his patriotism (he thought the biscuit should stay in England), to his defense of Scott (his 2004 book Race to the Pole is dedicated "to the families of the defamed dead"), and perhaps to the power of food as symbolism. One lonely biscuit in a tent full of starved and frozen men might represent the discipline and self-abnegation required to traverse a continent of ice. Or it might be, as Douglas Mawson once feared while his emaciated body dangled above the eternal blue prison of a crevasse, merely a lost opportunity to eat: "After having stinted myself so assiduously in order to save food, I should pass on now to eternity without the satisfaction of what remained."

Tournados of Seal Portugaise

Seal steaks as required
Butter, seasoning
Mixed herbs
Sauce
2 ounces butter
1 tablespoon flour
Tomato sauce
Milk
Salt and pepper to taste
Garnish
Tomatoes (approximately 2 per person)
Green peas
Croutons of bread fried in butter

To prepare the meat: Wipe the meat dry and cut into neat round pieces approximately three-quarters of an inch thick. Season well a few moments before cooking and fry quickly in butter.

To prepare garnish: Drain off the juice of a tin of tomatoes and heat the tomatoes in butter for a few minutes until hot also the peas.

To prepare the sauce: Put the butter in a small saucepan, melt and bring to the boil. Add the flour and cook for a few minutes, stirring all the time. Add the milk slowly, keeping the pan off the stove, or rather the heat and stir in enough to make the sauce the consistency required. Season to taste. Next add sufficient tomato sauce to give a nice sharp flavor. Return to stove, heat again but do not boil.

To serve: Place each tournado on a crouton of bread and garnish with the tomatoes and green peas. Top each with the tomato sauce and pour the remainder around the sides. Serve with sauteed potatoes.

The Syrup of American Comfort

8

I first arrived in Antarctica in Winfly of 1994. I left Maine in early autumn, transitioned through a cool New Zealand springtime, then landed on what was the cusp of Antarctic summer but looked like an eternal winter. Everything was new, confusing, and cold. The windchill sunk to negative triple digits. McMurdo felt like a college campus but resembled a derelict Alaskan industrial park.

The weirdness had a social center: Building 155, the huge two-story community hub built in the late 1960s. It has several offices and dozens of dorm rooms, but its primary function has been kitchen and cafeteria to the parka-clad masses. Though always referred to as the galley, its official name is the McMurdo Station Dining Facility. Still a segregated eatery when I arrived, the E-side (enlisted dining area) was large and plain with rows of rectangular tables, while the O-side (officers' room) was a more intimate chamber with collegial round tables. I was, like so many before me, disappointed to find the same food served in both rooms.

If I wasn't working or sleeping or exploring, I was eating and observing in the galley. Many of the exhausted winterovers kept their distance from the cheerful new arrivals. Tensions swirled through the E-side and O-side along with the odors of industrial food. It was an intense transition time, with storms heralding the return of the sun, darkness receding, and pale and distant people waiting for their ticket home.

Some lucky ones had left with the Winfly flights, but many had to stay another month or two. A winterover nicknamed Rhino lived down the hall from me and was as gruff as his name suggested, not least because he was at his wit's end about a woman back home who had abandoned him. He wanted out, but no planes were flying. He needed to eat, but wanted to be alone, so he stood in the long line on the E-side wearing a large homemade cardboard sandwich sign with a scrawled request: DON'T TOUCH ME, DON'T TALK TO ME, DON'T EVEN FUCKING LOOK AT ME. Which mostly worked.

I could walk out of the galley with a bowl of freshly baked brownies topped with soft-serve ice cream, grab a bottle of wine at the little station store, and shuffle across the gravel parking lot to my dorm, dodging forklifts, all the while staring out at a frozen sea and glacier-drowned mountains tinged with the thousand colors of a polar sunset. McMurdo was a hive of bustling weirdness plunked down in a silent icescape unchanged for millennia. I was comfortable — if I ignored the –25°F temperature hardening my soft-serve — and didn't really know why.

I learned eventually what Rhino knew, that life in McMurdo is often about navigating the feeling of being in two places at once.

may not be as delicious as you hoped

The typical Antarctic narrative begins with some kind of arrival saga, a descent over the lines of latitude to the strangeness of the southern continent. What was once the stuff of legends—dogs and bags of coal washed overboard from overcrowded wooden ships—became hearty flight-of-passage stories in the post-IGY decades of navy aircraft making treacherous landings. And now, in an era of more comfortable flights, it's merely an amusing trope for blogs or magazine articles. *Oh, what a long strange flight I had*, a writer muses, before he or she dons sunglasses, picks up their USAP-issue orange duffel bags, and steps off the plane onto the eternal ice to board a warm shuttle bus. If there was cell-phone reception over the Southern Ocean, everyone on southbound planes today would send texts and tweets about icebergs, boredom, and lousy flight lunches. The hardship for new arrivals now is that they must wait to send those iconic tweets until they land in McMurdo and connect to Wi-Fi, chatting to the world via the swarm of Starlink satellites encircling the globe.

One stark tale from Winfly of 1983, recounted by Jim Mastro, tells of three Hercs that arrived together above McMurdo just minutes after an intense blizzard obscured the airfield. As the whiteout worsened and fuel ran low, the pilots were forced to land blindly on an empty patch of sea ice. Passengers were so frightened that a chain reaction of puking spewed flight lunches all over the cabin. "Vomit was everywhere, and the cabin reeked," Jim wrote. "Old Antarctic hands knew there was trouble, and they were scared. New people were terrified."

When my wife, Heather, heard Jim's story she said, "Well, yeah, those flight lunches deserved to be puked up." Flight lunches have rarely been popular. Opened sometime after a flight reaches cruising altitude on the long voyage over the

Southern Ocean, those brown bags, reeking of cheap peanut butter and jelly on white bread, give this astonishing journey to the end of the Earth the aura of an elementary-school field trip. For new arrivals, it's their first taste of Antarctic culinary deprivation.

Karen Joyce, a twenty-year veteran of McMurdo, described a scene, circa 1990, when everyone on board her flight, "as if on silent command," dug into their heavy flight lunch not because they were hungry but because they wanted to know what the hell was in it. Everyone, she wrote, discovered the following:

- One sandwich: white bread, 1 slice pink baloney, 1 slice orange processed American cheese
- One sandwich: wheat bread, peanut butter and grape jelly (thinly spread)
- One 4-ounce round white cardboard container: mixed green salad
- One 4-ounce round white cardboard container: canned fruit salad, including one-half maraschino cherry and one seedless grape, each
- One packet of impossible-to-open condiments: mustard, ketchup, mayonnaise, "Kraft Italian Salad Dressing," plastic utensils, and Handi-Wipes
- One package of six small cookies, of the kind found in vending machines on the Pennsylvania Turnpike ("Never Go 'Round Hungry!")
- One Red Delicious apple, tough of skin and applesauce-mealy of flesh
- One full-size American candy bar, various: Milky Way, Mars, Snickers, or Three Musketeers
- One 2-ounce bag of Fritos or Potato Chips, crushed to dust

- One package of two (2) Saltine crackers, completely pulverized
- Two 6-ounce cans of fruit juice, apple and grape, three years past their "Best if Used By" date
- One 8-ounce carton of real milk: particularly precious, as it was the last real milk anyone would see for the next five months

This "1960s-era school-lunch-on-steroids," as Karen called it, was meant to satiate navy personnel not just for the five-hour trip to McMurdo, but also for the inevitable turnaround flights, which might take twice as long. Also known as a "boomerang," a turnaround flight occurs when mechanical trouble or bad weather in Antarctica forces the airplane to turn back. Each Antarctic flight has a PSR, a Point of Safe Return, the last point at which a flight still has fuel sufficient to return to its point of origin. (The navy term used to be PNR, the Point of No Return, but it scared the civilians.) Once the Herc pilots fly past PSR, about four hours out of Christchurch, they are committed to McMurdo, bad weather or not.

Larger air force cargo jets, such as the C-141, C-17, and C-5, fly faster than a Herc and have fuel ranges that allow them to fly the full distance to McMurdo and back again to New Zealand. The bad news is that a passenger who boomerangs on one of those planes spends up to ten hours going nowhere. The consolation prize for turning around is a return to the fine restaurants and cosmopolitan cafés of Christchurch, New Zealand, with a pocketful of government per diem money. But there's only enough time to find dinner and a drink before heading back to bed for another 4:00 a.m. wake-up call to do it all again.

I boomeranged twice in my first deployment. I lingered eight days in Christchurch, eventually worn out from turnarounds or cancellations announced after a day of waiting at the airport. The first boomerang came three hours into the Herc flight, after the pilots heard a bad weather report from McMurdo. I gnawed distractedly on my flight lunch, thinking of the good chowder and better beer I'd consume in Christchurch that night. The second turnaround was more dramatic, since it happened *after* we passed PSR. The radar wasn't working, and the panicked crew wouldn't fly without it. Nine hours after takeoff, we landed with just a few minutes of fuel left in the tanks.

The curated shelves of Robert Falcon Scott's Cape Evans hut

In October of 1998, the flight group ahead of mine tried for fifteen days to reach McMurdo. Several times the C-141 pilots, with the same tightly packed scrum of 120 poor souls aboard, chose to fly all the way down to circle McMurdo just in case the weather improved. It never worked. Meanwhile, I was throwing down bundles of per diem cash on bottles of Australian shiraz.

When that 4:00 a.m. call does come, it's a minor saga of shuttling out to the airport, dressing in a red parka, white rubber "bunny" boots and other ECW (extreme cold weather) clothing, despite the warm New Zealand weather, checking in with your orange bags, being sniffed by a drug dog, lounging around for a few hours (after shedding your ECW gear), then finally standing in line on the tarmac where, as visiting Australian journalist Roff Smith experienced it in 2000, you look like a "conga line of 93 department store Santas that Uncle Sam was about to airlift to the wrong pole."

Inside, these military aircraft have none of the façade of commercial planes. Aside from the drab green color and exposed tubing, what this means is noise so loud that earplugs are necessary for the entire flight. The noise makes it difficult to think and nearly impossible to talk.

It's important to bring a book that is plot-driven enough to entertain your tired brain. *The Brothers Karamazov* may not be a good choice, as Traci Macnamara, a writing-teacher-turned-snow-shoveler, discovered in 2003 on her first Antarctic flight. She found herself so bored that she dug into her flight lunch just to read the questions on the bag of Pams Ready Salted Flavour crinkle-cut potato chips.

Pams Chippie Trivia Quiz entertained her with questions about the weight of a giraffe's brain, the wing speed of a gnat, and the ant-carrying capacity of an anteater's tongue, until suddenly she realized that she'd eaten her entire lunch, with hours left to fly.

Four years later, first-time South Pole sous-chef Michèle Gentille, known in the blogosphere as Ms. Tomato of *Harriett's Tomato*, was more amused than curious about her lunch. It bore this strange label: "May Contain Organic Products!" Perhaps, Gentille pointed out, it should have said, "May Not Be as Delicious as You Had Hoped!" Not dismayed that "the tuna salad had an aura of feline cuisine and the raisins tasted slightly chemical," she was well traveled enough to appreciate it as part of "the grand adventure." With better cuisine on her mind, she glanced out at the approaching continent as she flew over the Ross Sea, declaring—as perhaps none before her had done with such culinary flair— that her new home appeared to be "an entire continent made of Italian meringue."

oreos versus plankton

Antarctica, in fact, is 99.6 percent icing and 0.4 percent stony cake. Ice is everywhere, covering all but that 0.4 percent of exposed land. Its ubiquity is strange and overwhelming. Once first-timers stumble off their plane from Christchurch into the blue-white freezer, they momentarily contend with the idea that this mineral—frozen water—they know best from mixed drinks and ski slopes has engulfed their lives. They know that to live within such a landscape must mean living with the threat of an icy death, or at least on the razor's edge of survival—until they ride that warm shuttle into McMurdo, that is, where a strange land gives way to a stranger community.

"McMurdo exists alongside Antarctica rather than in it," wrote Roff Smith on his first visit. "After all, in Antarctica, you don't withdraw 20 bucks from a Wells Fargo ATM and then swing by the convenience store to pick up a packet of Oreos, a bag of Fritos, and a six-pack of Bud and kick back to watch a Cornhuskers football game on TV. But you can in MacTown. And a lot of people do." Indeed, today's McMurdo Station would be unrecognizable even to the post-IGY men of the 1960s and 1970s.

McMurdo is an anomaly, the Antarctic metropolis. Once a small orderly cluster of one-story buildings, McMurdo now consists of more than a hundred buildings (plus fuel tanks and cargo yards) spread across as many acres. When I arrived in 1994, the USAP budget was about $200 million per year, nearly as much as the Antarctic budgets of Russia, New Zealand, France, Australia, the UK, Italy, Norway, and Japan combined. Fourteen two- and three-story dormitories housed up to 1,200 people. Building 155, our central community structure, was pierced by Highway 1, the busy hallway with the store and ATM that Smith mentioned, providing a veneer of American familiarity to this Antarctic outpost.

Tromp upstairs from Highway 1 to the galley today, and instead of the two windowless, E-side and O-side dining rooms of old, there is one sunlit, handsome facility, completely redesigned in 2000. The old dishroom is gone, and with it what one writer maligned as "a too-cold non-sterilizing dishwasher . . . as effective as deep-tongue kissing everyone on base in spreading the annual plague known as the Crud." One of the few remaining traditions from 1960 is the four-meal schedule—breakfast, lunch, dinner, and midrats (midnight rations).

By the late 1980s, the navy no longer considered the ice a hardship post; thus, no more filet mignon on the regular

Sunday menu. When John Behrendt, who began his ice career in 1957 gnawing on Meat Bars and avoiding Finn Ronne, overheard new arrivals to McMurdo in 1995 complaining about the lack of fresh eggs *for a whole week*, he just looked at them and said, "Yeah, life is tough in Antarctica!" Eight years later, though, Behrendt saw the writing on the wall, literally, for his nearly fifty-year Antarctic career when he noticed with chagrin that one of the old Meat Bars was "in a display case of ancient Antarctic artifacts."

Rear Admiral George Dufek, leader of the navy's IGY effort, wrote a relentlessly upbeat book for young readers in 1960 called *Through the Frozen Frontier*. His chapter "Antarctica in the Year 2000" accurately predicts satellite communications and face-to-face TV-style messaging, like Skype. But his prophesies about planes arriving year-round at speeds of five thousand miles per hour, or guided missiles bringing light cargo and third-class mail, were a bit misguided.

Most food in Dufek's future McMurdo would be grown locally "in a mixture of native soil, refuse of penguins, sea life, and chemicals," or sucked out of the ocean. Machinery on shore and ships would harvest plankton and separate it "according to vitamin content." Some would be kept for local human food, chicken food, and greenhouse fertilizer while the rest was shipped off at a handsome profit for worldwide medicinal use.

That today in McMurdo we eat Oreos rather than plankton seems the natural choice, but we can hardly blame Dufek for proposing to the children of the baby boom the ancient human virtue of living off the land. Though his vision was mostly a pie-in-the-sky nuclear-powered technological utopia, the admiral at least offered up a culinary dream of Antarctica-as-home, rather than still, fifty years later, an outpost to which we ship little bags of industrial garbage called snack food.

ʃ assume your guests are tired and hungry ⅄

When Karen Joyce arrived at McMurdo's end-of-the-world outpost in 1990, she was hungry. She rushed to her first galley meal only to find the guy ahead of her in line "glopping some orange mush onto his prison tray." It turned out, she later wrote, "to be the first of many meals that leveled hunger but left another kind of longing in their wake." *At least it's free*, she told herself.

This was Karen's introduction to the dichotomy of McMurdo food. On one hand, we could come in shivering from Antarctica and eat to our heart's content. Against the historical backdrop of starvation and scurvy, we were satiated, perhaps even spoiled. But all that free and easy food in a makeshift town "thoroughly drenched in the syrup of American comfort," as Karen put it, made us wonder how hard it would be to make the food good.

In a comedic novel I wish she had published — *The Winter of My Discount Tent* — Karen's characters debated whether the galley food was tasteless: "Oh, I don't know," said Josh, "there's plenty of flavor here: high notes of freezer burn, subtly entwined with undercurrents of over-used Galley grease, grandly overarched by the stench of rotting seafood."

As we've known since the days of Rozo and Lindstrøm, a good cook makes all the difference. In what Jim Mastro remembers as "a magical winter" in the late 1980s, the head chef was an ex-submariner who "took real pride in making his food as good as it could be." McMurdo residents ate beautiful meals night after night. But summer arrived and with it a new head chef: "One day it was a joy to go to the galley, the next it was a nightmare." It could have been worse: On one occasion in the 1970s, the navy supply officer simply shut down the food line during a meal. He told the kitchen staff that the food was unfit for human consumption and demanded that a replacement meal be made immediately.

But the story behind a bad McMurdo meal has always been more complicated than just the work in the kitchen. The navy galley received bulk quantities of mystery meats from low-quality military suppliers in the United States, and long-term planning is difficult because the vast tonnage of food is delivered just once per year on a single cargo ship plying its way through the ice of the Southern Ocean.

Freshies too are erratic, arriving by plane in small, irregular batches through the summer. What the cooks, good or bad, have on hand is all they can count on. If they run out of something, that's it. This is as true today as it was under navy leadership, which was phased out department by department through the 1980s and 1990s, with food services going private in 1992.

If the twenty-first-century galley is an improvement over the navy days, that's due in part to Sally Ayotte, who transformed the USAP food experience. Ayotte, known from 1996 to 2008 as "Sally in the Galley," was an executive chef on a mission. "Food is love," she was fond of saying. "If you can't put love into it, it's going to taste bad."

Cooking with love may be a cliché in American kitchens, but in the lonely confines of Antarctica the idea had resonance. Under Ayotte's leadership, the strangeness of Antarctica and the weirdness of McMurdo found a counterbalance in the comfort food made by a loving kitchen.

"The only way to make hundreds of people feel special and loved," said Sally, "is to treat them as dinner guests, so we throw a dinner party four times a day. We must always be in a good mood and smile when we cook. If we're not, the food's flavor and presentation reflect it. Frown, and the pot roast will burn." Probably because Sally's fine food and relentless enthusiasm surprised visiting reporters with expectations of a grumpy frontier camp still fed on pemmican, the media loved her, praising her as the queen of an oasis in the wild icy desert. Again and again, Sally's message was clear: "Morale is big around here," she told MSNBC, "and of course food is morale." Another motivational phrase on her office door was more pragmatic: "Assume your guests are tired and hungry and treat them accordingly."

Sally honed her philosophy in the perfect Antarctic crucible: cooking the midrats meal for the nightshift at the South Pole. Isolated not only from the world but also from the majority of the small South Pole population, she had a revelation: Her Antarctic friends' happiness was in her hands. She was responsible for the most important feature of their lives that could be controlled. Working conditions were difficult, but food — her food — could make it better. She never looked back.

For the next five summers she was in charge of all South Pole food, supervising a dozen kitchen staff while on a mission to make the end of the Earth a happier place. In 2002, she became executive chef of the entire USAP and spent half the year in McMurdo, managing eighty cooks and kitchen staff at McMurdo, Pole, and Palmer stations. During the rest of the year, Sally worked in the corporate office in Denver, massaging a multimillion-dollar USAP food budget and convincing the powers-that-be to increase the per-meal allowance for McMurdo. It's a classic recipe for better meals: more money spiced with happier cooks.

Sally also planned the yearlong McMurdo menu (based on a five-week meal rotation) and created the massive annual food order to supply it. Her task was in the tradition of the heroic age expedition leaders who planned for two-year journeys, but at a scale and complexity that would have blown Shackleton's mind.

Her order included seventy thousand pounds of beef, fifty to sixty thousand pounds of poultry, and twenty thousand pounds of seafood. Antarctic logistics made it more complicated, because the food she ordered at the end of one summer didn't arrive in McMurdo until the end of the next, when a cargo ship could reach the base. It's really not possible, Sally said, to make adjustments on the ice: "Menu changes are rare at the bottom of the world, and if we run out of an ingredient, it's gone—there's no 7-Eleven down the street to pick up some butter or salt."

While there's no supermarket within 2,400 miles, there is food down the gravel road in McMurdo's three food-storage buildings. Like most of McMurdo's older architecture, they are nondescript structures sheathed in corrugated metal and known by their old Cold War navy nomenclature—Building 165, Building 157, and Building 120—but are otherwise known as the freezer, unheated storage, and DNF (do not freeze) storage.

Every week in the summer, about thirty pallets of food are pulled from the warehouses for galley use.

On a warehouse tour, visiting writer Gretchen Legler compared it to "walking down the canyon of a Manhattan street lined by skyscrapers, only these were bulging cardboard monoliths full of pork and beans, chili and canned pears."

She was lucky, while among the food canyons, not to encounter the ghost in the freezer, a legend that arose because of the corpses stored there after a horrific Air New Zealand crash on Mount Erebus that killed 257 people. Ever since, galley workers have been haunted by mysterious clouds of breath.

Legler was, however, shown some living-dead ketchup — ten years past its sell-by date — that once had the great purpose of glazing the vast navy cache of hot dogs that if laid end-to-end would, according to rumor, stretch the 843 miles to South Pole.

Under Sally's guidance, the Antarctic menu became less divorced from the warm reality of home. For American vegetarians in particular, Antarctica entered its golden age. Selections such as pumpkin lasagna, veggie stir fry, or miso soup became commonplace.

Even McMurdo flight lunches included a vegetarian option. A registered dietician for twenty years, Sally also put sauces on the side for fat-conscious eaters and removed trans-fat oils from the deep fryers.

Roff Smith found five vegetarian selections in the galley when he passed through in 2000, something that might have perplexed the blubber kings of the heroic age.

ᛦ cooking is a terrible way to see antarctica ᛦ

The single best thing Sally could do to improve the quality of food for such a large operation was to hire first-rate people. In part, this meant hiring staff that reflected her philosophy. Everyone, from the chefs to the lowly DAs (dining attendants, nicknamed "galley slaves" around McMurdo), was expected to project a positive attitude. One McMurdo sous-chef said, "I think she hires more for attitude than aptitude. If your attitude's right you can learn."

I'm reminded of Douglas Mawson in 1912 interviewing young scientists about their willingness to cook. Though Sally risked hiring cheerful second-rate Unconventional Cooks, like Mawson she believed enthusiasm was more important than experience, simply because cooking in Antarctica is so unpredictable. How, for example, do you plan a meal when planes full of new arrivals may well boomerang back to Christchurch? When I asked Sally about this, she said simply that "the key to life is a good Plan B."

One of her first duties while training a new McMurdo cook, Sally told me, was helping them adjust to an all-electric kitchen. Because of the risk of fire, there are no gas appliances. Buildings made tinder dry by Antarctica's extremely low humidity are ripe for conflagration, and extreme caution is necessary in a community with nowhere else to go.

New staff also struggle with the unpredictability or outright absence of freshies. The Thanksgiving feast in 1997, for example, served no freshies at all, because nearly every flight from Christchurch had been turned back by a month-long pall of fog. "A lot of cooks," Sally told an NPR reporter, "that come from restaurants to here are used to dealing with high-quality produce every single day." Sally ordered roughly 5,000 to 7,000 pounds of freshies per week during the summer. This may seem substantial, but among 1,500 residents, 6,000 pounds (minus pallet weight, packaging, and waste) come down to fewer than four pounds per week per person, perhaps just two oranges, a couple of salads, and a few fried eggs. And while some cooks might be frustrated by the lack of produce, others who wanted consistency or who found it easier to open a can had a different perspective. "How do you spell freshies?" asked a former Pole cook: "W-O-R-K!" The cooks, facing a hungry and opinionated clientele, must decide whether freshies should be served raw — a rare gift in Antarctica — or cooked up in entrées that might not excite the masses.

Another hiring challenge is that many McMurdo kitchen workers look for other Antarctic jobs after just one season. Cooking is still one of Antarctica's most psychologically demanding jobs. For all of the philosophical pleasure Sally's cooks might derive from comforting tired and hungry Antarcticans, it's hard for galley staff to feel that they're having an adventure if they work indoors in windowless kitchens washing pots for five months. Today's prep cooks are as cut off from the glories of the ice as poor Axel Andersson was in the sooty annex to the Swedes' crude stone hut on Paulet Island in 1903. Food services is a high-turnover department because many people who take the job just to see Antarctica find that cooking is a terrible way to see Antarctica. Transient work invites mostly transient cooks, and only a few of those, the Rozos of each generation, will choose to bless this frozen backwater with their culinary gifts. Even Rozo disappeared after one journey with Charcot.

Our work here is by contract. We work half-year or year-long stints before leaving for greener pastures. Because the USAP attracts adventurous souls who can find Antarctica on a map, many entry-level positions are filled with overeducated and underqualified people. In an online Antarctic jobs forum, a galley worker explained that on his McMurdo midrats crew six out of ten coworkers had master's degrees, but none were in culinary arts. Throughout McMurdo, he said, "There are attorneys, judges, pharmacists, and PhD's working as mechanics, janitors, galley slaves."

What these snow-shoveling pharmacists and PhD-toting shuttle drivers want from the cooks, Sally says, is comfort food that resembles home cooking, like real mashed potatoes, steak, pizza, and grilled cheese with tomato soup. Other crowd-pleasers are Reuben sandwiches, fish and chips, fresh-baked sourdough, roast pork tenderloin, and ethnic-themed meals (Mexican, Italian, or Asian). But perhaps the most important comfort food is homemade dessert. We eat more sweets on the ice, partly because the desserts are good, free, fresh, and available, but also because our bodies, moving in and out of the cold all day, begin to crave the sugar. Few jobs in McMurdo actually burn sufficient calories to justify the extra sugar, but brief exposures to hard cold and freezing winds trigger the desire to fatten up.

Although we no longer eat seal blubber or penguin breasts to stay warm, one local animal is still served up for the holidays. One-hundred-pound specimens of Antarctic cod just happen to outlast their usefulness for research around Thanksgiving and Christmas and so end up on the serving platter. Though called cod, *Dissostichus mawsoni* is actually Antarctic toothfish, a slow-moving, deep-dwelling mass of what Sally describes as "sweet, creamy, fatty, yummy" flaky white flesh: "Some of the most tasty fish I've eaten," she said, "and I've eaten a lot of fish."

As is typical in Antarctic cuisine, food in McMurdo is at its best during the holidays, featuring extra freshies and New Zealand cheese ordered from Christchurch, along with special treats like candied grapefruit rind and mascarpone. For Sally, it wasn't just about making a fantastic meal. Some people "definitely get a little on edge" during the Thanksgiving and Christmas holidays. Certainly, the galley staff gets stressed out. But in the tradition of expedition solidarity, some McMurdo residents volunteer to help, since the quantities for a Thanksgiving meal are formidable: twelve hundred pounds of turkey, four hundred pounds of roast beef, two thousand dinner rolls, five thousand pounds of mashed potatoes, three hundred fifty pounds of root vegetables, three hundred pounds of asparagus, one hundred pounds of cheese, sixteen gallons of salad dressing for two hundred pounds of salad, one hundred forty pies (pumpkin, pecan, apple), and one thousand pieces each of pumpkin cheesecake and chocolate cake.

Still, the truth is that even under good leadership like Sally's, day-to-day galley food can be hit-or-miss. One person's comfort food is another person's mush. Cooks frown. A pot goes unwatched or a pan of lasagna sits too long on the warming tray. People on restricted diets still face challenges. Ira, a tall, ravenous coworker of mine with a gluten allergy, was sometimes reduced to heaping his plate with mounds of a single canned vegetable. Usually there's *something* satisfactory among all the options the galley staff has sweated to provide. Cardboard pizza crusts dabbed with tomato paste and topped with a single forlorn pepperoni may sit next to the saving grace of a delicate miso soup. Fine spanakopita and a warm slice of fresh olive bread might salvage a dinner otherwise made of gluey mac-and-cheese and an undercooked chickpea salad.

And who are we to complain? We forget that our own long flight south was just a taste of the much greater voyage made by nearly every ingredient in the meal. McMurdo is full of suburban employees confused by their attraction to the end of the Earth. They claim the honor of living where explorers perished but prefer to do their claiming over fine café cuisine.

harsh continent

With some Antarctic culinary wisdom, then, we sit down to meals hopeful but not judgmental, exhibiting the patience and forgiveness necessary in a strange, cold settlement fed from the dark corners of warehouses and a kitchen 2,400 miles from the nearest farm. We remember that despite the implied normalcy of the McMurdo work-eat-sleep triangle, we are still living a back-of-beyond life. "We do not," as Roff Smith said, "really occupy any more of Antarctica than our boot soles."

After visiting a few small, typical Antarctic bases, Smith was stunned by the scale of McMurdo, where the galley boasted "a vast assortment of condiments, juice machines, and soft-serve ice-cream makers. Chefs in white jackets and classic checked trousers grilled burgers and carved roasts. Kitchen hands scurried to replenish salad bowls and Jell-O molds."

On a continent larger than the U.S. and Mexico combined,

there is no other place that resembles McMurdo. We are a (relatively) large population, isolated together amid an Antarctic wilderness we are both obsessed with and separate from.

Amid that isolation, the galley is our primary shared space, both public square and kitchen table. Arguably, the galley's role in feeding social interaction is as important as its kitchen full of warm food. There are seventy-seven dining tables around which up to three hundred twenty coworkers, friends from various departments, or a mix of friends and strangers congregate to talk and eat. Tables are usually available for couples who want a little private time and for someone who prefers to eat alone.

Each new arrival mills around with a full tray, looking for their spot. Though McMurdo is a world of working adults, all the dynamics of high school or college cafeterias lurk beneath the surface. We may steer toward a table full of beckoning hands or stare blankly at our tricolor pasta salad as we weave toward an unoccupied corner.

The usual compulsive lunchtime topics for a thousand adults in an Antarctic work camp are, of course, work, Antarctica, and other Antarctic workers. Rumors and gossip about affairs and freshies drift through the galley faster than any scent from the kitchen. Employees talk about supervisors, supervisors grumble about management, and everyone has an opinion about the food. The green continents drift away, and Antarctica becomes our entire world.

You could see this in the 2000–2001 Antarctic ice cream flavor–naming contest sponsored by Ben & Jerry's (because a friend of theirs was working in McMurdo), which spawned a pile of suggestions that would make little sense anywhere else. This included Freshy Fantasy Fiesta (vanilla ice cream stuffed with pieces of antiscorbutic fruit) and references to the heroic age like Shackleton's Salvation and Antarctic Hoosh (vanilla "blubber chunks," shortbread "sledging biscuit" pieces, and dark chocolate penguins). At the far end of the obscure were Chocolate-Raspberry Antarctic Treat-ee, one of only a few submissions linked to the IGY era, and Harsh Continent—a reference to an ironic USAP cliché used whenever something goes wrong in our comfy Antarctic life, as in "Dude, no more fresh eggs? Well, it's a harsh continent." According to its inventor's description, a pint of Harsh Continent is just a pile of ice cubes.

The winning flavor was Roald Almonds-en, a name my friend Dave Weber and I came up with, but for which he created a better flavor (chocolate ice cream with toasted almonds, toasted coconut, and chocolate chips). The flavor was never actually made, but Dave and I split the award: a year's supply of ice cream (fifty-two Ben & Jerry's coupons).

Some of my less marketable ideas include Absolute Amundsen, a pint of pure vanilla ice cream with a layer of red candy dogs at the bottom, Scott's Tent (same vanilla pint with three chocolate bodies in caramel sleeping bags), or Mertz's Surprise (little candy dog livers and a fingertip).

Otherwise, the submissions were dominated by the expected flock of cute penguin flavor names—like Polar Tuxedo and Penguin Paradise—all of which included little chocolate penguins. There was even Penguin on a Stick, though it was meant to describe a penguin hugging the South Pole rather than being skewered over a blubber fire.

Skuas made it in, but not a single seal flavor was entered, an outcome that contradicts the basic facts of Antarctic culinary history.

In the rare moments when news from back home became part of McMurdo daily life, our response was likely to be as satirical as serious. At a Sunday brunch during the time of the O.J. Simpson murder trial, some sardonic DA put signs on the two orange juice dispensers, one — Nicole — signifying the victim, and the other — OJ — the accused.

By meal's end, as at the trial's end, Nicole was empty and OJ untouched.

Sunday brunch, the most popular meal of the week, is the best time to see just about everyone on base, from the lowly GAs (general assistants) to science PIs (principal investigators). Sunday is our one-day weekend, and the whole community gathers to eat, say, a leisurely omelet with hash browns and some fresh fruit on the side, taking time to gossip about work and life in the USAP. That conversation might be a joyful recounting of our incredible luck in being paid to experience the beauty of Antarctica, but often is nothing of the sort.

More likely, the chatter is punctuated by complaints about coworkers or the policies of the NSF and the government contractor running the USAP. When the entire winterover community is hit with an unexplained cut in their bonuses, or when the NSF suddenly bans drinking alcohol at dinner or criticizing the USAP in personal blogs, there are reasons to talk.

Nicholas Johnson, author of *Big Dead Place*, created an underground satirical newspaper, the *Symmes Antarctic Intelligencer*, to feed on and feed into the McMurdo zeitgeist, satirizing management and USAP culture in an effort to make it more honest. The *Intelligencer* was popular because it was clever and because it addressed the problems many of us talked about. During the two summers we were roommates, Nicholas and I rushed into the galley on Sunday just before brunch to distribute copies of his paper, which offered diners headlines like "Magic Elf Appears at Pole; NSF Refuses Shelter" and "Disposable GAs, DAs Introduced to Workforce."

Nicholas had begun his Antarctic life as a DA, documenting with sardonic wit the habits of Antarctic authority from his vantage in the galley. When a snail was found crawling through some New Zealand lettuce, other DAs hid it from their supervisors out of fear that it would be killed.

When U.S. senators and other distinguished visitors were toured through the USAP to encourage their support for program funding, Nicholas noted that they received special banquets in the galley with dishes never offered to workers, like "creamy feta and red pepper roulade and stuffed chicken breast with rum-lemon glaze and green beans amandine, with fresh shrimp flown from New Zealand." And if that wasn't enough, DAs were "yanked from the dishroom to serve them."

Inevitably, the galley itself is a cause for gossip, and not only for its food. The most famous galley tale is the "hammer incident," still an infamous moment in McMurdo's gossipy history. A bereft winterover cook borrowed a hammer from the housing office on Highway 1, walked up to the kitchen, and popped his supervisor (allegedly his ex-lover) in the head, apparently for refusing to let him leave on a Winfly flight. According to legend, he was found shortly thereafter singing "Mary Had a Little Lamb" on Highway 1, having returned the bloody hammer.

And sometimes the galley workers do the gossiping. Female dishwashers in the old E-side galley were stuck behind a low window through which everyone threw their dirty glasses, silverware, and sloppy five-compartment trays. The job made them nameless and faceless, but one summer some realized they could become the objectifiers rather than the objects. They learned to identify men by the bulge in their pants.

All of these galley stories, however dark or light, together with Sally's management, reveal a theme: Whatever its faults, McMurdo is a tightly woven community in which we all intimately observe each other. Whether it's a room full of sharp eyes noting the success or failure of romances, sharper male eyes watching a table of laughing women, the mutual scrutiny of management and workers, or Sally and her staff adjusting the five-week meal rotation because no one was eating the Blazin' Redfish, little goes unnoticed in a self-absorbed end-of-the-world population sitting down to eat together.

ᘒ home cooking ᘓ

After a few summers of feeding and gossiping three times a day in the busy galley, I began to cook for myself in my room. Other long-time McMurdo residents showed me the wonders of reclaiming self-sufficiency with an electric tea kettle, rice cooker, and electric wok. Instant oatmeal and tea at home were fine on the mornings I didn't want to rush off to scoop up some powdered scrambled eggs. Lunches I often ate in the galley, unless I had leftovers from the night before.

None of my dinners were elaborate, usually vegetarian nori rolls or Thai and Indian meals made with bottled curry pastes. I didn't cook all the time but had enough food to break up the monotony. After a few summers, I had a nice kitchen set-up: cutting board and knife, spice rack, plastic containers (for gathering ingredients from the galley), and a few key appliances.

Some home-cookers used a microwave or toaster oven to make or reheat simple meals, while others imported luxuries like a small pizza oven. These appliances were either mailed from home, stored between summers in secret McMurdo locations, or handed from friend to friend between summer and winter contracts.

Jim Mastro and his wife, Lisa, were deeply invested, setting up everything from a Crockpot to a tortilla maker. They scarcely showed their faces in the galley except for Sunday brunch and a few select dinners per week, when the menu the galley had posted ahead of time looked good. Their room was stocked like a grocery store, Jim told me, with "cereals, pasta, rice, beans, olive oil, garlic, spices, tortilla flour, and the like."

Milk and orange juice came courtesy of the galley, in bottles they refilled as necessary. They made tortillas and filled them with beans from the Crockpot for lunches. Dinner might be rice or pasta boiled up in the rice cooker, topped with sautéed garlic and peppers.

Home-cookers either "just couldn't stand another galley meal," as Jim put it, or they were avoiding the crowd. Antarctica may consist of wide-open space, but McMurdo, particularly the galley, can be claustrophobic. Tending to food with a friend or in the hush of your own company is a simple but rare pleasure. More commonly, non-home-cookers make their escape too, filling up a plate or bowl at the galley and scurrying home to the dorm.

For me, the process often started in Maine, where I dehydrated slices of tomatoes grown in the garden before I bagged, boxed, and mailed them to myself in McMurdo. The tomatoes were popular with friends, including my roommate in 1998, Berndt, who ate them like antiscorbutic candy whenever I turned my back. I also did last-minute shopping at a supermarket and Asian foods store in Christchurch, picking up fine New Zealand cheese, coconut milk, and rice noodles or whatever looked good. I squeezed these into my duffel bags or camera bag or parka pockets for the flight south and completed my shopping in McMurdo's "skua piles."

Skua piles, named after the South Polar Skua, a kleptoparasitic seabird, are a USAP tradition and the clearest sign that we are a transient community. Departing people leave behind their excess stuff in a heap near their dorm recycling area, and arriving people grab what they need for the season. If you're in the right place at the right time, you can find anything: homemade bookshelves, insulated work clothes, flannel sheets, half-filled shampoo bottles or, less usefully, broken pencils, used batteries, and sex toys of unknown provenance.

Skua piles are so fundamental to McMurdo culture that "skua" is as common a verb as it is a multipurpose noun. Stuff is skuaed, the wise go skuaing, and so on. That said, many of the skua food items are galley condiments people are too lazy to return or odd things that no one really wants to eat but are unwilling to throw away.

I saw the same can of fiddlehead ferns from Maine

disappear and reappear over several years. Dusty jars of nearly flavorless spices that I twice claimed, never used, and returned years ago may still be snatched excitedly each summer by a desperate home-cooker. But again, anything is possible in the skua piles; I have stumbled upon troves of cooking supplies and a new electric teakettle that someone didn't feel like mailing home, as well as quick-cook oats, rice, and other staples.

For me, dinners often weren't worth making unless I could also score freshies. At first, this meant a trip to the McMurdo greenhouse. The greenhouse experience was as valuable as its food: Leaving Antarctica by walking through the door of a windowless shack into greenery and warm, humid air was one of the world's unique pleasures. It stirred senses not activated since the final 4:00 a.m. departure from a Christchurch hostel. Inside, ten separate hydroponic loops — one each for tomatoes and peppers, two for greens or lettuce, and three each for herbs and cucumbers — percolated while a sea of greens waved in the fan-driven breeze.

McMurdo Station greenhouse, circa 1988

Many people visited just to look and smell, others snipped a few herbs for home cooking, and some came in to drink wine and snuggle in the greenhouse's hammock, while a rubber snake wound through Edenic vines. For some purists, though, a step into the greenhouse was an unnecessary one. Julian, my partner on the Odell Glacier, had a policy of avoiding it: "Hell, if I was in Antarctica for the greenery," he told me, "then I may as well stay home!"

Built by volunteers from salvaged materials in the summer of 1988–89 and closed by the NSF in 2011, McMurdo's greenhouse was, like most of the base's small buildings, a freezer used in reverse, a sealed and insulated structure keeping out the cold it was designed to keep in. Inside, forty-one high-intensity lamps were reflected by foil-lined walls. At just 649 square feet, the facility grew only enough to supplement the tons of New Zealand freshies flown in during McMurdo's overpopulated summer, but in the winter, it really came into its own. At peak production, the greenhouse could pump out two hundred fifty pounds of produce a month, which meant a salad every four days for each winterover, plus some herbs, fruit, and vegetables for the cooks to incorporate into meals. Typical produce included lettuce, arugula, peppers, chard, cucumbers, tomatoes, herbs, and edible flowers.

I always felt guilty clipping cilantro, cucumbers, or cherry tomatoes from the lush vines of this Eden-in-a-box, and in later years I found the best course of action was to go to the galley and ask the kitchen staff if they had enough freshies to justify donating some. I'd walk away happily with whatever they handed me—ideally an onion or two, a carrot or pepper, and a cucumber. With everything but the cuke chopped up for Thai vegetable curry, the rice cooker rattling, and my dried tomato slices rehydrating in warm water, I was just twenty minutes away from dinner.

ᘓ soup and sausage point ᘚ

Where there is food, there is food waste, particularly in an industrial-scale food operation serving satiated Americans. Food packaged in the United States and shipped down to McMurdo's warehouses might sit for months or years before being processed into a single day's meal and then scraped off a plate into plastic-lined bins. In the early 2000s, McMurdo discarded on average about 320,000 pounds of food and leftovers per year, about 875 pounds per day (though most food waste is produced in the summer). South Pole Station added an additional 115,000 pounds each year, temporarily stored each summer alongside McMurdo food waste in the old Fortress Rocks landfill site. Full bags of food waste are thrown into large plastic-lined triwalls (heavy-duty cardboard boxes), which are eventually loaded into refrigerated shipping containers for the return voyage to the U.S. by McMurdo's annual cargo vessel.

Upon arrival in the United States, having crossed the world's oceans without rotting, these two hundred tons of pleasantly cooled scraps are treated by an anxious USDA as pest-ridden imports, unsuitable even for composting. Every triwall, plastic and all, is incinerated.

I'm not sure which is stranger: that a carrot canned in California years before it's ignored in a McMurdo casserole is sent back to California as garbage, or that the forlorn carrot is treated as a threat to California agriculture.

Although McMurdo still throws away an "amazing amount" of food, according to Sally Ayotte, things are better than they used to be. When I first started in the program, the combination of bad cooking and those five-compartment trays made us cornucopias of food waste. When the galley switched in the late 1990s to a flat, blue tray on which we could place a plate or two and a glass, food waste decreased dramatically. Still, Sally thinks, even the blue trays should go. The best way to decrease food waste is to make food the community won't throw away, but a large tray will always lead to excess.

Not all food waste slides off a lazy diner's plate. Food products, particularly seafood, stored too long beyond their use-by dates must be discarded. In 2006–2007, a clean-out of the McMurdo freezer warehouse pushed the station's food waste output up to 401,584 pounds. And a newer waste stream, called SOUP by the Waste Management department, collects greasy liquids directly from the galley, which in the past were dumped down the drain and into the sea.

McMurdo finally completed a sewage treatment plant in 2003, which releases only clean water into McMurdo Sound. It was a long time coming, given that our sewage had significant ecological impacts on the local underwater environment. (Underwater video footage from 2000 showed a sea urchin on the edge of the sewage outfall pile attempting to camouflage itself with a mottled white panty liner.) Sewage treatment has its limits, though, which is why the USAP sends its excess fats and oils in barrels back to the U.S.: The bacteria have as much trouble digesting galley grease as we do.

Bizarrely, explosives used in early construction of the sewage treatment plant in 1999 revealed a vein of meat running through McMurdo's substratum. Nicholas Johnson described how the operator of a large rock drill "struck a noxious pocket of primeval sausage slime that squirted onto his face."

The source of the slime was the forgotten old landfill site along the shores of Winter Quarters Bay, where the excavation revealed a few tons of decades-old buried sausage. Per order of NSF, Sausage Point, as it became unofficially known, was cleaned up by underlings who were, wrote Nicholas, "dispatched into the feeding swarms of skuas to separate the meat from the rock" and pack it for shipment home.

Winter Quarters Bay and the seabed of McMurdo Sound, however, remain as polluted as ever. A survey by New Zealand researchers of fifty acres of McMurdo Sound counted fifteen vehicles, twenty-six shipping containers, and more than six hundred fuel drums.

Worse, research has shown that healthy fish brought in from the clean waters of the Ross Sea to the chemical soup deep in Winter Quarters Bay develop diseased gills and liver tumors when left in live traps in the harbor for just two weeks. Still today, no effort has been made to clean up this toxic mess.

Now that food waste is well handled, times are tough for the skuas who lived through the golden years of trash buffets at the Fortress Rocks landfill. Only the odd trifle from an open food dumpster or a damaged triwall makes its way into a skua's iron beak. But back in the McMurdo summer of 1990–91, when Greenpeace lived next door and was busy shaming the USAP toward an environmental philosophy, there was a grand finale of sorts for the skuas of the Hut Point peninsula. It is a tale as weird as anything in McMurdo history, and weaves together many of the usual threads of USAP storytelling: food, work, management and bureaucracy, and the wildness of life on the ice.

◖ the day it rained chickens ◗

Though Karen Joyce would become a computer maestra for McMurdo researchers, back in 1990 she was working as a general assistant (GA). The underpaid and overworked underclass of the McMurdo labor pool, GAs do whatever incidental work needs doing around town. (In early decades, GAs were known as GFAs, general field assistants or "good for anything.")

Shoveling snow is their job guarantee early in the summer, but later the possibilities range from chipping frozen urine to inventorying drywall screws to assisting a cook in a deep-field camp.

Karen and the other GAs were mucking around at the landfill on a midsummer day when a galley forklift showed up with two large triwalls containing five hundred pounds of whole chickens, left to thaw too long on the galley deck and now discarded. Guster, their "wizened little cowboy of a boss," as Karen described him, opened the top flaps of the reeking triwalls and suggested letting the skuas take care of it. Skuas are thieves and consummate survivors who devour everything from seal placenta to baby penguins to each other. Guster's idea was logical but not rational.

Uneasy, the GA crew debated while walking down to eat lunch in the galley. They were little better than indentured servants in the McMurdo hierarchy, and Guster could make an already difficult life hellish if they bucked his orders. But they knew that the Antarctic Conservation Act, the U.S. law enacting the new environmental protocol of the Antarctic Treaty, forbade altering the behavior of wildlife. In fact, the ACA includes a ten-thousand-dollar fine for such violations (though it has never been applied).

The irony of being prosecuted by the authorities who for years had created and ignored the skua banquet at Fortress Rocks was not lost on them, but that would be poor consolation if they were fired or fined. Unhappy with either option, they hoped no one would notice the feeding frenzy. The moment they left the galley, though, they knew they were in trouble.

What seemed to Karen to be "a dark, undulating shadow that was moving across the sky above the landfill" soon revealed itself to be a writhing black cloud of skuas called in from every nest on the peninsula. Up close, it was "a seething, protean mass of avian fury, fascinating and sickening as a mass of spiders."

The large predatory gulls, with wingspans as wide as the triwalls, converged on the top layer of putrescent chicken bodies. The bodies were too heavy to lift easily, especially as dozens of other birds snatched at them in midair.

Each carcass dropped to the ground became the object of a "giant atomic feather-ball."

Nothing could be done to stop the feeding once it began, and so Karen and her fellow GAs slunk off to work elsewhere.

But curiosity got the better of them, and they ran back up to the scene of the crime, which she said "had escalated into a skin-crawling horror, a writhing mass of annihilation. Feathers, birdshit, and chicken parts carpeted the area." For

Karen, whose non-Antarctic life included time in a law firm, this was a problem: "Everything about this bizarre fracas of birds beak-deep in a largesse unprecedented in the history of Antarctica, nose-diving in the egregious waste of McMurdo and hardwired to fight for their lives on the raw edge of starvation, spelled trouble for us—the complicit GAs."

It got worse. They woke the next morning to find a town littered with chicken parts. Karen described utility poles and wires, rooftops and trucks "festooned with swinging chickens." Skuas successful in flying away with carcasses did the natural thing, sitting on the high points of McMurdo's landscape to gobble them down. Only Karen, her compatriots, and the conniving Guster, knew the truth. "We've . . . uh, kind of opened what you might call Pandora's Triwall Boxes up here, heh heh!" said their panicked supervisor, as he demanded their silence.

The GAs' options were limited. "American labor law," Karen noted, "has a long tradition of being suspended down here." USAP employees work overtime every week without compensation. The Occupational Safety and Health Administration and other regulatory agencies have no jurisdiction. Application of regulations is spotty, depending on what best suits the bottom line of the bureaucracy and its contractors. When an employee acts up or acts out, the authorities usually have a simple answer: Get out. Troublemakers, whether drunk or merely interrogative, are sent home every year. There is no reprieve.

But there are shining moments when, like skuas arguing over raw flesh, authorities looking for scapegoats turn on each other. Just as the GAs walked glumly away from the corpse-strewn gravel of Fortress Rocks, a truck full of NSF officials hailed them for directions to any possible source of chicken bodies. Moments later, the truck pulled up to little Guster under the shadows of his scavengers. Guster, much to his minions' pleasure, was sent home on the next flight north.

Karen and the GAs celebrated only as long as it took someone else to assign them the month-long cleanup of the chicken pieces spread across the McMurdo wasteland.

Morrie Fisher drinking at Mawson Station, Christmas 1957

"How to Cook Pig at the South Pole: Bring in from outer berms on a ski-doo. Thaw for approximately seven days in the thaw box. Serve with tortillas and salsa and chopped onion if you have it . . . whoops, don't have any of that, well then, mashed potato made from flakes."
–Michèle Gentille, Harriet's Tomato blog

A Cookie and a Story 9

The hardest day of work I've ever done was at the South Pole. It was late October, 1999. I'd flown in from McMurdo with about a hundred others to help open up the base for the summer season. My job was to help a coworker set up a fueling system by the skiway so Pole (the Amundsen-Scott Polar Station) could either provide fuel to, or take fuel from, the Hercs that supplied the station. It was an essential task that had to be done right away. No more flights would arrive until the system was running.

The fifty or so folks who had just spent eight months isolated from the rest of Earth were overwhelmed by us. Many of them had paper-pale skin, worn and often oil-stained clothing, a winter's growth of beard or long hair, and eyes that shifted uncomfortably from new face to new face, no matter how polite they were with us or how glad they were to be leaving. We'd disturbed their lunar seclusion.

My first workday was sixteen hours long, with thirteen hours of it outside at –60°F. The light breeze made it feel like –80°F. But the cold wasn't the main problem. We'd flown up from sea level to 9,300 feet (which because of air pressure felt like 10,000 feet), and without acclimating, had to manhaul 1,500 feet of heavy fuel hose, lungs sucking for air as we went. I felt like I was doing sit-ups with a freezer on my chest.

The hose was stiff as a glacier, as was the pump, and as were our faces and hands. My glasses and goggles constantly fogged and froze. New gaskets shrunk in the cold and old gaskets took up to fifteen minutes to chip out of the hose ends. Our hands had to be free enough to handle nuts and bolts, so we shed our mittens to work with thin glove liners. We'd work until our hands were wooden, then swing our arms like windmills to move warmer blood into the estranged fingers.

Everything needed direct heat to work, including us. Because the hose had to be softened to put fittings on, we borrowed a portable heater, which we hugged when we could no longer feel our hands or when we began to shiver without relief, all while struggling to get enough oxygen.

Even after a hot meal, by the time I went to bed my core temperature was still low enough to make me shiver violently (fully dressed, with a wool hat) for the first two hours under very warm blankets. Fever and fever dreams worked me for the next three hours. But Pole is a workcamp with extreme conditions that Polies take pride in acclimating to, despite not being paid a penny more for the "same" work done in McMurdo. Sixteen-hour workdays are not uncommon. Paper-pale skin or not, the winterovers had been working in temperatures down to –100°F or worse in the depths of a six-month-long winter night. I had nothing to whine about.

⟨ gremlins in the baking 🐧

There's little else to do at the South Pole but work. The station is a high-tech refuge from the highest, driest, most isolated and lifeless environment on Earth, with an average year-round temperature of –56°F.

There's nowhere to go, no neighbors to visit. Life is hard,

strange, austere, and if you can handle it, amazing. The microsociety at Pole consists of more than two hundred people in summer and about sixty in winter. It has ample margins of safety and a nice array of creature comforts, but residents exist to work, need to sleep, and love to eat. Sally Ayotte calls these the Big Three. The cooks pride themselves on taking care of fellow Polies during their intensely difficult life. Sally became famous doing it, not least because of the difficulties of the job. Like everyone else at Pole, cooks must reinvent their livelihood to succeed in this extraordinary place.

Simply put, cooking at the South Pole is weird. Start by making spaghetti and see what happens. Water boils at 189°F, 23 degrees lower than normal; the water may be boiling, but the food within it is not as hot as it should be. Cooking times are seriously prolonged. "Pasta," Sally has said, "can be a great challenge for a first-time cook at Pole." A soup big enough to serve the lunch crowd can take up to four hours just to heat up. The problem is the high altitude (9,301 feet) and low air pressure, which together make life at the South Pole feel like living on a mountain peak above ten thousand feet. James Brown, another long-time South Pole executive chef, has felt the pressure altitude climb above 11,500 feet. Air pressure fluctuates throughout the year, altering heat flow in the ovens and acting like a gremlin in the baking.

Baking at the Pole seems a heroic art. When water boils at a lower temperature, casseroles and custards finish more slowly and pies brown on top before the fruit within is fully cooked. Cakes may crust over before cooking through. Moisture evaporates quickly from a batter or dough, so the ratio of liquids to solids is altered, increasing sugar and fats.

It doesn't help that South Pole air is extraordinarily dry, with a humidity even in the kitchen of just 1 to 3 percent. Dry air means that drier flour requires additional liquid for a batter or dough. Baking at altitude also causes leavening bubbles to expand faster, making it likely that breads, soufflés, and cakes will rise too fast, overflow their pans, or collapse. Yet when I asked James Brown about this, he was proud to say that his high-quality Pole staff avoided such baking disasters, though crème brûlée tended to be "temperamental and experimental each time we try."

Still, what happens once the ingredients are mixed for breads or sweets is hard to predict. "I always tell the new baker the first week to not bother making muffins," Sally said. In general, the rules for altitude baking are: Increase flour and liquid, decrease sugar, fats, and baking powder or baking soda. But these are guidelines, not a hard science, and new cooks just have to figure it out. Patience is required. "A lot of bakers come here and can't make their favorite recipes," Sally explained, "and they get all worked up when an angel food cake falls or a Danish pastry doesn't rise." Nonetheless, Sally was known throughout the U.S. Antarctic Program for her cookies, and Herc flight crews often delayed departure until they got some.

There are other difficulties. Although ingredients everywhere on the ice are limited to what's on hand, a Pole cook stands at the end of the longest supply chain on Earth. While McMurdo is dependent on what groceries arrive from the United States or New Zealand, Pole is dependent on what makes it onto a Herc from McMurdo. It's a process not unlike the International Space Station waiting for whatever fits onto the Earth-origin freighters. Moreover, the summer flight schedule at Pole, only four months long, is often interrupted by blizzards and fog in McMurdo. And still, no matter how overbooked the Hercs might be with science cargo, construction materials, and sufficient fuel for the eight-month winter, they must deliver a year's worth of food.

A typical annual food order includes about thirty-five thousand pounds of meat (beef, chicken, pork, and seafood), seven hundred pounds of tofu, eight hundred dozen tortillas, and a ton of chocolate chips. Freshies and eggs are rare commodities. Pole serves no fresh cream and only powdered milk.

What can be frozen is stored outside at temperatures that range from $-10°F$ to $-110°F$ and will need about five days in the thaw box. Hard-frozen number-ten cans (about three quarts) of fruit or veggies take a full week to thaw, while large slabs of meat can take twice as long.

South Pole cooks figured all this out long ago. And despite the difficulties, fine food has been served under these conditions for decades. This is part of the longstanding effort to provide better cuisine as recompense for harder work, but much of the success is due to one strange fact: Many people love working at Pole. Chefs return to the end of the Earth more often than they do to McMurdo, just as crews maintaining the station under horrendous conditions come back to work year after year. Polies take pride in their work ethic and hardass reputation and have little regard for the easy life in metropolitan McMurdo. Friendships made at Pole often run as deep as the latitude.

James Brown says that Pole's most popular meals are Christmas dinner (typically beef Wellington and lobster tail), Steak Night (every Friday), and Filet Mignon and King Crab

Nights. Pole's comfort foods include meatloaf, tamale pie, burgers, hot turkey sandwiches, and grilled cheese with tomato soup. While the quality of the food may be better because of the smaller operation, the main difference between McMurdo and Pole, says Brown, is how *much* people eat. In a typical winter, the average consumption of beef per person might be eighty-five pounds, along with twenty-four pounds of French fries, and eighteen pounds of butter.

South Pole Food Growth Chamber

That kind of calorie consumption has been standard since Chet Segers served up meals in the original IGY (International Geophysical Year, 1957–58) Pole station. Those buildings and Segers' galley still exist, though buried deep beneath the crushing weight of accumulated snow and ice. Like the South Pole garbage which, in the old days, was simply bulldozed into large snow dumps, the once-warm refuge of the hundreds of Polies who occupied it from 1957 to 1974 is pancaked several meters below the surface and drifting outward with the ice toward the coast.

For many years, it was still possible (if against the rules) to sneak down a secret snowy shaft into the haunting dark and frost-covered remains of Old Pole, where one visitor noted that, among signs of a hasty departure, the "plywood floors were strewn with T-bone steaks, white beans, and a fine gravel of frozen broken eggs." There were plastic bags of hot dogs, a can of Piels Real Draft Premium Beer with "a permanent head of frozen foam," and a bowl of cereal on a galley table, "flakes in a puddle of ice."

The second incarnation of Pole Station existed from 1975 until 2003, where all cooking and eating took place in an undersized galley in a warren of small buildings protected by a massive geodesic dome. Sally's Galley, as it was known during her reign, was described by Roff Smith in 2000 as "a cramped and crowded little eatery . . . [like a] truck stop café along the Alaskan Highway." It couldn't fit even half of summer residents in one sitting.

Life was just as crowded behind the serving line. As Sally described it then: "There is not enough elbow room. There is not enough refrigerator space. There is not enough anything." Staff had little defined workspace and often bumped into each other, but one cook who didn't mind was Don Highsmith, an ex-navy cook who spent seventeen years working on submarines for months at a time, always in uniform, with minimal freshies and no women around. "There is no comparison," Highsmith said. "The South Pole station would win hands down."

In that tiny galley, men and women in USAP-issued

Carhartt work clothes took turns chowing down hearty breakfasts of bacon and eggs, breakfast burritos, sausages, pancakes and syrup, fresh-baked muffins and scones, and bread and cookies. Lunches and dinners were no smaller, with the galley staff determined to feed everyone at least 5,000 calories a day. Leftovers were available in a refrigerator, reducing food waste and giving everyone easy access to extra calories. And they need those calories. Crews working outside usually lose about fifteen pounds a summer, regardless of how much they eat. Part of the problem is the thin air, since low oxygen content at altitude makes it harder for the body to fully metabolize fats.

But few complain, particularly about the quality of the food. Pole, with a longstanding work-hard-and-play-hard culture, is not for complainers. In the tiny galley, if someone were foolish enough to gripe about food made under difficult conditions, one of the galley staff rang the WHINER ALARM bell to alert the other diners. As Chef Mark Lehman recounted:

> Once, the alarm rang in response to a construction foreman who complained loudly about his freshly baked hamburger bun, which was topped with sesame seeds. "What am I?" he demanded, "A freaking bird?" DING! Later in the same season, someone shouted, "Can't you people ever serve chicken without bones?" DING! And on another occasion, a young woman showed us her angry face and hardly touched her bowl of soup, saying "Hey what *is* this? It doesn't taste like Campbell's at all!" DING!

Everyone else in the galley, men and women who knew a good thing when they ate it, would then laugh, boo, and hiss the whiner back to their seat.

✎ a free cup of coffee and a boot in the ass 🐧

Though it has no neighbors, the South Pole sees a steady, summer-long trickle of tourists, adventure tourists, and true adventurers. The distinctions between these categories has to do with *how* they arrived, best expressed by the ratio of cash to sweat. Pole workers don't give wealthy tourists, who fly in for a brief visit to the galley and the South Pole souvenir store, a second glance.

Those who "ski the last degree" (that is, ski from a private camp at 89° South latitude to the Pole) don't earn much attention either. Polies do enjoy the steady trickle of odd arrivals marking their small places in history, like the British-Icelandic team that drove a modified E-series Ford van, the tourists arriving via Russian "snow bugs" (odd vehicles with six balloon tires), and the first female Indian skydiver to make the leap over the Pole.

They particularly respect the hardcore skiers who, in traversing the continent, have worked even harder than Polies to earn their place at the bottom of the Earth.

National Science Foundation policy remains aloof to all visitors, like the owner of a massive estate through which cuts a necessary public road. They worry about costs to U.S. taxpayers for feeding and rescuing tourists. In their role as the estate owner, the NSF consents to brief stopovers as a sort of noblesse oblige. The official line was rephrased in gentler terms to me by Chef James Brown: "All adventurers who come to Pole, either on skis or as day-trip visitors by plane, are very happy to receive a fresh cookie and tell their story."

No doubt this is true for those who haven't worked too hard to arrive. But there is a lingering question in the minds of some adventurers, many of whom have dedicated years of their lives and much of their savings to reach the Earth's south polar nexus. In the words of veteran Polie Kathy Blumm, if Antarctica belongs to everyone, then why should someone who arrives self-sufficiently at the Pole be limited to a cookie, "a free cup of coffee, a hero shot at the Pole, and a boot in the ass to get out?"

For those skiing the full distance to Pole or across the continent, self-sufficiency has included some minor revolutions in camp cookery. Just as Victor Czegka modified the Nansen stove for the mechanical age, today's camp stove has reached new levels of efficiency, absorbing much more of the energy given off by the burning fuel. Rune Gjeldnes, a Norwegian who in the austral summer of 2005–6 made the longest unsupported crossing of Antarctica by traveling from Queen Maud Land via the Pole to the Italian base at Terra Nova Bay, used an ultra-efficient device he calls the "Willy" stove. Designed by Willy Gautvik, the cooking system weighed just 810 grams and utilized up to 70 percent of the stove's heat energy, far better than the 40 to 45 percent efficiency of a typical outfit. Gjeldnes used a mere fifteen liters of fuel in his ninety-day crossing.

Less time cooking means more time skiing or sleeping, and less fuel needed means less weight carried, the gold standard of adventure travel. Such a cooking system, even if available only on the return trudge, might have saved the lives of Robert Scott's Pole party.

Expedition food has continued to evolve as well. The industrial modification of pemmican that began in the heroic age has reached extraordinary levels. Today, we find polar adventurers buzzing about brand-name energy bars, energy drinks, and other vitamin supplements common in ultrasport athletics.

While pemmican and hoosh are nowhere to be found, there are still simple foods available, though sometimes in modern guise: oatmeal and thick slabs of chocolate, salami, freeze-dried chicken curry, and freeze-dried porridge.

Typical options for would-be adventurers can be found on the website of Expedition Foods, a British company. The site is full of freeze-dried food, including vegetarian (Vegetable Tikka) and gluten-free (Beef and Potato Hotpot) options.

There are also expedition-ready nutritional supplements (GU Energy Gel) and camp kitchen items to make heroic age hoosh-eaters like Mawson and Shackleton jealous, particularly the Unbreakable Spoon.

But it's the ease of applying for sponsorship from companies like Expedition Foods (just email them) that would have especially excited Shackleton and other leaders. They spent years begging for funding before boarding their ships.

What if it had been so simple? Gather your men and dogs, pack your pemmican and energy gel, plan and train like crazy, email the sponsorship pages of related companies, and strap on the skis, dude!

When I see these casual offers to provide funding for interesting adventures, I'm tempted to apply as Carsten

Borchgrevink with a bold plan to spend the first winter on the ominous shores of the unmapped southern continent.

❦ elevated and spoiled ❧

The Amundsen-Scott South Pole Station was once again reborn in 2003 as a massive elevated station on thirty-six columns ten feet above the snow surface. This new architectural tactic addresses the unending battle with accumulating snow. Undisturbed areas around the Pole receive only nine inches of drift per year and negligible precipitation, but any human disruption to the flat surface of the ice cap — buildings, machines, cargo lines — will quickly be buried by wind-driven snow. For every one foot a building rises above the snow surface, the snow will drift twenty feet downwind.

By the end of its time, the fifty-foot-high geodesic dome was half-submerged, despite massive annual plowing efforts. Snow will mostly travel underneath the new station, but when necessary the structure can be jacked up another twenty-four feet. The dome and the cluster of small buildings it sheltered for twenty-eight years are gone. Excavated, torn down, and shipped back to the States, all that's left of Sally's Galley and thirty years of extraordinary life are memories and a smoothed-over patch of snow. No future writers will sneak down into a warped, subnivean dome to discover rock-hard slabs of pumpkin lasagna.

Aside from infrastructure that cannot be elevated — the power plant, fuel storage, garage, cargo areas, and extra housing at Summer Camp — the new $153 million, 65,000-square-foot structure holds everything the community needs, including 154 beds, a gym, a library, lounges, medical and lab spaces, and a lovely window-lined galley. The new kitchen measures thirty-five by eighteen feet, twice the usable space as the old one. Although former Executive Chef James Brown sometimes missed the personality of the difficult dome kitchen and bemoaned the hiking up and down stairs to pull food from storage, he would not have returned to the old days.

The hypermodern upgrade includes the new South Pole Food Growth Chamber (SPFGC). This "oasis of loveliness," as Chef Michèle Gentille called it, is a 392-square-foot climate-controlled greenhouse lit by twelve one-thousand-watt, water-jacketed, high-pressure sodium lamps. It is capable of automated, atmospheric carbon-dioxide enrichment, hydroponic nutrient delivery, and acid injection. The SPFGC is linked by Argus Satellite to the University of Arizona, which maintains it remotely. Built as a possible model of growth chambers to be installed someday on the moon, the high-tech greenhouse successfully grows tomatoes, peppers, cucumbers, lettuce, strawberries, and a variety of herbs. What the SPFGC lacks, in contrast to the old aluminum-foil-lined South Pole greenhouse, is a portable tanning bed.

Perhaps in recompense, the kitchen in the new elevated station brought in a long list of new equipment that excited the staff. Head Chef Jon Emanuel raved about his giant tilting skillet ("You can do pot roast for 150 in one of those," he said, whereas before they used three large roasting pans in three separate ovens), a deep fryer that filters its oil with paper and diatomaceous earth, a double-stacked convection oven, and a twenty-quart steam-jacketed kettle.

And, as strange as it may sound, the South Pole kitchen acquired a freezer for the first time in fifty years. Most frozen foods remain outside at the ambient East Antarctic temperature, which is too low for quick thawing. With the new freezer, cooks gained the flexibility of a kitchen back on Earth. "I feel spoiled," Emanuel said. Spoiled also because the new four-well steam serving table will add some rare humidity to the kitchen. And when they take a break from cooking, the crew can stroll into the dining area and gaze through the windows across the ice cap from their noble pedestal.

One essential utensil from the dome kitchen that survived the transition is the WHINER ALARM bell. "The Polies are trained to boo and hiss—the entire dining room," Emanuel said. "It's a beautiful thing."

a sixty-six-dollar bag of cool ranch doritos

The truth about cooking, says Chef Michèle Gentille, "is that about 50 percent of the culinary arts consists of cleaning up ugly messes, packing and unpacking, schlepping, being generally uncomfortable and exhausted, and using up food products one wishes neither to eat nor serve to others, often because of that thing called 'the budget.'"

She learned this on culinary travels that took her from fine French cooking schools to Mediterranean yachts, from remote Pacific atolls to the homes of Hollywood celebrities before arriving at the Pole where, at least in terms of schlepping, exhaustion, and unexpected cuisine, the culinary art was extraordinary.

As her alter ego, Ms. Tomato, of her now-defunct *Harriett's Tomato* blog, Gentille discoursed upon all things culinary.

Often she referred to herself in the third person in a self-described "tea-and-roses style prose," creating that lovely distant sense of self that we associate with finicky eaters: "We can't stop saying things like, 'I can't believe I'm at the South Pole eating a fresh donut!'"

At the new elevated station, where she summered in 2007–8 and wintered in 2009, Gentille was distinctly down-to-earth, a survival skill at that singular latitude. Starting her day at 4:30 a.m., she donned her chef's uniform, padded overalls, a layer of fleece, and a South Pole parka, all just so she could hike to the bathroom. And her Brooklyn vegan diet lasted only one day after reaching the ice. Slowly she reached for some bacon and then never looked back. The work was too hard, the days too long, and the altitude too high for such a delicate diet.

Other survival skills she mentions: using superglue — which sold out from the little Pole store in the first week of summer — to patch fingers split in the dry, deep cold, and having patience while heating soup at Pole's low boiling point for four long hours. Michèle had to accustom herself to the completely electric galley, where frying takes twice as long and, because adjusting the temperature of electric coils is slow and awkward, "there is no such thing as sautéing."

In her first summer, she was one of three sous-chefs working alongside the executive chef, three cooks, one breakfast chef, and a baker. "The baker," she said, "as chief Sugar Purveyor, is most adored." In a workspace "half the size of [her] Brooklyn one-bedroom," the sous-chefs made the usual four meals a day for two hundred fifty hungry Polies.

A typical comfort-food lunch from mid-November included hamburger soup, shrimp fajitas, pasta with pesto cream, rice and beans, green peas, green salad, and butterscotch bars.

Like most Antarctic cooks, Michèle saw little of the polar world outside the galley aside from her twice-daily walks between Summer Camp and the station.

Pole was not without its own syrup of American comfort, particularly at Thanksgiving. "They will not do without turkey and stuffing," she observed. "Some things are nonnegotiable." So Michèle and her comrades got busy, working through the holiday, as cooks have throughout Antarctic history, while everyone else relaxed and prepared to feast. James Brown deep-fried eight turkeys, smoking eight more on the back deck (in an ambient temperature of –50°F), and roasting some others.

Another sous-chef cooked up vats of real mashed potatoes and "buckets of root vegetables." Volunteers peeled potatoes and made pies—apple, pecan, and pumpkin. Mounds of stuffing were cooked in the massive tilt skillet, stirred with a five-foot paddle, and then emptied by hitting the electric tilt switch.

"You practically have to crawl inside to clean the thing," Gentille said, "but in a situation such as this, it is an invaluable tool." They laid out appetizers—smoked salmon, tapenade, and baked brie en croute—and watched nearly unrecognizable friends and coworkers, freshly showered and well dressed, show up to eat. It took three seatings to feed everyone, with volunteers waiting on tables and pouring wine.

Afterward, much of the station gathered to dance all night—"these are not conventional folks," Ms. Tomato gently reminded us—and then gathered again at the traditional Sunday brunch. Only a few personnel, including the breakfast cooks, were sober at breakfast.

As in McMurdo, booze, beer, and wine are readily available for purchase, all of which make a tidy profit for the contractor. And as expected from a hard-working frontier town set in the "visual Alcatraz" of East Antarctica, with transient citizens who have the dual responsibility of working hard and maintaining strong social bonds, drinking is both necessary and common.

The party scene varies from season to season, but as Nicholas Johnson noted, it might involve monthly slushy parties using the world's cleanest snow or the usual tequila-fueled revelry.

Perhaps Sally Ayotte should have expanded her list to the Pole's Big Four: eating, working, sleeping, and drinking. In a few short weeks, Michèle and the crew did it all again for Christmas. Instead of Santa's sleigh, the holiday was ushered in by that year's ITASE (International Trans-Antarctic Scientific Expedition) traverse, a multiyear project traveling around the Antarctic to take snow and ice samples.

Like overworked elves, the twelve ITASE personnel had lived in small sheds towed behind two tracked vehicles, traveling 880 miles in two months without a day off. The ITASE cook, Gentille noted, was equipped with just two burners, a two-foot-diameter dining table, and a slosh bucket sink. Suddenly her half-a-one-bedroom-Brooklyn-apartment-sized workspace seemed palatial. The kitchen crew put it to good use, offering up a feast of beef Wellington and lobster tails before another late-night dance party filled with cross-dressing construction workers: "Those who work hard DANCE hard," Gentille wrote.

The kitchen seemed bigger a year later, when Michèle returned to Pole for the longest, darkest, coldest winter on

Earth. As sous-chef, she was one of just three chefs responsible for feeding forty-three souls for the next eight months. She explained what it takes to survive such a winter: "One cannot come here and hope to be taken care of and entertained. . . . So first-timers here tend to end up either very disappointed, or very resourceful and creative. Ms. Tomato grew up locked in her bedroom most of her youth (not her choice) and had a good deal of early training in the ways of self-amusement. Therefore we like to think of ourselves in the latter group."

Freshies quickly disappeared, minus the occasional greenhouse salad. She could only hope that in October the first flights would bring "a few oranges to stave off encroaching scurvy." In the meantime, she diligently blogged about the winter's events:

March 4, 2009: Bacon bars from the 1980s were found, though she refused "to place the contents on her tongue."

April 15, 2009: Green beans and other mixed veggies brought in from –100°F shattered "like glass" when they hit the floor, or froze together in freeform sculptures when dumped out of the bag.

May 3, 2009: The last carrots on station — minus the amputations of rot — were divided equally among the forty-three residents. The windchill reached –120°F. Vodka left outside froze solid in an hour. Winter was well under way.

May 11, 2009: Jalapeños arrived from the greenhouse, thus a belated Cinco de Mayo was celebrated with a jalapeño-eating contest, one scientist against another. But it was no competition; one ate twenty hot peppers, a mix of red and green, "like they were so many apples." The other choked on his thirteenth (all green) while attendants ran for a bucket.

June 21, Midwinter's Day, 2009: As usual, a large feast and celebration were held. The highlight was the Midwinter Auction, in which the last snack-food items from the little South Pole store were put on the block.

The last Snickers bar went for $10. The last Dr. Pepper? $20. Ms. Tomato herself paid $3.50 for the last bit of nonculinary chocolate on station: a bag of peanut M&Ms. "But the crowning glory, the most inane buy of the evening," she wrote, was the $66 thrown down for a bag of Cool Ranch Doritos: "For that price, we hope he at least slept with it first."

July 4, 2009: Charred pig, burgers, hot dogs, barbecue chicken, darts, poker, chilled beer—and then red, white, and blue cupcakes. "Happy Birthday, USA!"

July 26, 2009: She looked at a photo of herself and was unimpressed: "Yeah, Ms. Tomato bears a fierce resemblance to her grandmother here. And she's dead. . . . The zombie effect comes from working long and arduous hours in the dark. We are, actually, becoming newts."

September 23, 2009: Finally, sunrise, and it's "gorgeous, glorious, and something to be wildly celebrated. . . . Naturally we throw a big dinner." Indian food and beef Wellington were the two vote-getters in the station poll for the sunrise dinner, so both were served.

The appetizers included pakoras, samosas, and baguette toasts with dips: romesco, tapenade, stilton, and arugula pesto. The beef Wellington in red-wine raisin sauce was served alongside vegetable coconut curry and chicken tandoori, saag paneer, lamb biryani, and dahl. Mango lassi and gin sours washed it down, and the cooks topped the meal off with sweet ginger rice pudding.

Cherry tomatoes from the greenhouse made the meal exotic

by South Pole standards, but Ms. Tomato was even more excited about the "cheesy paper pineapples," which reminded her of the green world and "chirpy birds" they hadn't seen for most of a year.

Everything about the sunrise and the meal had them looking outward to the planet they'd left behind. In less than two months, Gentille wrote, they would "descend upon Christchurch, New Zealand, and raid the pantry."

Gentille reminds us that, at its best, Pole is a joyful workcamp *in extremis*. The work can be extraordinarily difficult, and the isolation (in winter especially) is so stark that NASA has studied Pole's community dynamic as an analogue for life on spacecraft and off-Earth bases.

I'm glad I had my little experience of it—enough to be deeply impressed by residents' enthusiasm for life—but it didn't entice me to return for a full season. Walking around outside, gazing at what should have been the emptiness of ice, the blank 360° horizon was interrupted everywhere by buildings, cargo lines, and antennas.

Pole was too busy. But I didn't want to be stuck in McMurdo either.

What I wanted was to be in the hinterlands without crowds or infrastructure. If that meant I'd experience the heart of the Antarctic without beef Wellington or crème brûlée, so be it.

Peppermint Chicken a la State

Brush your teeth using a peppermint flavored toothpaste. Spit out the rinse water into a clean fry pan (it must be spic and span, hygiene is of utmost importance), then leave it outside in −4f to freeze (if you are not in the Antarctic, put it in your freezer).

Take a frozen chicken from the food box and thaw it slowly by heating it in a camp oven with some hot water, then cut it into pieces.

Fetch your fry pan from outside with the frozen toothpaste water and cook the chicken pieces in it, adding some oil, salt, and pepper to taste.

Gives a delicious peppermint flavor.

—John Long, *Mountains of Madness*

Sleeping with Vegetables

10

In my first season in McMurdo, rumors swirled among us greenhorns about the high quality of field-camp food. Those lucky souls in the wasteland ate some mysterious better-quality scientist food provided only to them, we were told. We wondered about their options and how much tastier they might be than the galley's mass production, and we dreamed that the dining experience — sharing a simple, intimate meal in the backcountry — would be a nobler, nicer affair.

But I scarcely left McMurdo that first season. Some of my friends in Waste Management spent weeks cleaning up the remnants of Cape Hallett, the old IGY station plunked down in the midst of a large Adélie colony. They came back to the clutter of McMurdo glowing with tales of camping amid tens of thousands of penguins against an incredible backdrop of mountains and glaciers. Aside from a half-day trip by helicopter to a distant nunatak (the peak of an ice-drowned mountain), I was confined all summer to gravel streets tinged with exhaust fumes and to galley food tainted with the navy kitchen's ample supply of liquid smoke.

While on my little helicopter trip, however, I noticed a filthy, oil-stained guy working at Marble Point, a three-person helicopter refueling station on a small peninsula sixty miles away from McMurdo. He seemed a native of a different culture, isolated in this quiet corner of the coast. No dorms, no cafeteria, no crowds. As intrigued as I was, I had little idea that I would be that filthy guy in less than a year, that Marble would become a second home, and that I had a decade of even greater adventures ahead of me.

Social distinction among support staff in the U.S. Antarctic Program is often defined by mobility, by who goes into the wilderness versus who stays tethered on their McMurdo leash. When McMurdo residents ask each other what they do or what department they work in, the implicit question is often *Where have you been?* We venerate people with double-digit years of McMurdo or South Pole ice time, but most USAP personnel are travelers who want to see more of Antarctica than McMurdo's industrial arena or Pole's lunar modules. Usually nothing comes of this desire but a mix of awe and frustration. The hinterlands are more idea than reality, more horizon than foreground. McMurdo has a splendid view of what most support staff will never experience.

Science personnel, on the other hand, fill up the deep-field camps, most of which exist specifically for research purposes. The camps vary in size from two guys in a tent to a mix of several dozen researchers, grad students, technicians, and support personnel settled into a small tent city. Many of the smaller science parties work autonomously, sleeping in backpacking tents and eating trail food. They are set up, dropped off, and serviced by air (helicopter, Twin Otter, or Herc) as necessary, but are otherwise on their own in a high-pressure scramble for data.

Paleontologist John Long recounts in *Mountains of Madness* two field seasons of fossil hunting among the peaks of the

Transantarctic Mountains, during which his small team's time seemed equally divided between long days of hard-earned finds on steep terrain and long, frustrating days of storm-bound tenting. In camp, they devoured stews or freeze-dried meals, sometimes in experiments born of hunger and boredom. Mixing some curry powder, soup mix packets, and lemon-flavored drink crystals made a "jazzy sauce," but they also devoured less jazzy meals of corned beef curry and cake tainted with kerosene.

As a thorough scientist, Long created a short appendix in *Mountains of Madness* to proudly note the team's culinary experimentation. He highlighted their Deception Irish Cream, a thick slurry of full-cream milk powder, sugar, and some "cheap and nasty" whisky, as well as his tentmate Brian Staite's Peppermint Chicken à la Staite, a simple pan of chicken pieces fried in oil, salt, pepper, and that morning's spit-out peppermint toothpaste. While not the first time that toothpaste was used to flavor an Antarctic meal, it was probably the first time a chicken recipe entailed so much saliva. "Just make sure you have a good brand of toothpaste," Long cautioned, "or it could taste awful!"

Another way for a roaming science party to make a meal taste awful is to update it every day with random ingredients. Charles Lagerbom, part of a three-man glacial-geology team working in the Dry Valleys in the summer of 1990–91, told me that their "Who-Hash" (as in "Who knew what was in it?") was part stew, part camp challenge: "We just kept adding things to it on a daily basis and then used the leftover as a base from which to add more. When necessary, we added pasta or rice when it became too liquidy, and spaghetti sauce or Raro [a sugary juice powder] or anything that came to hand when it became too stiff!" It was a game, one in which hard-earned hunger dictated that no matter how much they played with their food it would still be wolfed down. Their longest run of Who-Hash was sixteen days, ending only when the geologists had to move their tent camp elsewhere in the valleys. Now, Lagerbom says, "My stomach churns when I think about it."

A few small science parties work out of semi-permanent shelters in areas of long-term study, sometimes with a mountaineer or cook on hand. In old Australian Antarctic parlance, these were "cut-lunch explorers," derided for their luxury of dashing back from a hard day's work to an easy home rather than shivering in a cold tent. Around McMurdo, such work takes place in the ice-free Dry Valleys or up near the crater rim of Mount Erebus. In the Erebus hut—at twelve thousand feet—the long-standing king of the volcano, volcanologist Phillip Kyle, reigned for more than four decades. His notable addition to Antarctic cuisine—burying Thanksgiving turkeys in hot ground near the volcano's summit—seemed more Hawaiian than polar. After several hours, the birds emerged "brown and succulent and tender," but only if he had picked his hot spot carefully. There was a difference "between slow cook and fast rot." One badly cooked turkey fell apart in Kyle's arms, leaving the king to reign the remainder of his volcanic summer reeking of sulfur and rotten bird.

The big-ticket deep-field work is done from larger camps set up and maintained by USAP personnel in the empty quadrants of East and West Antarctica, with a population that ranges from ten to more than fifty. These camps might have a life span of several summers, depending on what kind of projects have been funded. At the start of each science season, carpenters, equipment operators, fuelies, and other camp staff are flown out to resurrect Jamesways (large sectional canvas-over-wood-frame tents), build a landing strip, create fuel and heating systems, and generally prepare for a busy summer.

The cooks are there on day one, feeding the cold, hungry construction crew long before a proper kitchen is established or science teams show up to work. Those cooks will rely on McMurdo, which sends out supplies on irregular Herc and Twin Otter flights. Food comes from three sources: Galley warehouses provide large bulk items (flour, sugar, number-ten cans of carrots, etc.), New Zealand sends a few green morsels, and the aptly named Food Room—part of the field-support services provided by the Berg Field Center (BFC) and the source of the magically-different menu I heard about when I first arrived on the ice—is responsible for everything else.

no cafeteria, no crowds

I signed up with Fuels for my second Antarctic summer (1995–96) and was given a three-week stint out at Marble Point right away. Suddenly there were no more meals cooked for a thousand. One of the rare manned stations that does no science, Marble consists of a few small weather-beaten buildings and some fuel tanks plunked down on an undulating coastal moraine wedged between a massive glacier and the sea ice of McMurdo Sound. Marble exists solely to fuel the helicopters that move science parties and their cargo around the Dry Valleys. Off and on throughout the day I'd hear the *Apocalypse Now* thumping of the navy's old single-engine Hueys approaching over the glacier, and I'd step into my boots and head out to fuel them. Otherwise, I busied myself tending to equipment or happily scoffing down home-cooked food.

The other two people at Marble were there for the full season: the camp manager and the cook. In my first Fuels summer, these two positions were filled by a husband and wife, the first laconic and laid back, and the other so remarkably uptight that she asked me, as I reached for the bread knife a few minutes after my arrival, "You know how to cut bread, right?" This did not bode well. But I was my diplomatic self, and we got along. I pressed firmly yet sawed gently on her still-warm loaves. I put utensils and dishcloths in their places, and she ensured that hearty soups, cookies, and bread were always available.

McMurdo was a thirty-minute helicopter ride away, but it seemed as far from Marble as it was from New Zealand. I spent my off-work hours exploring the area, marveling at the relative abundance of life: small clumps of moss, lichen, algae, springtails and mites (hidden in the moss), seals, and skuas. Free of McMurdo's restrictions—no solo travel and only on marked trails—I walked alone for miles across hills and sea ice with granola bars and sandwiches stuffed into my bag.

In 1996–97, my third Antarctic season, Marble had new staff and I had a partner in crime. Jamie Pierce, the cook, began his career as a professional chef but abandoned the kitchen to become a mountaineer. By the time I met him, he had led climbs all over the world. His entry into Antarctic work was through the kitchen at Palmer Station, where one of his adventures involved—ice axe in hand—a dramatic ascent of a frozen mass of "post-Vietnam-era food boxes" to secure some ancient corn dogs. Fridays, he told me, were Fried-days, "meaning hotel pans were laden with fried cheese, French fries, onion rings, and much more," despite the protests of vegetarians in the new era of what Jamie called "a more refined Antarctic diet of nutritious self-righteousness." At Marble, he produced perfect cookies and roasts and tried to teach me how to make roux and fine simple soups, all the while sighing and shuffling from window to window to stare out at the peaks he wanted to climb. He and I set out whenever we could, circling icebergs on foot and discovering mummified seals miles away from the sea.

In later seasons, Jamie guided science groups. He worked for a while with Antarctic meteorite hunters, tossing off gourmet versions of camping gruel for his companions after each day of scouring the fields of ice for the crumbs of space.

In my fourth and fifth seasons, still in Fuels, I was sent out again to Marble, but also traveled a few times to camps in West Antarctica, and once for that brief, difficult stint at the Pole.

My longest journey was a seven-week job at Siple Dome in West Antarctica. Siple was big, with several large Jamesway tents and a village of small dome tents for its fifty-odd people. Most of them were ice-core drillers, the rest a mix of science groups and USAP staff. I wasn't supposed to be there, but the young fuelie who preceded me had partied with the drillers and allegedly sprawled half-naked in the snow, which annoyed the camp manager.

So I was sent at a moment's notice to replace her. Aside from fueling aircraft and filling heater tanks, I helped out where I could and played Scrabble during my off time with a Scottish grad student.

We devoured homemade cookies in the galley Jamesway and argued over his arcane and probably fictional synonyms for mutton.

Thanksgiving at Siple Dome, 1997

Siple had three cooks, two of whom built the menu, managed the back stock and food orders from McMurdo, and provided lunch and dinner. We ate well, especially at Thanksgiving, and always had access between meals to sweets, homemade bread, leftovers, and the microwave. There was a sense of home, even in that dark green military-surplus tent silhouetted against the twenty-four-hour sunshine, and even during the twelve-hour, round-the-clock shifts of the men and women extracting cores of ancient ice from deep within the ice sheet. We were all gathered in the empty landscape for the same purpose and broke the homemade bread together.

Shelley was the third cook at Siple. She was the nightshift, a loner in the kitchen during the quieter half of summer's constant daylight, doing much of the baking for the big crowd in camp. Shelley was also the most birdlike woman I've ever known, a swallow flitting from counter to cupboard, flickering smiles across the kitchen tent, moving with a quickness belied only by the slow, determined kneading of her various doughs.

For her, I invented the double-Ziploc technique for preserving baguettes. Instructions: Take two two-gallon Ziplocs and turn one of them inside out. Insert the baguette into one and pull the other over the exposed baguette end. Seal the bags *to each other*, and voilà, no fine French bread turning overnight into a giant crouton in Antarctica's incredibly dry air. This on-the-spot survival thinking is exactly what Antarctica requires, though Shelley was otherwise content to fit them into a single bag by breaking the bread into two forlorn wings.

the food room

By my sixth season, I was determined — and lucky enough — to finally chew through my leash completely and become a field-camp guy. I had come up a little in Antarctic society. I was an old hand around McMurdo and had traveled throughout the USAP empire as a fuelie. I had left town for many trips to Marble, seven weeks at Siple, three other trips to West Antarctica, a few weeks at South Pole, overnight trips on the Coast Guard icebreaker, and even an hour at Russia's fabled Vostok Station. As a thirty-three-year-old poet with diesel-stained Carhartts, I still didn't have a résumé that mattered up north, but on the ice I had some credibility.

When I grew tired of Fuels, I had to make a decision: go back to life in the real world or deeper into Antarctica. So I leapt at the opportunity to learn another arcane skill: making skiways on the two-mile-thick East Antarctic ice cap at –30°F.

In January of 2000, I was offered the job by a drunken friend at an end-of-season party. Kip reeled across the floor of McMurdo's darkened carpenter shop and shouted over Pink Floyd a slurred version of the question we all ask at the end of an Antarctic contract: "Hey man, are you coming back next year?" When I shrugged the shrug of the restless, he yelled an eager if unpromising offer: "You should come back and work for AGO next year. It's crazy!" AGO (pronounced like the end of "Winnebago") was the Automated Geophysical Observatory program, notorious for hard work at high altitudes. Each four-person team, made up of two skiway groomers and two engineers, flew out to three remote sites where automated science equipment lived through the year on power generated by thousands of gallons of propane. The engineers downloaded data and fixed what had failed over the winter while the groomers prepared a two-mile-long skiway for another propane delivery. Kip had graduated to management and would be doing the hiring.

This was my first real Antarctic camping trip. My AGO team had to pull together all necessities before setting out, which meant that one of our main tasks in McMurdo was to show up at the BFC's Food Room to "discuss food requirements, make a menu, and fill out the food list," as explained in our instructions.

Unlike British, New Zealand, and Australian field parties,

who are handed their standard boxes of rations before deployment to the field, USAP field parties are the beneficiaries of a generous ten-page, 550-item à la carte selection.

One of the reasons the Food Room offers such lavish options is that many of its clients are researchers who, if badly fed, can complain to the federal authority that oversees the USAP. So the "beverages and juices" category offered, among other things, Gatorade (lemon-lime or grape), V-8, pineapple-juice concentrate, and fifteen flavors of herbal or black tea.

The handout had a dozen more categories: baking supplies, pie fillings, and puddings; grains, pasta, dried beans, and potatoes; canned stews, meats, and seafood; sauce mixes; canned vegetables; canned fruits; jams, jellies, and peanut butter; cookies, crackers, and snacks; freeze-dried meals; condiments and sauces; herbs, spices, powders, and flavorings; and frozen foods, which included everything from Florentine mixed vegetables to chiles rellenos and halibut steaks. It was a little overwhelming.

On the first page of the food list was some old-fashioned advice: "The food you take to the field can have a critical effect on the morale of your field party, so the careful preparation time you spend in town will be well worth the effort once you get to the field." My AGO team would be out six days for each trip, unless (as was quite likely) bad weather or flight delays kept us out for weeks. We had to consider how hard we wanted to work to make our meals, and whether variety was more valuable than simplicity. Both sounded good to me, but the process looked daunting. Luckily, Joe, lead engineer and our team leader, was an old hand at this. Bella, the lead skiway groomer, was new to AGO but had many months of fieldwork behind her. Although I knew McMurdo inside and out, I could only follow their lead in planning field camp food. And then there was our other tech, an electrical engineering grad student whom I'll call "Rudy," who was a complete novice.

I was also fortunate that my good friend Deb Baldwin was the maestra of the Food Room. She was the nexus between local supply and remote demand. She shepherded every field-camp cook or field party through the initial food selection and responded to requests from the field throughout the season. If a carrot or a cake-mix box arrived at a camp by helicopter, Twin Otter, or Herc, its journey started with Deb. Veteran cooks and researchers came to her hoping that their every culinary wish might be granted. Groveling greenhorns came to her hoping that she would prepare their menu and pull their food. And my AGO team, modest and efficient, came to her hoping, like everyone else, for extra portions of frozen scallops and Cadbury chocolate.

Deb's was an odd monarchy within the science-support world. She worked autonomously and with great responsibility, but her realm was a weather-beaten second-floor metal chamber in a rusting, forty-year-old Quonset hut, through which windblown snow melted and dripped onto the shelves and floor. It had been the repository of field food for about fifteen years, during several of which Deb had been in charge. In that time, she'd had a first-hand view of a little-known history: the clash between McMurdo's navy, civilian, and science personnel, with the Food Room at the center of it all.

Deb first held the Food Room job in 1988. Back then, she was a science-support civilian struggling against navy antipathy toward scientists and the scientific mission. McMurdo was mostly a navy town, and Deb describes the daily scene inside the galley as "a sea of green." Galley management "hated to deal with anything related to food for science." In fact, the head of the galley once told her, in all seriousness, that "this base would be a great place without science here," forgetting that science was the professed purpose of the entire Antarctic program.

Meanwhile, the other civilians in town, mostly "big bearded guys in Carhartts" working in the construction and maintenance departments, didn't get along well with the ruling navy hierarchy. Even so, they shared with the navy what Deb describes as a righteous anger at the scientists they believed were "a bunch of spoiled brats who got the good food and never had to do any real work."

What makes this situation so remarkable is that, for the first time in Antarctic history, trail food was more desirable than base food. The unhappy civilian and navy personnel, many of them children of the new suburbs, expected culinary conditions rivaling those at home. As the Food Room manager in a strangely stratified society, Deb was targeted because she was perceived as "part of a conspiracy to withhold food that rightfully belonged to the McMurdo population." There was no conspiracy, but Deb admitted that there was reason for revolt: "The galley food sucked. There was always a hot chocolate shortage, which enraged people. The Food Room had everything everyone wanted: Chocolate bars, tortilla chips, salsa, cookies." It sounds like an unlikely cause for a folk revolution, yet it did lead to occasional break-ins during the winter when the Food Room lay cold and unused.

There were other problems. Deb ordered small cans of fruit or condiments but instead received huge items, like number-ten cans of peaches that she was expected to dispense to a four-person research party. Also, she says, "McMurdo was a dumping ground for navy suppliers" of ugly meat products she never ordered, like pigs' feet and "weird, noodly, nasty-looking meat-type stuff."

Because the navy refused to give her reasonable access to the warehouses, Deb had trouble supplying food to field camps. She learned to hide the leftover frozen food brought back from the field so she could reissue it on her own, but she needed a way to guarantee access to the freezer warehouse, where "rows upon rows of stacks of teetering triwalls" held the food that should have been issued to her weeks earlier.

It was then that she had her great revelation. As an innocent among the cynical, it had taken some time for her to realize that she had a real source of power, a high-value commodity: Deb had the best food in the USAP.

She'd also figured out that while the navy ran the show, the civilian construction department "was considered kind of the mafia in town." Nothing got built or fixed unless Construction was ready to do it. In exchange for steaks, drink mixes for parties, and some candy bars, they built spice shelves and a table in the Food Room and helped with her supply problem by, when necessary, hiding some of her Food Room cargo from the navy.

Deb also leveraged her food wealth to sneak behind enemy lines. At midnight on a Saturday, she met a galley worker in the kitchen, where civilians were unwelcome. Some rare treats were exchanged.

Together they used the galley's band saw—the equipment

says something about the cuisine — to slice masses of frozen hamburger and forty-pound slabs of frozen chicken parts into nice, manageable six-inch blocks of meat. The scientists, she says, "got a charge out of those."

On another late-night mission, she surreptitiously met a guy at the door of the freezer warehouse. He keyed her in and gave her a quick lesson on the forklift. She handed over some candy bars. He left. Then Deb spent the entire night moving boxes and organizing the summer's worth of food before the morning shift arrived. It was all going well until the forklift started acting erratically. She looked behind her and found she had snagged a whole frozen pig wrapped in burlap (intended for a celebratory pig roast by the Maori members of a New Zealand subcontractor) and was dragging it around the entire warehouse. If she wasn't so sleep-deprived and hypothermic, she might not have laughed hysterically all alone in the freezer. But she did. And she had the last laugh, too, by getting the food she needed to do her job.

rich southern cooking

As my AGO team prepared to fly out, Deb was busy too. If she wasn't placing buckets to catch drips from melting snow, she was bustling back and forth between the shelves of dry goods and her computer, answering questions from us or other foraging groups, and shooing me away from the Cadbury. We had checked off everything we wanted on the food list for each of our trips, which she then modified according to the limitations of her stock.

Joe, Bella, and I packed dry goods, cans, teas, and spices

into boxes for separate trips, but frozen food remained in boxes labeled for us in a walk-in freezer out by the loading dock. We had to buy our liquor at the McMurdo store. Freshies, if we were lucky, would be picked up along with the frozen food on the morning of our flight.

But we had a problem. Rudy, our whiz-kid neophyte, had become increasingly erratic, often disappearing for parts of the day. Among other quirks, he had changed his name en route to the ice and made a speech in McMurdo's coffee house about how humans can communicate with each other in a shared dream-state. Rumors swirled around town about Rudy's plan to look for aliens out on the ice cap — something he had neglected to mention to us. In general, he seemed a bit detached, which is not an ideal characteristic for a coworker amid the hazards of life on an ice cap.

Reluctantly, Joe asked the Science Support manager to interview Rudy and determine his mental fitness for the journey to the remote AGO sites. Despite his protests, Rudy was found wanting and remained behind in McMurdo until some weeks later when his delusions apparently took over. He walked from table to table at lunch in the galley explaining to everyone that the mothership would arrive at noon on Thursday to pick him up. Thursday was a sad day for everyone but a few cynical and chuckling spectators, some wearing alien masks for the event, when a bewildered Rudy waited for deliverance in a parking area between the galley and Medical.

Our disheartened trio flew out to our first AGO site on two Twin Otter flights packed to the roof with thousands of pounds of cargo. I stared at the jumble of gear bags and food boxes haphazardly strapped down. In a crash, flames and melting snow would turn it—and us—into an ugly, instant hoosh.

Despite the initial shock of arriving into –35°F with a freshening wind and subsequent ground blizzard (dense snow moved laterally by the wind while the sky remains blue and clear), life at the AGO site was relatively easy. A tough field camp veteran, Bella preferred her tent, while Joe and I lived in the AGO box, a shipping container (eight by eight by twenty-four feet) elevated and converted into a little Spartan lunar base big enough for a few bunks, some shelves, a counter to cook on, and lots of electronics. As ascetic as it may sound, the luxury of stepping off a plane into a weatherproof cube in East Antarctica changes everything. We were safe and comfy on the far side of the moon.

I helped Bella turn ten thousand feet of wind-sculpted, rock-hard snow into a landing strip, using only a snowmobile and a four-foot-wide tow-behind groomer, and assisted Joe in rebuilding the station's thermoelectric generator. Long days made us hungry for our richest food, particularly scallops and pesto on angel-hair pasta. And despite hard work in profound cold and the noble history of starvation on similar terrain, we gained weight.

We remained at the AGO site for ten extra days ("camping for cash," as it's called), because we lacked Rudy's electrical engineering expertise and because bad weather in McMurdo cancelled our flights. I was annoyed that we were going to miss the big Thanksgiving feast in McMurdo, but it was a good reality check: Antarctica was in charge. We were fine, enjoying a space-age life that had everything the heroic age lacked: extra food, a warm shelter, and communication with people who *might* be able to reach us in an emergency.

In *The Heart of the Antarctic*, a starving Ernest Shackleton speculated whether "the people who suffer from hunger in the big cities of civilisation felt as we were feeling, and I arrived at the conclusion that they did not, for no barrier of law and order would have been allowed to stand between us and any food that had been available."

For Shackleton, a sense of noble purpose made all the difference: "The man who starves in a city is weakened, hopeless, spiritless, and we were vigorous and keen." Joe, Bella, and I, on the other hand, were the future of Antarctica: soft, vigorous, and satiated.

When Joe, a thin man who grew up on rich Southern cooking, announced one night after dinner that "the South is really bad for a person's figure," he was talking about Antarctica, not Alabama.

Two weeks later, I was back in the Food Room preparing for our second AGO trip when Steve Dunbar, the manager of Science Support, came by to talk with me.

A good friend of Deb's from Idaho, Steve was also the guy who had interviewed, then contained Rudy. A genius for logistics, Steve was on the USAP fast track from mountaineer to management. At that moment, though, I thought he was crazy.

He asked if I was interested in being pulled from my AGO team to lead a short two-man trip to a short-term camp called Seismic Center, another blank spot on the high ice sheet. The job was to groom a fifteen-hundred-foot skiway for an electronics-laden Twin Otter and set up a fueling station with seventy-six airdropped barrels of fuel.

Deb laughed later about my deer-in-the-headlights expression, which I thought I'd disguised as thoughtfulness.

Suddenly six years of dreamy notions of flying off to my own Antarctic camp were just a *yes* away from realization.

"What about Joe and Bella?" I asked. "We're already having a hard time without Rudy." Steve had already talked with Joe. The BFC would loan the AGO team one of their people for the second trip and I'd be back "in a week, max" — plenty of time to help with the third.

But I never rejoined Joe and Bella, or saw another AGO site. With the help of Ryan, a young, upbeat, and rugged GA (general assistant) from the carpenters' shop, I put together the food and gear for Seismic Center in two days and, once on site, had the job completed in another two days.

Still, despite Steve's assurance of "a week, max," various delays in McMurdo extended our Seismic trip to two weeks. But my AGO trip had taught me to be patient and to pack plenty of extra food.

Ryan and I ate lots of bagels and burritos, drank some whisky, and entertained ourselves competing in the Seismic Center Olympics, in which a large can of refried beans served as both shot put and soccer ball. I still have dents in my shins.

When we got back, Steve loaned Ryan to the AGO team and surprised me with another offer, a "quick two-man trip" to set up an emergency runway on the Odell Glacier. The New York Air National Guard (NYANG), which had taken over all LC-130 Hercules operations from the navy in 1999, desperately wanted an alternative landing site away from McMurdo. Ideally, it would be somewhere high in the mountains, free of the weather that commonly shuts down McMurdo, and where wheeled aircraft could land safely. The Odell is a blue-ice glacier, so windswept throughout the year that only small patches of snow exist on the ice. This would provide, in theory, a good hard surface for a plane on wheels.

Over the next three weeks, I made two trips to the Odell in an attempt to set up the runway. Working and playing in the gorgeous, dramatic peak-and-glacier landscape was a rare joy, but otherwise both trips were failures. In the first two-man attempt, the tow-behind groomer I'd used at AGO and Seismic Center either bounced harmlessly off the rock-hard patches of snow or stuck fast, throwing the driver into the windshield. On the second trip, I returned with three men and three tons of food and gear, including a small Kubota tractor. We chopped, excavated, and transported several tons of snow for a week before NYANG inspectors and Steve Dunbar—an amateur pilot at home—decided to come out and actually look at the site. (I had never been told that the initial inspection was done by glancing at it from a helicopter.) The verdict wasn't good. "I wouldn't land my Cessna on this," said Steve. "What were they thinking?"

The boys and I rolled our eyes, thinking of our wasted effort. Luckily, there was a smoother, if shorter, possible site on the lower glacier. We threw in a few flags to outline it, then left for the season.

Steve asked me to plan on building and maintaining that runway for the next summer season. I spent the next several months back home learning everything I could about blue-ice runways—they exist only in Antarctica—and arranging details for next year's full-season trip with Julian Ridley.

My research led me to the foremost Antarctic glaciologist, the oft-cited Dr. Charles Swithinbank of the British Antarctic Survey. On his first trip south with the 1949 Norwegian-British-Swedish Expedition, Swithinbank had noted that wheeled aircraft might be able to land on these windswept blue-ice areas. Decades later, he wrote a comprehensive study of them.

Coincidentally, Swithinbank had written in one of his Antarctic memoirs about both Julian Ridley ("a young field assistant who confided that he was a grandson of Lieutenant William Colbeck") and Deb Baldwin ("a wisp of a girl who was a top-class whitewater canoeist when not in the realms of ice").

Swithinbank passed through McMurdo in 1988 and, when foraging in Deb's Food Room, never gave the ramshackle qualities of the building a second thought. Having begun his Antarctic research in the age of pemmican and grilled seal brains, he knew what was important. For him, Deb's chamber of plentiful food, where "gluttony was to have free reign," was like Aladdin's Cave.

Whether he was referring to the storied cave of *The Arabian Nights* or the ice grotto of the same name—with its three frozen oranges and a pineapple that saved Douglas Mawson at the end of his tragic 1912 trek—is unclear.

farmers of the odell

Lieutenant Colbeck's great-grandson and I got busy as soon as we deployed from Christchurch to McMurdo in October of 2001. Before we began Julian's "100 Days after 100 Years" on the Odell, we had to spend a few weeks racing around the station putting our camp together. We tested communications equipment (VHF and HF radios, plus a satellite phone), set up tents, collected our illicit sourdough bread from Rob the baker, helped rebuild two old snowmobiles and tore apart a brand-new Kubota tractor for shipping in pieces to the Odell, attended field-safety classes, and much more. We checked off lists and then made more lists. We had to imagine all the problems that might arise from work and weather. When you're heading into a landscape that requires logistics for everything but the air you'll breathe, it's important to plan well. It's embarrassing to send the plane back for a can opener.

Steve Dunbar upped the ante by reminding us we'd better plan on one hundred days of self-reliance, as he had no idea if there would be Twin Otter or helicopter flights available to bring us anything. We could not fail to properly plan for more than three months of meals, snacks, and drinks. Julian and I were both tall, hungry men with fast metabolisms. I'd never planned a camp menu for longer than three weeks, and even then I didn't do a very good job. You can't really suffer from a mistake in quantities in just a few weeks, but I shuddered to think what we'd have left to eat at the end of the third month. I was getting lost somewhere between planning specific meals and adding up the three-month quantities of individual items.

Deb took care of me. She coached me in imagining meal plans and computing different units for different foodstuffs. I was calculating bars of chocolate, bags of pasta and egg rolls, smaller bags of sugar and dehydrated vegetables, pouches of freeze-dried food, boxes of tea and granola bars, cups of loose rice, cans of smoked oysters (not nearly enough, sadly), buckets and packets of instant soups, bottles of sauce, and much more. Julian and I packed everything into the biggest cardboard boxes we could carry to and from a plane.

Deb also caved in—after daily wheedling—and allowed us more than our fair share of the items labeled "limited" on the order form: New Zealand cheese, Cadbury chocolate, roasted cashews, Sambal Oelek sauce, and frozen scallops. This was crucial for our morale, after all.

I reminded Deb that Antarctic history teaches us happiness begins in the belly. Needless to say, we were not suffering for variety. During the brain-curdling selection process, I felt like I was suffering *from* variety, but what we carried out into the field would keep us happy for many weeks. And should a plane or helicopter ever come our way during the summer, we'd have an opportunity to order whatever we'd forgotten or eaten too quickly.

After a few rushed good-byes to friends in McMurdo, we shuttled out to the Twin Otter at the ice runway. To me, this aircraft was an extraordinary machine central to the delicate calculus of our survival, but to the Canadian pilots it was just a station wagon with wings.

Its ancestor, the single-engine Otter, was used in the IGY and described in 1957 as able to carry "ten passengers and a crate of oranges 1,000 miles at about 110 knots." Now, its twin-engine successor had only to carry two passengers, zero oranges, and a ton of stuff for 120 miles. The pilots hurled our future sustenance into the plane and told us to jump in with it. When we arrived, Julian and I were two miles from the campsite—which was as close as the Otter could land—and possibly one hundred days from a shower. At our altitude of 5,500 feet, the temperature was a balmy 0°F, 20 degrees colder than McMurdo, but the wind made it feel about –25 °F. Julian looked around at the windswept wilderness of ice, rock, and sky, then looked at all our stuff and said, in a bit of understatement either British or Californian, "Well, I reckon this will keep us busy for a while."

Within an hour, I had almost knocked him senseless. As we motored up over a steep three-hundred-foot slope on the glacier, the heavily laden sled I'd hastily hitched to my snowmobile rattled free and raced down the ice toward a garden of boulders.

The sled contained all of our essential camping equipment, including the propane cook stove and survival gear. Julian nimbly brought his machine up against the lower side of the sled to slow its descent. Less nimbly, I dropped down to pin the sled between us but came too fast, slamming into it hard enough to send my companion sprawling across the hard ice. I carefully clipped the sled back onto my hitch, Julian saddled back up, and we headed off to build our new home.

As it turned out, we were so busy it was several hours before Julian remembered the crisis, and by then even he thought it was funny. That first night, we huddled around the stove and ate some modern hoosh—a fatty, cheesy, gloopy, freeze-dried concoction optimistically called Leonardo da Fettuccine—straight out of the bag. Like the Northern Party in 1912 who spent an unplanned winter hunched over in their small ice cave, we later developed our own version of "igloo back."

The highest point of our Endurance tent, an eight-by-sixteen-foot living space, was just tall enough for me to stand up straight in my socks. At six foot five, Julian was out of luck.

Like Victor Campbell's crew and their blubber stove, we spent the next three months hunched over the two-burner propane Coleman stove, cheerfully melting snow and making meals. Unlike the Northern Party, though, there was no dysentery, smitch, or singing.

We gathered snow for drinking water from the edge of the

glacier. Sand blown onto it from the Allan Hills ensured we got a daily dose of minerals. We kept two large, clean trash cans filled with chunks of snow just outside the tent door and had an oversized melting pot on or near the stove at all times. All of our food sat on the ice just ten feet outside the tent door in two lines of boxes aligned with the prevailing wind, anchored to the glacier by ice screws and heavy-duty cargo straps. Most of our kitchen supplies came in the standard-issue BFC kitchen box, a carefully packed pile of pots, pans, dishes, utensils, and the like that we could never repack properly.

Much of what we ate was standard-issue car-camping cuisine. Breakfasts usually amounted to bagels or English muffins, as well as cereal for Julian or packets of instant oatmeal for me. Favorite lunches, and often dinners, included ready-made frozen burgers, vegetable egg rolls, and cheese burritos.

I also made dinners of pasta, quesadillas, Thai curries, or sautéed factory-farm chicken breasts with frozen Oriental mixed vegetables. Baking was a problem, since the oven consisted of a collapsible Coleman device that sat on the two-burner stove. Its metal was thin, and the tent was cold. I managed to heat up pizzas on ready-made crust, and one night I stayed up late after Julian went to bed to secretly bake thirty-nine chocolate chip cookies for his birthday, using frozen dough swiped for us from the McMurdo kitchen by Rob the baker.

Throughout the summer, we rationed out the luxuries we'd coaxed from Deb: pesto, scallops, halibut, and salmon steaks. Our primary culinary habit was devouring Cadbury bars, which we had tucked away in parka pockets, pants pockets, sleeping bags, and under snowmobile seats. We lounged with red wine now and then, too, though it was always chilled and sometimes slushy. A better choice for the climate was whisky, though it didn't necessarily pair well with grilled cheese or refried beans or just about anything else on the menu. Some friends at the BFC joked about us being the "Farmers of the Odell" and had decorated our kitchen box with a barnyard sketch. Sometimes Julian took up the theme while chatting idly by radio with MacOps (McMurdo's communication center) when they weren't busy talking to other camps:

"MacOps, MacOps, this is the Farmers of the Odell."

"Farmers of the Odell, this is MacOps. We have you loud and clear. What are you growing out there?"

"MacOps, Odell: Well, the usual things: snow peas and iceberg lettuce..."

Our first few weeks were spent in long days clearing areas of rock-hard snow from the runway with the Kubota tractor and drilling hundreds of holes in the ice for marker flags. Within a month, we had an adequate last-chance airfield for any Herc that could not land in McMurdo. But the NYANG was leery of the runway they had demanded we build. They inspected it, buzzed it at high speed, but they never landed on it. In fact, in a bit of perfect military logic, they declared that they'd never use it, but insisted we should stay there and maintain it just in case.

So, after completing the job, we settled in for a long, fine, exploratory summer on the Odell. Every day was a wonder, a privilege, a dream come true. Aside from occasional maintenance on the runway, we spent our time eating like kings and exploring by foot or snowmobile our empire of rock and ice. We climbed unnamed peaks and ate lunches of cheese and chocolate, gazing over enormities of breathless land. With sandwiches, smoked oysters, and up to four Cadbury bars per day, we cruised around nunataks and made a pilgrimage to a stone arch through which winds descending from East Antarctica surged like the sea.

Other men had preceded us. In a valley littered with two-hundred-million-year-old petrified wood, we stumbled across a forty-year-old New Zealand man-food box still packed with items like Cadbury's Bourneville Cocoa, Maggi Scotch Broth soup mix, a one-pound tin of butter, and a generic five-ounce beef-and-pork Meat Bar. We were respectful enough (and so well fed) that it didn't occur to us to sample the historic rations.

Our only overnight visitors were two mountaineers from the meteorite-hunting team who wanted to inspect the runway area for fallen stars. One was Jamie Pierce, my old friend from Marble Point, and the other was a legendary thirty-year veteran Antarctic guide named Johnny Schutt. Johnny has probably found more meteorites than any person in history, notably meteorites from the Moon and Mars. In two days of looking, they found nothing, but weeks later and farther downglacier, Julian and I found a meteorite the size of a grapefruit. There are few things more astonishing than being the first person to see and touch an object from deep space that is 4.55 billion years old, the same age as the Earth.

When we met him, Johnny was perhaps the last believer in the old Antarctic trail cuisine custom of never washing his mug. Like Jean Charcot and his filthy hoosh pot back in the heroic age, or like John Behrendt on his IGY traverse, Johnny reasoned that since the leftovers enhanced the next meal's flavor and the cup froze germ-free right after every meal, washing dishes was a waste of time and water. I didn't know about Johnny's habit until the end of our first dinner together. As Julian got ready to do the dishes, Jamie sidled up to us to advise against touching the encrusted mug. There was philosophy mixed in with those dregs. Not that we were overly delicate. Early in the summer, Julian had a repulsive habit of drinking the first dose of water he swirled around his dirty dinner bowl, and "by day thirty," he reminds me, "you too were enjoying it and wondering why you waited so long to embrace the convenience."

We did not suffer. Nor were we abandoned to any culinary monotony determined by my food-ordering mistakes. In fact, we ended up with so many incidental helicopter and Twin Otter flights bringing us bits of gear and food that Julian called us the Billionaire Boys Club. So much for one hundred days without resupply.

And rather than being freshie-less, the summer turned into a primavera romp. One flight mistakenly delivered forty pounds of vegetables and fruit intended for several people at a stormed-in Siple Dome. Suddenly the two of us possessed an unlikely proportion of Antarctica's fresh food, sharing our freezing tent with cabbages, carrots, onions, basil, a twenty-pound bag of New Zealand potatoes, and much more. We fought a three-week battle to protect this manna from the cold heaven from which it had descended, but witlessly lost half the raw potatoes to freezing. Too late, Jamie suggested over the radio that we should cube, parboil, and freeze them for later use as hash browns. We stuffed everything that could fit into our sleeping bags with us when we slept. I took herbs, tomatoes, and carrots, while Julian took oranges and asparagus and began a platonic relationship with a two-foot-long, shrink-wrapped English cucumber.

Aside from culinary luxury and the amazing good luck to have time to explore the landscape, our time at the Odell was defined by the wind. There is a reason that the Odell is a blue-ice glacier. When the katabatic gales kicked up for days at a time, we were stuck in tents that shook so badly we thought they'd break into shreds. When the winds really started howling, we stepped out to measure the wind speed and wondered aloud how much wind was necessary to knock us off our feet. In response, a gust knocked us off our feet and blew us like rags through camp. Down at the runway, nearly all the markers snapped like toothpicks.

That night, while we slept, some of our food boxes worked loose from their cargo straps in the fifty- and sixty-knot gusts and blew apart. We woke to a yard sale of scattered food and desperately followed a downwind trail of broken frozen pizza crust, prying pieces from underneath wind-carved rocks. We spent hours looking for other lost food, both of us distressed that we'd sent litter whistling through the cleanest wilderness on Earth. Big, airy potato chip bags just disappeared, probably reaching the Ross Sea forty miles away before we knew they were gone.

As for the fine sourdough breads covertly given to us by Rob the baker, these Julian and I rationed out slowly for grilled cheese sandwiches made with rich, sharp New Zealand cheddar and canned Alaskan salmon. In a moment of culinary rashness, I tried to make French toast by battering the bread with canned eggnog. The lousy meal that resulted was a sign of our surplus, not deprivation. In fact, we lacked for nothing at the Odell but the words to express our gratitude for the gifts granted us by Rob, Deb, each other, and the grand history of Antarctic occupation that led to our bountiful season on the ice.

Shackleton's well-preserved whisky

"How can you expect a man who's warm to understand one who's cold?" – Alexander Solzhenitsyn, *One Day In The Life Of Ivan Denisovich*

A Tale of Two Stations

11

With this century of stories in mind, how should I imagine the future of Antarctic cuisine? Will it be a high-tech science-fiction wonderland symbolized by the remote-controlled South Pole Food Growth Chamber? Will it be the Billionaire Boys Club writ large, with a constant flow of aircraft piercing once-impervious Antarctic weather to provide even the most remote camps with an endless supply of goodies and freshies? Will Rear Admiral Dufek's mid-twentieth-century dream of nuclear-powered, locally-grown, krill-fed agriculture ever come to fruition?

Since the era of sealers and Shackleton, of Rozo and roast penguin, Antarctic cuisine has ranged from fodder and flesh amidst scurvy and starvation to extravagant holiday meals. Mostly, though, Antarctic food has been adequate. And even today that adequacy is considered a triumph, with calories, vitamins, quantity, and flavor all accounted for. I have had fine meals and even great feasts but have never experienced truly extraordinary food served up daily. But I'm writing from an American culture whose greatest contributions to global cuisine are all industrial: Cool Ranch Doritos, anyone?

Antarctica may not have a cohesive continental culture, but culture still matters. There are as many imported cuisines on the continent as there are nations throwing citizens into parkas to claim their piece of the Antarctic pie. From Brazil's *feijoada completa* on King George Island to New Zealand's rum and rosehip syrup on Ross Island, menus vary wildly from station to station. Feasts are to be found in every kitchen in every base dotting the icy wilderness, and there are decades of culinary history from other national Antarctic programs — Korean, Chinese, Argentinean, South African, and many more — that I know nothing about.

But I will wager, having found nothing in my reading to compare, that no story of Antarctic cuisine can match the sumptuous epicurean repasts savored on a daily basis during the first winter at Concordia, a French and Italian joint-research facility in inland East Antarctica. If this is the future of Antarctic cuisine, I'm ready to move south permanently.

ʃ the best cook in antarctica Υ

How convenient that the continent's two most food-obsessed cultures joined forces in the new millennium to create, after the USAP's Pole and Russia's Vostok, Antarctica's third major year-round inland station. With the same inhuman combination of high altitude (10,607 feet), zero humidity, and harsh temperatures (including a winter low of –120°F), Concordia's working conditions are much like those of Vostok Station, officially the coldest inhabited place on Earth.

First inhabited in early 2005, Concordia consists of two three-story, eighteen-sided buildings linked by an enclosed footbridge. Within these sixty-foot-diameter structures are state-of-the-art facilities, stylish dorm rooms, and a spacious dining room with a fine high view of the ice cap. Equidistant from the coastal stations of Dumont d'Urville (France), Zuchelli (Italy), and Casey (Australia), Concordia has sophisticated aesthetics and a multinational ethic. The beautiful food served there is both a respite from difficult conditions and an expression of cosmopolitan culture. If any cuisine is capable of truly compensating for the working conditions in the heart of the Antarctic, it is the menu described by Guillaume Dargaud in that first winter of 2005.

Dargaud was already a veteran of six Antarctic summers and two winters, always in the company of fine French food at Dumont d'Urville. Situated in the midst of tens of thousands of nesting Adélies and other sea birds, French chefs at Dumont d'Urville had a tradition of working their culinary magic on local foods. To make a proper omelet from penguin eggs, for example, required removing two egg whites from every five eggs. For finer cuisine, the chefs might whip up a penguin *magret* (breast) or a penguin roasted on a rotating spit.

Even while living in temporary facilities at Concordia, as the new base was being built, Guillaume's Christmas dinner offered avocado with crabmeat and smoked salmon, farfel pasta with speck (juniper-flavored ham), rock lobster in spicy sauce with rice, millefeuille of tournedos with cream, artichoke bottoms, cheese, and marie charlotte with chocolate mousse and truffles. An ordinary Sunday meal was scarcely less fantastic. "I'm off to lunch where the usual seven-course Sunday meal awaits," Guillaume noted merrily in his blog. "Let's see what's for today: smoked salmon with caviar toasts, tortellini, Mirabelle sorbet *'trou normand,'* white sausage in brioche, duck à l'orange, cheese, and coconut chocolate pie."

Finally, the winterers moved out of tents and into the

livable but unfinished facility. Three of the twelve men and one woman in the crew conducted some research, while the rest took care of logistics and worked on completing construction. For the celebratory party, Guillaume describes Jean-Louis Duraffourg, a master chef with twenty-five years of Antarctic experience, serving "course after course of smoked salmon, fish pâté, oven-cooked oysters, tortellini, duck breasts in green-pepper sauce, and a lemon-meringue pie."

After the feast, for the first time in two months, Jean-Louis took a day off. An Antarctic veteran, he had already done ten winters and many more summers, devoting half his life to Antarctica, nearly all at Dumont d'Urville. The work at Concordia was the same, feeding the crew twice a day, but the setting was certainly different. For one thing, he said, it was much colder than the coast, and going outside was a shock: "One of the annoying things here is the time wasted dressing up each time you go outside, even just for a minute." As recompense he fell in love with the view. "Here," he said, "it's the republic of silence."

Like the scientists and builders, Jean-Louis had plenty of work and long-term planning to do. He had to decide how to arrange the kitchen, both for snug thirteen-person winter meals and next summer's sixty-person cafeteria meals. He had to improvise a menu without the three tons of potatoes mistakenly replaced on the supply traverse by an equal amount of Perrier (an absurd item considering they lived atop three kilometers of the purest ice in the world). And he had to clean and organize his brand-new storeroom, which was piled willy-nilly with tens of tons of supplies and sticky with the mess from frozen and now thawing cases of fruit juice,

Perrier, and—the horror—some of the thousand bottles of fine wines from Bordeaux, Bourgogne, Alsace, and Provence. (Another mistake: Someone had left the liquids in an unheated container outside.) Guillaume noted that the bottles that did not break had their taps pushed out by the ice, sometimes even through the cardboard boxes.

Capt. Scott's last birthday dinner - June 6th, 1911

Even so, they would have plenty of wine, and an astonishing array of meat to pair it with. The coffers were full, not just with beef, chicken, sausages, ham, and seafood, but also duck, lamb, veal, rabbit, venison, kangaroo, snails, and frog legs. They had 663 pounds of butter, enough for each person to have three and a half ounces per day. A few items from a typical birthday dinner illustrate their wealth of options: asparagus in mousseline sauce, mushroom pasta, frog legs, chicken en croute, grappa sorbet, and a version of Baked Alaska that Guillaume described as "a flaming volcano of ice cream and meringue that manages to not set fire to the station."

The Concordia crew worked Monday through Saturday morning. On Sunday, Jean-Louis served his seven-course meal; on Monday, the chef rested and each member of the crew took a turn filling in for him, just as they took turns washing dishes during the week. There is also a French Antarctic tradition to let the chef rest on May 1, based on La Fête du Travail (Labor Day), or what Guillaume called "I'm on strike" day in France. The French crew honor the holiday by cooking old survival rations over a camping ministove, which tends to scorch tables and plates.

The Monday cooks, some knowledgeable and others not (Roberto, for example, had never cooked so much as an egg), were not necessarily working from scratch. If they asked, Jean-Louis could prep meals ahead of time for them to simply heat and serve. Guillaume did it both ways on his first Monday gig, preparing a lunch of pasta all'Amatriciana and chocolate-pear cake to go with a main dish of roast veal with peas prepared earlier by Jean-Louis. For dinner, he made a cheese fondue.

Guillaume is a software engineer, but in Antarctica, "I'm more of a truck driver, snow shoveler, crane operator, translator, mover, and more." He speaks French, Italian, and English, which means when he wasn't maintaining experiments in atmospheric physics he was translating between coworkers who barely spoke each other's language. The Italians, Guillaume noted, distinguished themselves from the French in the way they gathered around the coffee machine after a meal, or when they talked through movies. The French wanted snails at every celebration while the

Italians would have, if possible, "pasta at every meal and pizza for breakfast." The French, he said, "act like they don't care about the pasta, but they eat just as much as anyone else."

Midwinter celebration in Antarctica is usually something akin to New Year's, with everyone toasting the solstice and the eventual return of the sun. But because the holiday fell on a Tuesday, the Concordia crew decided to make it Mardi Gras, or more likely, as Guillaume suggested, some sort of ancient pagan festival. They would party from Tuesday to Friday, with the weekend to help them recover. Each festival day had a new theme and new games. A week before the party started, the Concordia crew prepared different costumes and decorations for each day, while Jean-Louis worked on a magnificent meal, hanging a sign on the kitchen door "promising the worst tortures to whoever dares enter."

The crew gasped when they finally sat down Tuesday evening to read the extravagant menu. They gasped for air later on, as the meal took them four hours to consume. It included

- Porto-infused foie gras wrapped in pastry
- Venison pie with pistachio crust
- Smoked salmon on toast points with Uzbekistan caviar
- Lobster tails gratinée
- Scallops à la provençale
- Sautéed jumbo shrimp in curry
- Pear liqueur–flavored sorbet
- Vodka-flavored sorbet
- Whisky-flavored sorbet
- Frog legs and melted butter
- Escargots with garlic and parsley

- Oysters stuffed with champagne and cream
- Duck thighs slow-simmered in balsamic vinegar
- Beef filet in puff pastry
- Lamb's knuckles *aux quatre épices* (pepper, nutmeg, ginger, and cloves or cinnamon) and saffron couscous
- French and Italian cheeses
- Soufflé flavored with Grand Marnier
- Frozen vanilla-raspberry meringue
- Tiramisu with wild berries

Just like Mardi Gras, there were plenty of cross-dressers to compete in the "Miss Concordia" contest. The only woman on station wisely stayed out of it. A heavily bearded Guillaume appeared as the self-described "ugliest wet-nurse on the face of the Earth" and squirted milk onto the competition from his homemade set of plastic breasts.

The costume theme of the second Midwinter festival night was, appropriately enough, Gauls versus Romans. The main activities, besides eating mussels and fries and drinking, were games, including bobbing for ping-pong balls in water and then in flour, walking on cans, mock sword fights, and guessing the contents of mysterious mixed drinks. In the latter, while Guillaume and the others were "all lost in conjectures with our glasses in our hand," Jean-Louis stepped in, sipped each drink and named all the ingredients.

In keeping with Thursday's theme of Sailors and Pirates, Jean-Louis walked around with a bread parrot on his shoulder. The outdoor activity, sculpting snow blocks into the shape of Concordia, was short-lived because of –100°F temperatures under a sharp wind. They scurried back inside for an endless Italian buffet of pasta and pizza before a homemade game of Antarctic Pictionary. Awards were given out, including one for the best cook in Antarctica. It went without saying that Jean-Louis was the best, wrote Guillaume, "but it's also good to say it." On Friday, with everybody hungover and exhausted from a week of partying, they feasted on meat fondue and watched movies until 4:00 a.m. Jean-Louis served onion soup and more champagne to the seven survivors. The pagan festival was over.

The winter was not *all* fun and games. There were heroic tasks to perform in flooring, plumbing, and heating the whole of Concordia. There were nasty adventures outdoors in the dark polar night. Scientific instruments did not sleep, nor did the cold and ice that caused failures at inopportune moments. There were safety drills, particularly in training for the most dreaded threat to an Antarctic station: fire.

In one scenario, a blaze hypothetically broke out near the wine and liquors in Jean-Louis's food storeroom. The team heard the alarm and responded to the emergency, which included a staged medical crisis as well. "Jean-Louis tried to save a bottle of pastis and hurt himself in the process," reported Guillaume. "We find him laying down, still clutching said bottle. He's forcefully dragged out of the room and away from the 'fire.'"

Among Concordia's continuum of feasts was one celebrating the chef himself, who turned fifty amid the republic of silence. Jean-Louis agreed to have the staff cook a birthday meal for him, but only on the day *after* he cooked one for himself.

His Friday feast started with champagne, followed by "asparagus and smoked salmon toasts, crayfish donuts, pine tree–liquor sorbet, frog legs pie, steak filled with foie gras, and finally a meringue filled with raspberry and chocolate ice cream."

In the Concordia kitchen with Jean-Louis Duraffourg

Saturday's crew-cooked dinner began with a menu portraying Jean-Louis surrounded by his contemporaries: Antarctic dinosaurs. The staff feted their champion chef with champagne and appetizers, kangaroo pâté, cheese-and-walnut pies, scallops, then some wine sorbet made from sweet *vin de paille* before diving back into the dinner with main courses of foil-wrapped red mullet soaked in pastis and lamb loins encrusted with a salted pastry. Sides included artichokes and mashed green beans. Then, to finish, rhubarb ice cream with raspberry sauce.

Soon, miracle of miracles, the sun began to creep over the horizon to shine on this new pinnacle of Antarctic cuisine, while the naïf Roberto prepared on Jean-Louis's day off a chicken creole with vanilla and rum sauce. Anything was possible in the Concordia kitchen.

🐧 the whole romantic tale 🐧

Despite the culinary glories at Concordia, it seems likely that the future of Antarctic cuisine will continue to include leftovers of the storied past. The sheer impossibility of us truly occupying the lunar harshness of Antarctica, and becoming local to it, suggests that our capacity for eating well will be at least partially defined by the ice rather than wholly by our own warm desires. This is, of course, not necessarily a bad thing. There is value in the Antarctic struggle, whether for data or a good meal.

Sir Ernest Shackleton, Pole-seeker and poet of starvation, had (with his ghost writer, Edward Saunders) a talent for writing prose that transmuted hardship on the ice into song on the page. In *South*, he wrote on the pleasures of dispossession: "

Man can sustain life with very scanty means. The trappings of civilization are soon cast aside in the face of stern realities, and given the barest opportunity of winning food and shelter, man can live and even find his laughter ringing true."

Shackleton is gone now, as are his men, his ships, and his era. Little remains of that time but weather-beaten huts turned into shrines by those of us who think we know something about his stern realities. Visitors in parkas enter like hooded monks to marvel at the unadorned kitchens of the huts at Cape Evans and Cape Royds—perhaps unaware that conservators tidied them up years ago and, in search of a heroic-age ideal, redecorated shelves with a cute sampling of appealing foodstuffs found on site, like Bird's Egg Powder and Moir's Lunch Tongue. The evocative but artificial aesthetic helps us forget as much as remember. It's the classic problem of a museum trying to represent reality.

This was particularly true for Shackleton's whisky. In early 2010, conservators from the Antarctic Heritage Trust (AHT) were shocked to find three cases of Mackinlay's Rare Old Highland Malt Whisky, circa 1897 (and two of Hunter Valley Brandy from Australia) long embedded in ice beneath floorboards of the *Nimrod* expedition hut at Cape Royds. One case of the whisky was flown to New Zealand for meticulous thawing and preservation, and then, a year later, three bottles were sent by private jet to Whyte & Mackay (today's owners of the Mackinlay's brand) in Scotland for sampling. Those samples were extracted by syringe under full laboratory conditions and tested by "gas chromatography (CG), mass spectrometry, and CG olfactory analysis of fermentation-related congeners" before being nosed, tasted, and deconstructed by the Scottish distillers for a re-creation of a century-old lost recipe to be marketed in the glow of Shackleton's reputation. The character of the whisky, Whyte & Mackay discovered, was "surprisingly light and complex," less peaty and more modern than expected. (Full disclosure: I've drunk quite a bit of it. It's good.)

Weirdly, those three bottles were returned to the case, and the case was returned to Cape Royds to rejoin the others out of sight beneath the floorboards of the hushed altar the hut has become. A British official described the process as part of the "whole romantic tale" of Antarctic exploration.

The AHT, working under the aegis of the Antarctic Treaty, defines conservation as "the means by which the true nature of an object is preserved," yet in this case the true nature of the whisky seems to be symbolic. Great sums of money have been spent to preserve an austerity that Shackleton's men would scarcely recognize. If food and drink of that time have symbolic value, it is in the grateful and ravenous eating and drinking of it. I'm convinced that, rather than maintaining a cold museum with whisky hidden primly beneath the floor, the AHT should hire an actor in the guise of grumpy *Nimrod* cook William Roberts to serve tinned foods and whisky to tourists who have done four hours of chores outside the hut at −20°F.

Despite the curating of symbols and the telling of romantic tales, however, the old Antarctica is not entirely gone. Even snail-fed French Antarcticans honor the past by cooking survival rations on La Fête du Travail. Faint echoes of the heroic age are heard in every Antarctic program during every Antarctic season. Weather and geography have not changed, after all. Freshies freeze and storms sweep in. Tents shake and pasta overcooks. But beyond the occasional culinary *weltschmerz*, boomerang flights, and the shivers of otherwise comfortable twenty-first-century campers, there has been one place on the continent that still takes old-timey hardship for granted: Vostok Station.

I was lucky enough to visit Vostok, the rarest and coldest of Antarctic destinations, in January of 2000.

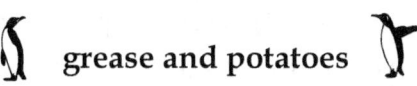

grease and potatoes

In 1997, Vostok unofficially bested its record temperature

of –128.6°F with an observation of –132°F. In 1963, a Vostok winter was described as so cold that "steel can shatter like glass, petrol can extinguish fire like water, and diesel fuel can be cut with a saw." It is also the most isolated base on the continent, a situation made worse over the last half century by a dearth of resources in Russia.

Until very recently, Vostok has been, to put it mildly, poorly funded. It was built in 1957, during the IGY, and scarcely updated over the next sixty years. Only three hundred fifty miles away from Concordia, the simple wooden facility bore little resemblance to the space-age elevated station fed on Perrier and kangaroo pâté.

But worn-out architecture has not meant poor food. Charles Swithinbank, passing through Vostok in 1963, thought the food was particularly good, a bonus for the intensely hard duty. For Bob Dale, an Antarctic veteran who was on the ice from 1959 to 1975, the Vostok diet seemed excellent. But he only sampled it during feasts given to American dignitaries, which featured lots of smoked salmon and caviar. "I was pretty sure they didn't eat like that often," he said, "but I never saw what they normally ate."

Exchange scientist Robert Flint did see what they normally ate when he wintered at Vostok in 1974. "In Russian fashion, it was quite plain for every day," he told me, "but truly outstanding for holidays and special occasions." His hosts fed him plenty of soups and stews made from slabs of Australian beef and canned vegetables, while he entertained them with his rudimentary Russian vocabulary. The Vostochniki (Vostok winter personnel) liked to pass around a clove of garlic from which each man could cut a thin slice for his soup. In a hilarious slip with dark echoes in Antarctic cuisine, Flint asked for someone to please pass the garlic, but "this was followed with peals of laughter. Instead of garlic (*chesnok*), I had said 'Please pass the puppy dog (*schenok*)!'" Some Sunday suppers featured "very satisfying" *oladi*, thick pancakes served with marmalade. Flint was particularly fond of the pickled herring served with cold peas, potatoes, and onions. Nearly forty years later, he said, "I still dream of it."

But the collapse of the Soviet Union made Russian Antarctic life even more austere. In 1990, Will Steger's expedition had their food dreams realized when the men of Vostok feted them with caviar, fruit, and champagne, but a U.S. scientist working at Vostok in 1990 described the daily meals as terrible, all potatoes and vodka. Meals apparently lasted just ten minutes. I'm reminded of the tasteless tinned dinners on Carsten Borchgrevink's *Southern Cross* expedition at Cape Adare in 1899, choked down quickly for sustenance and then abandoned.

Several years after Steger's visit, staff at Vostok was cut in half due to reductions in the Russian Antarctic program. The great tractor-train supply traverses from Mirnyy were limited to one per year.

All food and fuel necessary for winter survival had to come in on that single nine-hundred-mile journey, but the huge Russian World War II–era tractors, with bunks and kitchen inside, often broke down. When a 1995 summer convoy halted due to severe mechanical failure, Vostok closed for the winter and the USAP was asked to fly out Russian personnel.

By the summer of 1999–2000, fuel flights from McMurdo to Vostok were no longer unusual, and I got my chance to go. I felt like I'd won the lottery. No one travels to Vostok with a guidebook in their pocket. No one parades off a plane to *Ooh* and *Ahh* at the Russians' Cold War–era space station. It remains a strictly functional, if distant and tenuous, node in an aging empire's scientific network.

On January 26, 2000, I boarded the Herc with a dozen Russian Vostochniki, their bags, and two large air force pallets stacked with two tons of frozen home fries. Piled on top was a garnish of fresh potatoes, carrots, garlic, onions, and a few days' worth of fruit. These Vostochniki, fresh from the world, were about to winter under brutal conditions, not least of which was their cuisine for the next year: grease and potatoes, night in and night out.

Also on board the Herc were a few other Americans, including an administrator named Jim, a doctor sent to consult on a very ill Russian, and my friend Lena. Lena was bilingual and had been pulled from her job as a science tech to translate for the doctor.

My job upon arrival at Vostok was to help with the transfer of much-needed fuel from the Herc into the station's near-empty tanks. Without fuel, I had been told, the Russians would have to abandon the base. If I had time after the fuel offload, I might have a few minutes to run over to the base to look around. A fuelie who took an earlier trip had started his run to the station when the flight crew called him back to load up and sit down. All he saw of Vostok was the skiway.

But on the ground in McMurdo, I found myself in an ethical quandary. As I boarded, I was told by the Herc's loadmaster that this mission was for cargo only and would offload no fuel. I thought this was strange, as Vostok's fuel needs were critical.

I stood there hemming and hawing over whether I should

jump off the plane and get back to work in town.

The loadmaster solved the crisis for me when, over the growing roar of the turboprop engines, he came back and shouted a request: "We won't deliver any fuel, but there's a chance we'll want you to help us *take* fuel from the Russians!"

I looked at him as if he'd told me he hoped to squeeze blood from a snowball. This crew was new to the Antarctic, and they were unclear on the realities at Vostok. Although I explained to him in loud pantomime that we had neither the hardware nor the desire to suck up the dregs of Vostok's tanks and that the Russians couldn't afford to give it away, he remained unconvinced. He was the confused messenger with a confused message.

Sensing my opportunity, I decided my duty lay in preventing the aircrew from damaging their engines with unavailable bad fuel. Nodding to the loadmaster, I quickly sat down, put in my earplugs, and buckled up for my little adventure.

The faces of the Russians reminded me of stark American Civil War portraits staring out from sepia photos: carved and rugged, dark and impassive. Yet these were the men who had not yet spent their year on the ice; I wondered what the men we would bring back, those finishing their year, would look like. Then again, the lines on my companions' faces may have been from jetlag, since they had flown from St. Petersburg to Amsterdam to Singapore to Sydney to Christchurch to McMurdo on an epic one-way ticket.

By the time the Herc rose over the Transantarctic Mountains, most of our guests seemed to be asleep. Vostok's winter station manager, however, kept his eyes open, staring at the pale-green insulation lining the fuselage. His responsibility for the next year was to keep all twelve men safe and sane. Wintering in central Antarctica has always been considered a hardship duty *in extremis*. Even some winters at the comfortable South Pole Station have ended with a once-joyful community split into enraged factions. How much worse would it be within the thinner walls and deeper cold of a Vostok winter?

For three hours, we droned across part of an ice sheet the size of China, time zones passing beneath us like crevasses, until suddenly out of the endless snowy expanse a small speck appeared like a blister in East Antarctica's alabaster skin. We stepped out into −30°F air, 60 degrees colder than McMurdo. It felt like we'd landed in the clouds just below the jet stream. Around the extra-long skiway—necessary to build up speed for lift-off in thin air—was perfect whiteness under a perfect blue bell jar of sky. Breaking up the emptiness were an immense tower and the "BOCTOK" sign at its foot. Each seven-foot-high Cyrillic letter (red, of course) stood alone, like the Hollywood sign. The station itself lay hidden behind a rise built of years of plowed-out snow.

Lena and the doctor rushed off to find their patient. The rest of us pushed cargo pallets of home fries and baggage out of the plane by hand because Vostok's forklift had broken down. Then their thirty-year-old snowmobile began to ferry loads to the base.

One Russian arrival, with nothing before him but the fringe of the half-buried outpost, pulled off his hat, pulled out a pocket mirror, and checked his mussed black hair. I was reminded of the final moments of the *Endurance* journey, in which the haggard Shackleton, Crean, and Worsley, having arrived at Stromness whaling station after seventeen horrendous months, began to fuss with soot-caked hair and ragged clothes. Their concern was that there might be women. Here at Vostok, this was unlikely. There was only Lena, and only for a few minutes. Women have on occasion done summer science here, but no woman has ever wintered.

Once I confirmed that the Herc crew would not offload or, God forbid, try to take fuel, I set off over the white rise. Mostly submerged by accumulating snow, the station's several old, small buildings were sun-bleached and rusting. Slumped-over tracked vehicles littered the outskirts. Vostok, the world-class research outpost of an intellectual nation, had the hollow look of poverty. I can't say that Vostok felt more isolated than other camps — one raft in the ocean feels like any other — but the tenuous barrier this facility maintains against the cold unsettled my American mind.

Pushing through heavy wooden doors into the small, dark common room of the main building, I stepped into another world. Vostok's arriving and departing residents were gathered around an old billiards table, smoking their raw Russian cigarettes and talking quietly. They sat in dense smoke that had seeped into cracks in the billiard balls where it left a stain the color of dead grass.

The men about to leave with us, finishing their yearlong stint, seemed to laugh more easily than those arriving. In the U.S. program, the opposite is true. We arrive cheerful and energetic and leave pale and tired. Here at Vostok, the beginning of a harsh stint in an anteroom to deep space must bring a level of apprehension that participants in the U.S. program cannot fathom. These men still drop off the face of the Earth while we happily flirt with the edge.

When Lena entered after translating the doctor's

consultation, she was well attended but not harassed. Her language skills and beauty were the center of attention. Though the Russians were calm, it was interesting to observe their desire to speak with her. Some had not seen a woman for a year or more, and the others had that fate before them. Lena said later that they did not talk much of themselves but wanted to know about her. What I noticed was the occasional glance, or pause in their step, around Lena. What weight such a glance may carry, the last some of the men had of the warm world before slipping into the long Antarctic night.

Lena told me later that one of the men had boasted of his monthly salary to her, far higher than he could hope to find at home. When he asked Lena if she made good money too, she demurred. She had the compassion not to tell him that, as a young science tech on a U.S. government-funded aerogeophysical project, she earned his monthly salary in a week.

Murmured Russian syllables followed me into the empty dining room, presumably the same room in which Bob Thomson and his traverse crew had eaten their flash-frozen steaks in 1962. Spare and plain, the room was clearly Vostok's heart, a repository of culture and simple food so old that it seemed a survivor of ice ages and continental drift.

Years of smoke and grease had browned the high pale-yellow ceiling. Much of the paint on the yellow walls had long ago flaked off, and beneath it an older icy blue spread like frost, as if the snow outside the windows had seeped through.

Sepia light slanted through the left wall's dirty windows. Small framed paintings and photos, mostly rural and tropical scenes, gave a tilted hope to the worn room, while a dark polished grandfather clock stood ticking in the far corner. A pull-down movie screen hung empty.

Just then, USAP administrator Jim stepped in for a moment to say with awe that the room looked exactly as it did during his last visit, twenty-two years earlier, except that Stalin's portrait had come down. Perhaps it had been replaced with the large black-and-white photo of a pair of emperor penguins, which, even after a year in Antarctica, these Russians will never see. Vostok is farther from penguins than most American citizens are from the nearest zoo that puts them on display.

Withered herbs in window boxes stood silhouetted against the snow. In the dusty light, a mound of boiled eggs glistened in a large bowl like dabs of white paint. Six scuffed dark tables each held slabs of black bread, a brick of yellow butter, and a plate of sliced pink salami. On the sideboard, a massive cutting board and heavy cleaver wore the deep scars of the labor, hunger, anger, and celebrations of men living difficult, cloistered lives.

I'd walked into a Russian still life that seemed to breathe in its dark frame. A transient, I was still bundled up in my parka as I shuffled between the modest invitations on the dining tables. The strangeness of entering another culture in central Antarctica was dreamlike, in that I walked in from the palpable center of nowhere and found a stained wooden kitchen extracted from the pages of Solzhenitsyn.

The cook, with a blue-and-white broad-striped shirt and a broader smile, walked in from the kitchen to offer me tea. His arms were open, with a cup in one hand.

"Tea, for you?" he said (I think), in Russian.

"No, no, I'm just — I'm looking around. I — no, thank you," I said, lost in my thoughts.

A shrug and another smile said, "As you wish."

To this day, I wish I had accepted.

He was the only Russian at the camp I spoke with, and it lasted just a few seconds. I paused in my bustling exploration — so much to see, a mental map to make — to consider his kindness, then retreated to spend my last twenty minutes outside, taking bleak photos of old vehicles and the battle between utility and entropy. I wanted to frame Vostok's strangeness, as if I were the empty Antarctic.

Even as I clicked off my roll of film, I knew I should have sat with the friendly cook to sip some tea, eat an egg, and slab some butter onto the local dark bread. I had tried to see this strange place from the outside rather than taking the time to *taste* it.

Soon it was time to go. I trudged back to the plane and loaded up with the departing Russians as they began their descent into the warm latitudes. Onboard was the very pale patient and two silent men playing chess so rapidly it was obvious they had battled daily through their stark year of dark months and white months. The small magnetic board passed back and forth between them like a plate of endless hors d'oeuvres.

A year later I learned that the Russians we dropped off at Vostok emerged from the type of overwintering experience that should have ended a century ago with Shackleton. They had not received enough fuel to sustain them through the winter.

Distant Russian authorities in St. Petersburg had requested from the USAP a delivery of less than five thousand gallons, much less than Vostok needed. (South Pole burns that much fuel in five winter days.) It's possible these men suffered needlessly because my flight brought them no fuel.

The story goes that the dozen underpaid men spent the winter with the heat kept low. They used fewer rooms and those rooms were cold. They had a hard time, even by Vostok standards, with a thinner safety margin and no options for rescue. The station still ran on an old one-lung generator, coughing along through the blue-black winter months.

This was not the first heroic-age-type winter the Vostochniki have suffered. In April of 1982, a fire in the power plant killed one man and left the rest of the community without light or heat.

Only by restarting an old, discarded diesel generator they excavated from the snow did they get power again. "Their only heat," writes Jeff Rubin, "came from candle-like warmers they made by twisting asbestos fibers into wicks that they dipped in diesel fuel." For eight months, all twenty survivors lived like this in a single hut. They left the hut every day to do their jobs, too.

From my reading, I know of no similar winter experiences in Antarctica since the advance party of Fuchs and Hillary's 1956 Commonwealth Trans-Antarctic Expedition lived in their Sno-Cat crate. There has *never* been a winter like it in the USAP. We don't even imagine hardship like this anymore.

But finally, in 2024, the time came for Vostok to enter the twenty-first century. Funding for the Russian program increased again, and after decades of neglect, the station was entirely reborn.

Five large space-age modules were built in Russia before being disassembled and shipped to the ice. Vostok now resembles the new Pole and Concordia stations, with vibrant blue modules perched up on posts to let the ancient sweep of windblown snow pass underneath. Perhaps in response to the incredibly difficult winters that Vostochniki have experienced, the long-term strategy for the facility includes maintaining a two-year supply of fuel and food.

I do not know what will be carried up into the new station from the old dining room, whether the grandfather clock, scuffed tables, worn cutting board, and cleaver will make the transition to a brighter, shinier kitchen.

But I'm confident that the dark bread, pink salami, yellow butter, and black tea will be there, and that a generous cook will be there to share it.

EPILOGUE:
Not Under These Conditions

Ernest Shackleton told Frank Worsley, while crossing South Georgia at the climax of the *Endurance* saga, that he would never lead another expedition. But Antarctica had him in its thrall. "One gets the fever and can't stop going," he said, and later formed the *Quest* expedition. Frank Wild, second-in-command of the *Quest*, talked of the "little voices" that called him back to Antarctica. Other *Endurance* men had jumped at the chance to be with Shackleton again in the dangerous enchantments of the south, despite all they had suffered.

The mystical draw of the ice has always drawn us back. Axel Andersson, beleaguered cook of the 1901–4 Swedish Antarctic Expedition, was spotted by his old comrade Carl Skottsberg in the kitchen of a South Georgia whaling station just five years later. Julian's great-grandfather William Colbeck and his friend Louis Bernacchi swore off exploring after living a year with the insufferable Borchgrevink, but were back soon after.

I've been told that the Russians have a simple explanatory aphorism for the phenomenon: "Antarctica is not a place; it is a disease." Perhaps Raymond Priestley, survivor of the Northern Party ordeal, had the answer: "Half the fascination an Antarctic expedition possesses is to be found in the sharpness of the contrasts experienced during its course, for it appears to be true that a hell one day is liable to make a heaven the next."

Julian and I are part of the century of the enchanted. We returned to the ice over and over, long after family and friends wondered why, and long after the pats on the back that accompanied the usual comment: "Well, you might as well adventure while you're still young." Years passed, youth passed, as we stretched out that phase of our lives we may never truly leave behind.

Even now, when we're not on the ice, it informs our sense of what is real, what is difficult, what is beautiful. Antarctica defines us, because unlike any other time or place we have known, there is an otherworldly silence in the landscape, an unearthly depth to the horizons, and a somehow spiritual life in that absence of life. Antarcticans have generally been more interested in a warm drink or a good penguin breast than in God, but the ice continent is a mystical space and we love it, hunger for it.

In a final Odell adventure, Julian and I made a covert trip by snowmobile twenty-two miles to Trinity Nunatak, a sharp peak overlooking the mighty Mawson Glacier. Up on the summit, Julian broke out a hunger-inducing dice-like game called Pass the Pigs while I found a large piece of crusted snow to serve as a picnic table. The satellite phone sat nearby, as we waited for a call that would let us know if we were leaving as planned or staying an additional two weeks.

For some reason, neither of us could shake the image of a heroic-age sledging party manhauling their way up the heavily crevassed glacier below. Perhaps it was some combination of our godlike view of the Mawson and a growing sense of nostalgia for our Odell experience, but as we sat there munching on chocolate and drinking melted snow, we had one of those epiphanies particular to Antarctic fieldwork: All that exists in Antarctica is an abstract landscape of extraordinary beauty, a short yet remarkable human history, and a few inhabitants with a deep sense of wonder that they should be part of both.

For Julian and me, Antarctica imbued our ridiculous, unnecessary expedition with a grace and beauty that has left us, wherever we go in the world, hungry for that sense of belonging to a landscape that can swallow us up.

The greatest Antarctic deprivation we have ever experienced came not on the ice but after our departure from it. Antarctica is the great white menu, a blank list of options that feeds us only to make us hungrier for its beauty later on, when we're at home and bereft.

"Was there ever such heartbreaking work?" asked Gerald Cutland (another borrowed line from Stephen Lister) in *Fit for a FID*. "Who would be a cook?" Hours are spent toiling for results that are, as he wrote, "destroyed in an hour and forgotten in less." The monuments to a cook's labor disappear with little fanfare, and in Antarctica the work is harder, the result less monumental, and the fanfare less than adequate.

Thus, when at the end of the summer Julian and I flew back to McMurdo sunburned, happy, and cold, I presented Rob the baker with gifts of wind-carved rocks and stories of gales and meteorites and fossil leaves asleep under walls of ice. I also took the time to tell him he was a most excellent baker. He replied archly, "Yes, I am, but I'm an even better chef." I asked him why then, summer after Antarctic summer, he had signed on only as a baker or greenhouse tech. "Oh, he said. "I would never bother to cook under these conditions."

Acknowledgements

First to Heather, a better friend and companion than I can say. Thank you.

Among my many sources, I'm grateful especially to Julian Ridley, a fine friend to have at the end of the Earth; Jeff Rubin, for his generosity and expertise on all fronts; Nicholas Johnson, a hell of a writer and even better company; Michèle Gentille and Guillaume Dargaud, for the use of their remarkable blogs; Deb Baldwin, Karen Joyce, and Jim Mastro, for the gift of their great stories; Rupert Summerson, for sharing his intellect, aesthetics, and tales; Michael Robinson, for the support of an actual historian; Sally Ayotte and James Brown, for patiently answering lots of questions; Marjory Spoerri for showing up out of the blue with good information and great biscuit recipes; Roland Huntford, for his timely expertise; Lynne Olver at the Food Timeline, for her universal culinary knowledge; David Walton of Bluntisham Books and Crispin de Boos of Erskine Press for their devotion to Antarctic literature; and Charles Swithinbank, for a remarkable Antarctic life well-lived and well-told.

Other Antarctic sources and friends I am indebted to: Rob Taylor, Danielli Spears, Deb Lisman Smith, Mike Dixon, Dave Weber, Bob Dale, Steve Dunbar, Joe Kujawski, Kathy Blumm, Steve Kupecz, John Behrendt, Rune Gjeldnes, Robert Flint, Colin Monteath, Bill Spindler, Will Steger, Elaine Hood at Raytheon Polar Services, Sue Shephard of *Pickled, Potted, and Canned*, Paul Dalrymple and Charles Lagerbom of the Antarctican Society, Liz Brenna at Ben & Jerry's, various helpful souls at the New Zealand Antarctic Heritage Trust, Paul Ward of Cool Antarctica, Keith Holmes and David Simmons of the BAS Club, and staff at the British Antarctic Survey. If I've missed anyone, please forgive me.

The book would have been impossible without such support. Here at home, thanks also to Maureen Stanton for her writerly advice.

Images have been provided by the Royal Geographical Society, the National Science Foundation, the National Library of Australia, the Norwegian National Library, the Australian Antarctic Division, the New Zealand Antarctic Heritage Trust, the Byrd Polar Research Center, Carleton College, Crispin de Boos at Erskine Press, Seth White, Guillaume Dargaud, and David Simmons.

Thanks to the Archives and Special Collections Departments at the Queen Elizabeth II library at Memorial University in St. John's, Newfoundland, for the rare joy of looking through Victor Campbell's Northern Party diary. Thanks also to the Maine State Library and particularly to the staff at Skidompha Library in Damariscotta, Maine, for their assistance in the magical process of the interlibrary loan.

The essay that formed the seed for this book was first published in *Alimentum: The Literature of Food*. Other personal narratives excerpted and adapted for *The Roast Penguin Chronicles* were first published in *The Best American Travel Writing 2007, Antarctica: Life on the Ice* (edited by Susan Fox Rogers), *The Missouri Review, Virginia Quarterly Review*, and online in *The Smart Set, Endeavor*, and *World Hum*.

Finally, I'm grateful to Bob Mrazek of Compass Rose Publishing (among other claims to fame) for his friendship, his longstanding support of my work, and for his interest in giving this book another shot. Thanks also to James Bock, Thomas Hurd, and Diane Kane at Compass Rose for their hard work and high ambitions. I'm honored to be part of the Compass Rose story.

Author

Jason C. Anthony is the author of the Field Guide to the Anthropocene, a weekly Substack essay and newsletter exploring the transformed Earth. Among his awards, he was the 2014 Literary Fellow for Maine and a 2015 Macdowell Fellow. His essays have appeared in Orion, VQR, The Missouri Review, and in the Best American Travel Writing 2007. He lives and writes in Maine, "that state of grace wedged between the U.S. and Canada."

Photo Credits

PROLOGUE (Page 1) Herbert George Ponting/The Library of Congress

CHAPTER ONE (Page-12) © RGS-IBG
CHAPTER ONE (Page-19) from Amundsen, *The South Pole*
CHAPTER ONE (Page-31) © RGS-IBG

CHAPTER TWO (Page-37) courtesy of Erskine Press
CHAPTER TWO (Page-42) Herbert George Ponting/The Library of Congress
CHAPTER TWO (Page-45) © RGS-IBG
CHAPTER TWO (Page-49) from Amundsen, *The South Pole*
CHAPTER TWO (Page-56) Xavier Mertz, from the State Library of New South Wales
CHAPTER TWO (Page-66) courtesy of the Norwegian National Library

CHAPTER THREE (Page-68) Frank Wild, courtesy of the National Library of Australia
CHAPTER THREE (Page-79) the Frederick A. Cook Society

CHAPTER FOUR (Page-117) © RGS-IBG
CHAPTER FOUR (Page-123) UPI/Bettman, public domain
CHAPTER FOUR (Page-125) © RGS-IBG
CHAPTER FOUR (Page-131) State Library of South Australia
CHAPTER FOUR (Page-137) from Amundsen, *The South Pole*

CHAPTER FIVE (Page-146) from the papers of Admiral Richard E. Byrd, courtesy of the Byrd Polar Research Center Archival Program.
CHAPTER FIVE (Page-177) courtesy of David Simmons

CHAPTER SIX (Page-191) author photo

CHAPTER SEVEN (Page-214) © RGS-IBG

CHAPTER EIGHT (Page-248) Ralph Maestas, courtesy of the National Science Foundation

Selected Bibliography

Alexander, Caroline. *The Endurance: Shackleton's Legendary Antarctic Expedition*. New York: Alfred A. Knopf, 1999.

Amundsen, Roald. *Belgica Diary*. Huntingdon, UK: Bluntisham Books and Erskine Press, 1999.

My Life as an Explorer. Gloucestershire: Amberley, 2008.

The South Pole: An Account of the Norwegian Antarctic Expedition in the Fram, *1910–1912*. Translated by A. G. Chater. New York: Cooper Square Press, 2001.

Anthony, Jason. "AGO 1." In *Antarctica: Life on the Ice*, edited by Susan Fox Rogers. Palo Alto: Solas House, 2007.

"A Brief and Awkward Tour of the End of the Earth." In *The Best American Travel Writing 2007*, edited by Susan Orlean. Boston: Houghton Mifflin, 2007. First published online at www.WorldHum.com.

"The Heartless Immensity." *Virginia Quarterly Review* 85, no. 2 (Spring 2009).

"Hoosh." *Alimentum: The Literature of Food* 5 (Winter 2008).

"The Importance of Eating Local: Slaughter and Scurvy in Antarctic Cuisine." *Endeavour* 35, no. 4 (December 2011): 169–77. http://www.sciencedirect.com/science/journal/01609327.

"Seismic Center." *The Smart Set*, December 14, 2007. http://www.thesmartset.com.

"The Song of Hypothermia." *The Missouri Review* 28, no. 2 (Fall 2005).

Bagshawe, Thomas Wyatt. *Two Men in the Antarctic: An Expedition to Graham Land 1920–1922*. Cambridge: Cambridge University Press, 1939.

Barber, Noel. *The White Desert*. New York: Thomas Y. Crowell, 1958.

Behrendt, John C. *Innocents on the Ice: A Memoir of Antarctic Exploration, 1957.* Niwot: University Press of Colorado, 1998.

The Ninth Circle: A Memoir of Life and Death in Antarctica, 1960–1962. Albuquerque: University of New Mexico Press, 2005.

Belanger, Dian Olson. *Deep Freeze: The United States, the International Geophysical Year, and the Origins of Antarctica's Age of Science.* Boulder: University Press of Colorado, 2006.

Bickel, Lennard. *Shackleton's Forgotten Men*. New York: Thunder's Mouth Press, 2000.

Mawson's Will: The Greatest Polar Survival Story Ever Written. Hanover, NH: Steerforth Press, 2000.

Bonington, Chris. *Quest for Adventure*. London: Book Club Associates, 1982.

Borchgrevink, C. E. *First on the Antarctic Continent: Being an Account of the British Antarctic Expedition, 1898–1900.* London: George Newnes, 1901.

Bowden, Tim. *The Silence Calling: Australians in Antarctica, 1947–97.* St. Leonards NSW, Australia: Allen and Unwin, 1997.

Brown, R. N. Rudmose, R. C. Mossman, and J. H. Harvey Pirie. *The Voyage of the "Scotia": Being the Record of a Voyage of Exploration in Antarctic Seas by Three of the Staff.* Edinburgh: William Blackwood and Sons, 1906.

Burke, David. *Moments of Terror: The Story of Antarctic Aviation.* Kensington NSW, Australia: New South Wales University Press, 1994.

Byrd, Richard Evelyn. *Alone*. Covelo CA: Island Press, 1984.

Discovery: The Story of the Second Byrd Antarctic Expedition. New York: G. P. Putnam's Sons, 1935.

Campbell, David G. *The Crystal Desert: Summers in Antarctica.* Boston: Houghton Mifflin, 1992.

Campbell, Victor. *The Wicked Mate: The Antarctic Diary of Victor Campbell.* Edited by H. G. R. King. Huntingdon, UK: Bluntisham Books, 1988.

Carpenter, Kenneth J. *The History of Scurvy and Vitamin C.* Cambridge: Cambridge University Press, 1986.

Charcot, Jean-Baptiste. *Towards the South Pole Aboard the* Francais: *The First French Expedition to the Antarctic, 1903–1905.* Translated by A. W. Billinghurst. Huntingdon, UK: Bluntisham Books, 2004.

The Voyage of the Why Not? *in the Antarctic: The Journal of the Second French South Polar Expedition, 1908–1910.* Translated by Philip Walsh. London: Hodder and Stoughton, 1911.

Cherry-Garrard, Apsley. *The Worst Journey in the World.* London: Picador, 1994.

Cook, Frederick. *Through the First Antarctic Night, 1898–1899: A Narrative of the Voyage of the* Belgica *among Newly Discovered Lands and over an Unknown Sea about the South Pole.* New York: Doubleday and McClure, 1900.

Crawford, Janet. *That First Antarctic Winter: The Story of the Southern Cross Expedition of 1898–1900, As Told in the Diaries of Louis Charles Bernacchi.* Christchurch, NZ: South Latitude Research, 1998.

Cutland, Gerald T. *Fit for a FID: Or, How to Keep a Fat Explorer in Prime Condition.* Usk, UK: United Kingdom Antarctic Heritage Trust, 2010. Courtesy of the British Antarctic Survey, Crown Copyright 1957.

Darlington, Jennie. *My Antarctic Honeymoon: A Year at the Bottom of the World.* As told to Jane McIlvaine. Garden City NJ: Doubleday, 1957.

Davis, John King. *With the* Aurora *in the Antarctic.* Huntingdon, UK: Bluntisham Books, 2007.

Dayton, P. K., and G. A. Robilliard. "Implications of Pollution to the McMurdo Sound Benthos." *Antarctic Journal of the United States* 8, no. 3 (1971): 53–56.

Decleir, Hugo, and Claude De Broyer, ed. "The Belgica Expedition Centennial: Perspectives on Antarctic Science and History." Proceedings of the *Belgica* Centennial Symposium, May 14–16, 1998. Brussels: VUB Brussels University Press, 2002.

Drygalski, Erich von. *The Southern Ice Continent. The German South Polar Expedition aboard the* Gauss *1901–1903*. Huntingdon, UK: Bluntisham Books and Erskine Press, 1989.

Dufek, Admiral George J. *Through the Frozen Frontier: The Exploration of Antarctica*. Leicester, UK: Brockhampton, 1960.

Ellsworth, Lincoln. *Beyond Horizons*. New York: Book League of America, 1938.

Feeney, Robert E. *Polar Journeys: The Role of Food and Nutrition in Early Exploration*. Washington DC and Fairbanks AK: American Chemical Society, 1997.

Fiennes, Ranulph. *Mind over Matter*. New York: Delacorte Press, 1993.

Race to the Pole: Tragedy, Heroism, and Scott's Antarctic Quest. New York: Hyperion, 2004.

To the Ends of the Earth. New York: Arbor House, 1983.

Filchner, Wilhelm. *To the Sixth Continent: The Second German South Polar Expedition 1911–1912*. Edited and translated by William Barr. Huntingdon, UK: Bluntisham Books and Erskine Press, 1994.
Fuchs, Sir Vivian, and Sir Edmund Hillary. *The Crossing of Antarctica*. Boston: Little, Brown, 1958.

Gerlache, Adrien de. *Voyage of the* Belgica: *Fifteen Months in the Antarctic*. Translated by Maurice Raraty. Huntingdon, UK: Bluntisham Books and Erskine Press, 1998.

Giaever, John. *The White Desert: The Official Account of the Norwegian-British-Swedish Antarctic Expedition*. London: Chatto and Windus, 1954.

Gordon, Joanne. *Be Happy at Work: 100 Women Who Love Their Jobs, and Why*. New York: Ballantine Books, 2005.

Gould, Laurence. *Cold: The Record of an Antarctic Sledge Journey*. Northfield MN: Carleton College, 1984.

Gran, Tryggve. *The Norwegian with Scott: Tryggve Gran's Antarctic Diary 1910–1913*. London: HMSO Books, 1984.

Green, Bill. *Water, Ice, and Stone: Science and Memory on the Antarctic Lakes.* New York: Harmony Books, 1995.

Griffiths, Tom. *Slicing the Silence: Voyaging to Antarctica.* Cambridge MA: Harvard University Press, 2007.

Halsey, Lewis George, and Mike Adrian Stroud. "Could Scott Have Survived with Today's Physiological Knowledge?" *Current Biology* 21, no. 12 (June 2011): r457-r461.

Hamre, Ivar. "The Japanese South Polar Expedition of 1911–1912: A Little-Known Episode in Antarctic Exploration." *Geographical Journal* 82, no. 5 (November 1933).

Harrowfield, David. *The Tip of the Iceberg.* Christchurch, NZ: South Latitude Research, 1995.

Helm, A. S., and J. H. Miller. *Antarctica: The Story of the New Zealand Party of the Trans-Antarctic Expedition.* Wellington: R. E. Owen, New Zealand Government Printer, 1964.

Hillary, Sir Edmund. *No Latitude for Error.* New York: E.P. Dutton, 1961.

Hooper, Meredith. *The Longest Winter: Scott's Other Heroes.* London: John Murray, 2010.

Huntford, Roland. *The Last Place on Earth.* New York: Atheneum, 1985.

Shackleton. New York: Carroll and Graf, 1985.

Hurley, Frank. *Shackleton's Argonauts: A Saga of the Antarctic Ice-Packs.* Sydney: Angus and Robertson, 1948.

International Tin Research and Development Council. *Historic Tinned Foods.* 2nd ed. Middlesex, UK: International Tin Research and Development Council, 1939.

Johnson, Nicholas. *Big Dead Place: Inside the Strange and Menacing World of Antarctica.* Los Angeles: Feral House, 2005.

Jones, A. G. E. *Polar Portraits: Collected Papers.* Whitby, UK: Caedmon of Whitby, 1992.

Joyce, Ernest E. Mills. *The South Polar Trail: The Log of the Imperial Trans-Antarctic Expedition.* London: G. Duckworth, 1929.

Joyce, Karen. "My Continent, My Concubine." Unpublished manuscript, n.d., ca. 2000.

"The Day It Rained Chickens." In *Antarctica: Life on the Ice,* edited by Susan Fox Rogers. Palo Alto: Solas House, 2007.

"Snow Job." Unpublished manuscript, n.d., ca. 2000.

"The Winter of My Discount Tent." Unpublished manuscript, n.d., ca. 2000.

Knight, Stephen. *Icebound: The Greenpeace Expedition to Antarctica.* Auckland: Century Hutchinson, 1988.

Lansing, Alfred. *Endurance: Shackleton's Incredible Voyage.* New York: McGraw-Hill, 1959.

Laseron, Charles, and Frank Hurley. *Antarctic Eyewitness: Charles F. Laseron's* South with Mawson *and Frank Hurley's* Shackleton's Argonauts. Sydney: Angus and Robertson, 1999.

Legler, Gretchen. *On the Ice: An Intimate Portrait of Life at McMurdo Station, Antarctica.* Minneapolis: Milkweed Editions, 2005.

Lehman, Mark. "Food for Thought, Foods as Fuel." In *Antarctica: Life On the Ice,* edited by Susan Fox Rogers. Palo Alto: Solas House, 2007.

Lister, Stephen. *Fit for a Bishop; or, How to Keep a Fat Priest in Prime Condition.* London: Peter Davies, 1955.

Long, John. *Mountains of Madness: A Scientist's Odyssey in Antarctica.* Washington DC: Joseph Henry Press, 2001.

Macnamara, Traci. "LC-130." *Isotope: A Journal of Literary Nature and Science Writing* 6, no. 2 (Fall/Winter 2008).

Marr, James W. S. *Into the Frozen South.* London: Cassell, 1923.
Mastro, Jim. *Antarctica: A Year at the Bottom of the World.* Boston: Bulfinch Press, 2002.

Mawson, Douglas. *The Home of the Blizzard: A True Story of Antarctic Survival.* New York: St. Martin's Press, 1999.

Muir, A. L. "Ketonuria in the Antarctic: A Preliminary Study." *British Antarctic Survey Bulletin* no. 20 (1969): 53–58.

Murdoch, W. G. Burn. *From Edinburgh to the Antarctic: An Artist's Notes and Sketches during the Dundee Antarctic Expedition of 1892–93.* London: Longmans, Green, 1894.

Nearing, Helen. *Simple Food for the Good Life.* Walpole NH: Stillpoint Publishing, 1980.

Nordenskjold, N. Otto G., and John Gunnar Andersson. *Antarctica, Or Two Years Amongst the Ice of the South Pole.* London: Hurst and Blackett, 1905.

Orr, N. W. M. "Food Requirements and Weight Changes of Men on Antarctic Expeditions." *British Journal of Nutrition* 19 (1965): 71–91.

Oulie, Marthe. *Charcot of the Antarctic.* London: John Murray, 1938.

Owen, Russell. "Antarctic Trail: The Problem of Food; Byrd Party's Rations Fruit of Hard Labor." *Evening Post* 108, no. 129 (November 27, 1929): 11.

Parfit, Michael. *South Light: A Journey to the Last Continent.* New York: Macmillan, 1985.

Ponting, Herbert. *The Great White South: Being an Account of Experiences with Captain Scott's South Pole Expedition and of the Nature Life of the Antarctic.* London: Duckworth, 1921.

Priestley, Raymond. *Antarctic Adventure: Scott's Northern Party.* New York: E. P. Dutton, 1915.

"Inexpressible Island." *Nutrition Today* 4, no. 3 (Autumn 1969): 18–27.

Pryde, James, John Conner, Frances Jack, Mark Lancaster, Lizzie Meek, Craig Owen, Richard Paterson, Gordon Steele, Fiona Strangl, and Jacqui Woods. "Sensory and Chemical Analysis of 'Shackleton's' Mackinlay Scotch Whisky." *Journal of the Institute of Brewing* 117, no. 2: 156–65. http://scientificsocieties.org//jib/papers/2011/G-2011-0630-1168.

Pyne, Stephen J. *The Ice: A Journey to Antarctica*. Iowa City: University of Iowa Press, 1986.

Reader's Digest Services. *Antarctica: Great Stories from the Frozen Continent*. Sydney: Reader's Digest, 1985.
Richards, R. W. *The Ross Sea Shore Party, 1914–1917*. Cambridge, UK: Scott Polar Research Institute, 1962.

Rodgers, Eugene. *Beyond the Barrier: The Story of Byrd's First Expedition to Antarctica*. Annapolis MD: Naval Institute Press, 1990.

Rogers, Susan Fox, ed. *Antarctica: Life on the Ice*. Palo Alto: Solas House, 2007.

Ronne, Finn. *Antarctic Conquest: The Story of the Ronne Expedition, 1946–1948*. New York: G. P. Putnam's Sons, 1949.

Rosove, Michael H. *Let Heroes Speak: Antarctic Explorers, 1772–1922*. New York: Berkley Books, 2000.

Rubin, Jeff. *Antarctica: A Lonely Planet Travel Survival Kit*. 4th ed. Hawthorn, Australia: Lonely Planet, 2008.

"Train Oil and Snotters: Eating Antarctic Wild Foods." *Gastronomica: The Journal of Food and Culture* 3, no. 1 (2003). http://www.antarctic-circle.org/rubin.pdf.

Rubin, Morton J. *The Mirnyy Diary: 12 Feb. 1958–7 Feb. 1959*. http://www.antarctican.org. Last accessed April 17, 2010.

Rymill, John. *Southern Lights: The Narrative of the British Graham Land Expedition*. New York: Harper and Brothers, 1939.

Scott, Capt. Robert Falcon. *Scott's Last Expedition: The Personal Journals of Captain R. F. Scott, R.N., C.V.O., on His Journey to the South Pole*. London: John Murray, 1929.

The Voyage of the Discovery. New York: Cooper Square Press, 2001.

Sellick, Douglas. *Antarctica: First Impressions 1773–1930*. Freemantle, Western Australia: Freemantle Arts Centre Press, 2001.

Shackleton, Ernest. *South: A Memoir of the* Endurance *Voyage*. New York: Carroll and Graf, 1998.

The Heart of the Antarctic: Being the Story of the British Antarctic Expedition 1907–1909. New York: Carroll and Graf, 1999.

Shephard, Sue. *Pickled, Potted, and Canned: How the Art and Science of Food Preserving Changed the World*. New York: Simon and Schuster, 2000.

Simon, Alvah. *North to the Night: A Year in the Arctic Ice*. New York: McGraw Hill/International Marine, 1999.

Siple, Paul. *90° South: The Story of the American South Pole Conquest*. New York: G. P. Putnam's Sons, 1959.

Skottsberg, Carl. *The wilds of Patagonia; a narrative of the Swedish expedition to Patagonia, Tierra del Fuego, and the Falkland Islands in 1907–1909*. New York: Macmillan, 1911.

Smith, Roff. *Life on the Ice: No One Goes to Antarctica Alone*. Washington DC: National Geographic Society, 2005.

Smuul, Juhan. *Antarctica Ahoy: The Ice Book*. Moscow: Foreign Languages Publishing House, c. 1957.

Solzhenitsyn, Alexander. *One Day In The Life Of Ivan Denisovich*. New York: Frederick Praeger, 1963.

Steger, Will, and Jon Bowermaster. *Crossing Antarctica*. New York: Alfred A. Knopf, 1992.

Stewart, John. *Antarctica: An Encyclopedia*. Jefferson NC: McFarland, 1990.

Swithinbank, Charles. *An Alien in Antarctica: Reflections upon Forty Years of Exploration and Research on the Frozen Continent*. Blacksburg VA: McDonald and Woodward, 1997.

Foothold on Antarctica: The First International Expedition (1949–1952) Through the Eyes of Its Youngest Member. Sussex, UK: Book Guild, 1999.

Vodka on Ice: A Year with the Russians in Antarctica. Sussex, UK: Book Guild, 2002.

Thomson, Robert. *The Coldest Place on Earth*. Auckland: A. H. and A. W. Reed, 1969.

Uberagua, Jules. "True Point of Beginning." In *Antarctica: Life on the Ice*, edited by Susan Fox Rogers. Palo Alto: Solas House, 2007.

U.S. Navy. *US Navy Operation Deep Freeze Cruise Book*. Various issues, from 1959 to 1971.

Waldron, Commander James Edgar. *Flight of the Puckered Penguins*. http://www.anta.canterbury.ac.nz/resources/flight/index2.html. First published in 1996. Last accessed February 8, 2010.

Wheeler, Sara. *Cherry: A Life of Apsley Cherry-Garrard*. New York: Random House, 2002.

Wild, Frank. *Shackleton's Last Voyage: The Story of the "Quest": From the Official Journal and Private Diary kept by Dr. A. H. Macklin*. London: Cassell, 1923.

Worsley, Frank Arthur. *Shackleton's Boat Journey: The Narrative from the Captain of the* Endurance. Santa Barbara: The Narrative Press, 2001.

Notes

3 As Lieut. Kristian Prestrud of the 1910–1912 *Fram* expedition: From Roald Amundsen's *South Pole.*

4 In both Arctic and Antarctic: The Arctic reference ("and had both tea and 'hoosh' in little over the hour") is made in quotes but without explanation, indicating slang in common usage. Source is *Journals and Proceedings of the Arctic Expedition, 1875–76, under the command of Captain Sir George S. Nares, R.N., K.C.B.,* in House of Commons Parliamentary Papers Online.

1. ALL THINKING AND TALKING OF FOOD

23 a "hard, rough, jolly life": Quoted in Shackleton's *South,* 104-5.
26 "crazed by their privations": See Laseron and Hurley, *Antarctic Eyewitness,* 271.

2. THE SECRET SOCIETY OF UNCONVENTIONAL COOKS

34 The heroic age: The term seems to have originated with British explorer Duncan Carse in March 1956, writing in the *Times* of London about Shackleton, Crean, and Worsely — "three men from the heroic age of Antarctic exploration, with 50 feet of rope between them, and a carpenter's adze" — making the astonishing first crossing of South Georgia in 1916.
44 "Shackleton's men must have fed like turkey cocks": From Cherry-Garrard, *Worst Journey,* 624.
44 "Bobs' raucous voice": From Raymond Priestly's diary, quoted in Cherry-Garrard, *Worst Journey,* 42.
51 "in a princely fashion": From Tryggve Gran, quoted in Huntford, *Last Place on Earth,* 362.
60 "like six big maggots in a nest": From Meredith Hooper in her book *Longest Winter,* 221.

3. SLAUGHTER AND SCURVY

73 "kitchen garden where all good things grow": From James Collins, *The Story of Canned Foods*, quoted in Shephard, *Pickled, Potted, and Canned*, 247.

73 "rope-yarn": Schwarz's anecdote is from von Drygalski, *Southern Ice Continent*, 216.

74 "addition of a few delicacies": Macklin quoted in Wild, *Shackleton's Last Voyage*, 355.

75 "in his twenty years at sea": From Carpenter, *History of Scurvy and Vitamin C*, 29.

76 "embarked with nutritional deficiencies": Robert Feeney in his book *Polar Journeys: The Role of Food and Nutrition in Early Exploration*, 6.

76 "learned over again the lesson": Sir Raymond Priestley in an article entitled "Inexpressible Island," 18.

83 "Manna from heaven": From Jeff Rubin's excellent essay, "Train Oil and Snotters: Eating Antarctic Wild Foods," 39. The elephant seal stew described in the next paragraph is also derived from Jeff's essay (p. 44).

4. MEAT AND MELTED SNOW

106 "less than that provided": From Halsey and Stroud, "Could Scott Have Survived," R457-r458.

112 "dehydration is the critical deficiency": Personal communication with Roland Huntford, January 25, 2011.

112 "Contrary to what you may think": In an interview with National Geographic Adventure Magazine, February 2004.

115 Recent science suggests that fat and carbohydrates: From Halsey and Stroud, "Could Scott Have Survived," R458-r459.

121 Lieut. Kristian Prestrud stated: In Amundsen's *The South Pole*, 2:231.

124 One estimate suggests: From Reader's Digest Services, *Antarctica: Great Stories From The Frozen Continent*, 165.

124 According to another study: Cited in Orr, "Food Requirements and Weight Changes of Men on Antarctic Expeditions," 79–91.

124 an average of 6,500 calories: From Muir, "Ketonuria in the Antarctic," 53–58. Also published online at http://www.antarctica.ac.uk and cited by the Cool Antarctica website. Information comparing manhauling to competing in the Tour de France is from Halsey and Stroud, "Could Scott Have Survived," R458.

124 Amundsen and Scott both issued: Scott issued two different rations, the Barrier and the Summit; I'm discussing the Summit, for which I've found three different estimates: 4,586 calories (Feeney's *Polar Journeys*), 4,200–4,600 calories (from Reader's Digest *Antarctica: Great Stories From The Frozen Continent*), and 4,430 calories (from Huntford, *Last Place on Earth*).

124 The caloric deficit between the British team's needs: From Halsey and Stroud, "Could Scott Have Survived," R459.

126 "the goal of our desires": Olav Bjaaland quoted in Huntford, *Last Place on Earth*, 454.

127 "both damned the motor": From Cecil Meares's journal, quoted in Huntford, *Last Place on Earth*, 394.

128 Famed polar adventurer Ranulph Fiennes: In *Race to the Pole*.

129 After nearly five months and the expenditure of up to a million calories: From Halsey and Stroud, "Could Scott Have Survived," R458.

130 "One point which struck us all": From *The James Caird Society Journal*, no. 3 (Spring 2007), reproducing a 1909 piece by Shackleton called "In the Days of my Youth; My First Success."

5. How to Keep a Fat Explorer in Prime Condition

151 Commander Byrd was not: Much in this section is owed to historian Eugene Rodgers's remarkable book, *Beyond the Barrier*.

152 "perfect dollar waterfront whore": From Henry Harrison, quoted in Rodgers, *Beyond the Barrier*, 153.

156 Aside from the familiar planes: Sources include *Discovery*, the book by Byrd and his friend, reporter Charles Murphy.

168 Darlington's *My Antarctic Honeymoon*: Written with her ghost writer, Jane McIlvaine.

172 Glaciologist Charles Swithinbank: In his book about the experience, *Foothold on Antarctica*.

173 Maudheim, their base: One of the first priorities in building Maudheim was digging an outhouse hole. The glaciologists Charles Swithinbank and Valter Schytt took on the task, and the privy was afterward named the "schytt-house."

173 "I came to like the taste": He liked it so much, in fact, that at expedition's end he was allowed to loot sixty pounds of it to take home, knowing no one else in Britain, despite food shortages, would touch it.

176 "This is not, and does not pretend to be": Gerald Cutland's manuscript is the property of the British Antarctic Survey (archives reference no. ad6/13/4/1 to 3), and I'm indebted to them for giving me access to it. As noted in the chapter, the quote here is a direct borrowing from Stephen Lister's *Fit for a Bishop*.

177 "It should be noted for posterity": I'm indebted also to David Simmons, a bas Club member who contacted me to provide the back story on *Fit for a FID*.

6. INTO THE DEEP FREEZE

188 As Dian Belanger relates: A neglected part of Antarctic history, Operation Deep Freeze, the IGY, and the years that followed settlement deserve more study. Thankfully, there is Dian Belanger's excellent book, *Deep Freeze*, to which much in this chapter is owed.

203 Wildlife was scarcely on the menu: Moreover, Rear Admiral Dufek wrote that in order to protect the wildlife in "this faraway land down under," his sailors were forbidden "to molest the penguin colonies." They were, however, allowed to claim a penguin as a souvenir, which would be stored for taxidermy back in the US.

207 A navy pilot who shared his room with Wilkins: Commander James Edgar Waldron describes this scene in his online publication *Flight of the Puckered Penguins*.

209 Everyone but the whiner: Sources include Tim Bowden's *The Silence Calling*, Tom Griffiths's *Slicing the Silence*, and the Australian Antarctic Division (AAD). The "Hair Pie" section title is taken directly from the Jim Morgan story in the online annals of the AAD.

212 "thrown into the sea to drown": Morton Rubin's Mirnyy diary is available online at http://www.antarctican.org.

212 "Do we want to spread the disease of communism even to the penguins?": Quoted in Dian Belanger's *Deep Freeze*. Senator Dodd might have worried more about the Weddell seals had he known about their red flesh.

7. PRISONER-OF-WAR SYNDROME

218 "like long-lost cousins.": From Burke, *Moments of Terror*, 225.
218 "In this remote place": From Burke, *Moments of Terror*, 214.
220 "a warrior culture drinking blood": From Johnson, *Big Dead Place*, 31.
222 Antarctic cuisine has always made prisoners: This section is derived from Jim Mastro's *Antarctica: A Year at the Bottom of the World*.

227 He sampled the liver as well: Mawson's source, though, was husky livers; the vitamin A content of seal liver varies widely from species to species.

228 [Greenpeace] built their tiny base: During the construction period, a visiting U.S. Coast Guardsman from McMurdo strolled over to the Greenpeace base from his helicopter and said laconically, "So this is where my wife's $20 goes each year." Knight, *Icebound*, 90.

article from December 19, 1999, by Josh Landis, entitled "Testing Tainted Waters."

228 A 1971 study of the base's effect: Original source is Dayton and Robilliard, "Implications of Pollution to the McMurdo Sound Benthos."

229 The seabed of Winter Quarters: Among the sources for this information is an *Antarctic Sun*

229 "We are just screaming the problem.": From Knight, *Icebound*, 41.

231 International Trans-Antarctica Expedition: See Steger and Bowermaster, *Crossing Antarctica*.

236 He had pioneered: This is the same Fiennes whose impassioned defense (in *Race to the Pole*) of Robert Falcon Scott and his legacy I cite in chapter 4. The Transglobe story is derived from Fiennes's *To the Ends of the Earth*.

8. THE SYRUP OF AMERICAN COMFORT

245 "Vomit was everywhere, and the cabin reeked": Mastro, *Antarctica: A Year at the Bottom of the World*, 156.

246 Karen Joyce, a twenty-year veteran: In *Snow Job*, one of her wonderful (but unpublished) comedic novels about Antarctic life.

249 Pams Chippie Trivia Quiz: Traci Macnamara's essay, "LC-130," was published in *Isotope: A Journal of Literary Nature and Science Writing*.

251 "a too-cold non-sterilizing dishwasher": From an anonymous contribution by "Benny Arnold" to the "King Haakon VII Review" page of the Big Dead Place website, which often acts as a clearinghouse for commentary that might make trouble for employees.

252 "Yeah, life is tough in Antarctica!": Behrendt, *Innocents on the Ice*, 192.

252 "in a display case of ancient Antarctic artifacts": Behrendt, *Ninth Circle*, 177.

253 "glopping some orange mush onto his prison tray": From "The Day It Rained Chickens," Karen's essay in the anthology *Antarctica: Life on the Ice*.

255 "The only way to make hundreds": Sally Ayotte, from an interview with Joanne Gordon for her book *Be Happy At Work*, 137.

257 She was lucky: The pilots of a 1979 "champagne flight" had flown at full speed through the clouds into a 12,500-foot volcano because their misinformed computers told them to. All 237 passengers and 20 crew on Air New Zealand flight 901 died on impact. It was the world's third-worst air disaster at the time, killing far more people in that one moment than have otherwise died in Antarctica before or since. The first loads of what would amount to twenty-five thousand pounds of human remains were stored briefly in McMurdo's frozen-food warehouse before shipment to New Zealand, where some of the mortuary workers who received them thereafter became vegetarians.

258 "I think she hires more for attitude than aptitude": From an *Antarctic Sun* profile of Sally titled "Sally Serves Love and Laughter a la Carte," November 10, 2002.

258 "A lot of cooks," Sally told an NPR reporter: In an article by Daniel Zwerdling called "Food is Morale Booster or Breaker in Antarctica" (the article can be found at http://www.npr.org).

260 "There are attorneys, judges, pharmacists": From a jobs discussion forum on the Cool Antarctica website: http://www.coolantarctica.com/Community/find_a_job_in_antarctica.htm.

263 In the 2000–2001 Antarctic ice cream flavor-naming contest: Owed entirely to Deb Lisman (now Smith), a McMurdo housing coordinator, who had known Jerry and his wife for years. Here are the inventors of the flavors I mention: Freshy Fantasy Fiesta — Jeremy Sohlstrom; Antarctic Hoosh — Mark Sabbatini; Shackleton's Salvation — Devin Lamma; Polar Tuxedo — Michael Caldwell; Penguin Paradise — Chester Clogston; Penguin on a Stick — Tom Hamann; Chocolate-Raspberry Antarctic Treat-ee — Cathy Burns; Harsh Continent — Shawna DeWitt. **274 A survey by New Zealand researchers:** As reported in the *London Guardian*, November 17, 2001.

274 Research has shown that healthy fish: See Josh Landis, "Testing Tainted Waters, *Antarctic Sun*, December 19, 1999.

275 computer maestra for McMurdo researchers: Karen Joyce's story about the great skua feast of 1990 was published in the anthology *Antarctica: Life on the Ice* as "The Day It Rained Chickens."

9. A COOKIE AND A STORY

283 "Pasta," Sally has said: Recounted in Robert Lee Hotz, "Cooking at the Bottom of the World," *Los Angeles Times*, July 25, 2001.

284 I always tell the new baker": Hotz, "Cooking at the Bottom of the World."

284 "A lot of bakers come here": Told to Joanne Gordon, in *Be Happy at Work*, 136-37.

287 From 1975 until 2003: The dome galley never was meant to feed everyone during the busy summer season. Back in 1976, just after completion of the new dome station, there was also a larger, "bigger and better-equipped" satellite kitchen in Summer Camp, a cluster of housing units set apart from the dome. But that newly built kitchen burned down before it opened, in the largest fire in USAP history. For some reason, it was never replaced.

287 "There is not enough elbow room": Hotz, "Cooking at the Bottom of the World."

287 "There is no comparison," Highsmith said: From the *Antarctic Sun*, June 21, 2004.

288 Whiner Alarm bell: Mark Lehman's essay, "Food for Thought, Foods as Fuel," is in the anthology *Antarctica: Life on the Ice*.

290 "a free cup of coffee": Quoted in Johnson, *Big Dead Place*, 83.

293 "You can do pot roast for 150": Quoted in the *Antarctic Sun*, February 2, 2003.

294 "I feel spoiled," Emanuel said: From Howard Riell, "The Restaurant at the End of the World," *Foodservice Equipment and Supplies*, September 1, 2003.

294 "The Polies are trained to boo and hiss": From the *Antarctic Sun*, February 2, 2003.

294 The truth about cooking: This section is derived from chef Michèle Gentille's *Harriett's Tomato* blog.

295 a layer of fleece: Gentille's description comes from an article in the *Wall Street Journal*, April 15, 2008, entitled "Cooking at the End of the World."

297 the "visual Alcatraz" of East Antarctica: Nicholas Johnson's phrase, from *Big Dead Place*, 91.

10. Sleeping with Vegetables

306 Burying Thanksgiving Turkeys: The anecdote comes from Roff Smith in *Life on the Ice*, 126.

318 Thursday was a sad day for everyone: Roff Smith happened to be in McMurdo at this time, and later called the experience "disturbingly medieval," akin to bear-baiting.

325 "ten passengers and a crate of oranges": From Bellinger, *Deep Freeze*.

330 Suddenly the two of us possessed: We had some fun with our food wealth. In a stealth mission deep into the Allan Hills, we snuck into a geologists' camp (while they were out prospecting) to place an orange on their kitchen box.

11. A Tale of Two Stations

337 "I'm off to lunch where the usual seven-course Sunday meal awaits": The entire Concordia story is derived from Dargaud's remarkable blog of the experience, which is part of his even more remarkable website: www.gdargaud.com.

346 Shackleton's whisky: From the AHT website at http://whiskythaw.canterburymuseum.com.

346 "gas chromatography": Shackleton's whisky showed a distinctly modern set of highlights: pungent, peaty, dried fruit, sweet, woody, and spicy. The whole fascinating analysis, "Sensory and Chemical Analysis of 'Shackleton's' Mackinlay Scotch Whisky," can be read in the online annals of the *Journal of the Institute of Brewing*. See Pryde et al., "Sensory and Chemical Analysis," 156-65.

346 "whole romantic tale": From "Shackleton's Whisky Heads Home," in the *Financial Times* online, accessed March 30, 2011.

347 "the means by which the true nature of an object is preserved": From the AHT website at http://whiskythaw.canterburymuseum.com.

348 "steel can shatter like glass": As told to Charles Swithinbank, recounted in his *Vodka On Ice*.

348 "I was pretty sure they didn't eat like that often": Bob Dale, interview with the author, May 10, 2011, Brunswick, Maine.

348 "In Russian fashion": From personal communication with Robert Flint with the author, January 17, 2011.

357 "[T]heir only heat," writes Jeff Rubin: In the Lonely Planet *Antarctica* guide, 4th ed., 319.

357 hardship like this: Lena put it bluntly in an email to me: "The russians definitely have a MUCH higher suffering tolerance than the americans. While I've heard a lot of complaining about a lack of A-1 steak sauce and broken hot-tub pumps from our stars & stripes buddies, you ask the russians about a winter at vostok where they ran out of fuel, and they say, 'it was ok.'"

EPILOGUE

359 "One gets the fever and can't stop going," and "little voices": From Reader's Digest Services, *Antarctica*, 232, and Frank Wild's *Shackleton's Last Voyage*, 165.
359 "Antarctica is not a place; it is a disease": Something I heard while in the U.S. Antarctic Program.
359 "Half the fascination an Antarctic expedition possesses": From "Inexpressible Island," Priestley's 1969 article for *Nutrition Today*.